# IMPOSSIBLE MODERNISM

# IMPOSSIBLE

# MODERNISM

### T. S. ELIOT, WALTER BENJAMIN,
### AND THE CRITIQUE OF HISTORICAL REASON

## ROBERT S. LEHMAN

STANFORD UNIVERSITY PRESS
STANFORD, CALIFORNIA

Stanford University Press
Stanford, California

Printed on acid-free, archival-quality paper

Printed and bound in Great Britain by
Marston Book Services Ltd, Oxfordshire

Library of Congress Cataloging-in-Publication Data

Names: Lehman, Robert S. (Robert Scott), author.
Title: Impossible modernism : T.S. Eliot, Walter Benjamin, and the critique
   of historical reason / Robert S. Lehman.
Description: Stanford, California : Stanford University Press, 2016. |
   Includes bibliographical references and index.
Identifiers: LCCN 2016001497 | ISBN 9780804799041 (cloth : alk. paper)
Subjects: LCSH: Eliot, T. S. (Thomas Stearns), 1888-1965—Criticism and  interpretation. |
Benjamin, Walter, 1892–1940—Criticism and interpretation. | Literature and history. | Modernism
(Literature)
Classification: LCC PS3509.L43 Z69177 2016 | DDC 821/.912—dc23
LC record available at http://lccn.loc.gov/2016001497

ISBN 9781503600140 (electronic)

Typeset by Bruce Lundquist in 10/14 Minion Pro

*For Audrey*

One is soon forced to resort to paradoxical formulations, such as defining the modernity of a literary period as the manner in which it discovers the impossibility of being modern.

—Paul de Man, "Literary History and Literary Modernity"

# CONTENTS

# ACKNOWLEDGMENTS

The initial development of my arguments in this book benefited from the attention of my mentors at Cornell University. I want to start by thanking Jonathan Culler, Peter Gilgen, Douglas Mao, and Neil Saccamano. All were—and are—valued advisers, interlocutors, and examples of the sort of scholar that I hope someday to be.

Much of what made it into this book I learned through countless exchanges with teachers, colleagues, and friends. Any listing of names is bound to be incomplete; nonetheless, I want to thank Kevin Attell, Alexis Briley, Becky Colesworthy, Bradley Depew, Ben Glaser, John Hicks, Aaron Hodges, Jess Keiser, Tracy McNulty, Douglas McQueen-Thomson, Steven Miller, Julia Ng, Jeff Pence, Robert Ray, Robin Sowards, Danielle St. Hilaire (for Chaucer!), Phil Wegner, and Alan Young-Bryant; as well as all of the members of the Theory Reading Group and the Hegel Reading Group (in Ithaca as well as in Paris). Beyond any particular institutional context, Nathan Brown, Anna Kornbluh, Knox Peden, and Josh Robinson have been vital sources of intellectual energy Martin Hägglund provided invaluable advice and support during the completion of this project, especially in its final stages.

I completed this book as a member of the English Department at Boston College. For the warm scholarly welcome I have received there, I owe thanks to all of my colleagues. I am especially grateful for advice I received on this project from Marjorie Howes, Suzanne Matson, Kevin Ohi, and Frances Restuccia. Across the river, the Mahindra Seminar in Dialectical Thinking at Harvard

University has provided further intellectual stimulation, and for this I thank friends and co-organizers (past and present) Will Baldwin, Jamey Graham, Julie Orlemanski, Gordon Teskey, and Andrew Warren.

The final version of this manuscript has profited from the incisive comments of two anonymous reviewers, while my editors at Stanford University Press, Emily-Jane Cohen and Friederike Sundaram, have been helpful and responsive every step of the way.

My family in Ohio has always supported me. To my late grandparents John and Anne Chambers and especially to my mother Sally Chambers—thank you for all that you have done and know that I love you very much. Finally, and with all of my heart, I dedicate this book to my partner, Audrey Wasser, doubtless the better craftsperson, who scrutinized every page and without whom none of this would have been possible.

·  ·  ·

An early version of Chapter 6 first appeared as "Allegories of Rending: Killing Time with Walter Benjamin," in *New Literary History* 39.2 (Spring 2008): 233–250. Copyright © *New Literary History*, The University of Virginia, 2008; a portion of Chapter 2 appeared as "Eliot's Last Laugh: The Dissolution of Satire in The Waste Land," in *Journal of Modern Literature* 32.2 (Winter 2009): 65–79. Copyright © Indiana University Press, 2009; Chapter 5 includes some formulations that first appeared in "Finite States: Toward a Kantian Theory of the Event," *diacritics* 39.1 (Spring 2009): 61–74. Copyright © Cornell University, 2011.

# PREFACE

This book advances an interpretation of European modernism and, more specifically, of the relationship between European modernism and historical representation. I characterize this relationship as one of *critique*, not in the more colloquial sense of "assessment" but in the technical sense given to the term by Immanuel Kant and his successors, for whom critique describes an interrogation of the conditions of possible experience. My claim is that modernism's critique of history operates not (or not only) as the negation of tradition itself or as the extension of past forms through the creation of the new work of art but rather as a struggle to grasp and transform the formal conditions of historical experience, the conditions under which events come to appear as repetitions or innovations, as traditional or "new." More concretely, my contention is that when modernist authors struggle with history, they struggle not only with the massacres and wars that made the last hundred years "the most terrible century in Western history" (Berlin, qtd. in Hobsbawm 1) but also with the way that these events and others have been made meaningful. They struggle, that is, with history itself, with the way that, through the stories it tells, history secures the past and sets limits on the present. It is with this struggle in mind that I read the formal experimentation characteristic of modernist writing. Directed at the problem of historical representation, modernist experimentation is an attempt to imagine an alternative architecture of history, one open to artistic innovation or political transformation.

My particular focus is on the critique of history as it is articulated in the writings of two roughly contemporaneous authors: T. S. Eliot (1888–1965) and

Walter Benjamin (1892–1940). Despite their striking personal and political differences, Eliot—the self-proclaimed "Anglo-Catholic, classicist, royalist"; the
individual who was, perhaps more than anyone else, responsible for the shape
that the study of literature took during the last century—and Benjamin—the
"Marxist rabbi," forced into intellectual, then literal, exile, and driven finally
to suicide—shared for a time in what was fundamentally the same project: the
project of challenging an image of history regnant since the early years of
the nineteenth century, one that came into being in the wake of the French
Revolution and found its watchword in Leopold von Ranke's exhortation to
write history "as it actually happened" (*wie es eigentlich gewesen ist*; Ranke 57).
Against this image of history, Eliot and Benjamin tapped into a submerged tradition of thinking about the relationship between historical representation and
literary form, one that connects (via many intermediaries) Aristotle's elevation
of poetry over history in book 9 of the *Poetics* to Nietzsche's subordination of
history to life in the second of the *Untimely Meditations*. Fundamentally, they
took as their starting point an understanding of history not as a collection
of empirical facts but as something formed, something written; and so they
turned to specifically literary devices—devices such as lyric, satire, allegory,
and myth—to reimagine the shape of historical time and the possibility of historical change. This shared project developed over the course of their careers;
and it culminated in their respective masterworks—*The Waste Land* and *The
Arcades Project*—which stand as monuments to the possibilities and limitations
of a particularly modernist historical thinking.

My objective, again, is to understand how modernism—the sort of modernism exemplified in the poetic, critical, historical writings of Eliot and
Benjamin—addresses itself to historical representation rather than to a particular set of facts about the past. This particular topic has, I believe, been
neglected in the contemporary scholarship. A cursory glance at recent work
on modernism finds books dealing with modernism and the Great War, as
well as with modernism and the New Deal; with modernism and technology,
as well as with modernism and spiritualism; with modernism and fashion, as
well as with modernism and food. Most generally, these studies locate twentieth-century cultural texts—a heading that now cuts across the arts, high and
low, Western and non-Western—within their respective social, economic, or
political contexts. These texts are then interrogated with an eye toward how
they respond (critically, ideologically) to the givenness of historical facts,
which facts can be as undeniably significant as a war or as apparently mun-

dane as the closing of a music hall. The ubiquity of this approach has provided the inspiration for new book series and for major conferences in the field; and it underlies the "expansionist" rhetoric of what Douglas Mao and Rebecca Walkowitz have termed the "New Modernist Studies." My intention is not to deny the value of the historicist project, which has done much to fill in our picture of twentieth-century culture. And yet, I want to insist, in this project history itself remains a blind spot. By "history itself" I do not mean those objects or events that pile up at the feet of Benjamin's angel or accumulate in Eliot's wasteland; rather, I mean the historical worldview that continues to determine our representations of the past. In their eagerness to read modernism historically, critics have rarely paused to consider how history is read by modernism. As a result, they have not asked how modernism might encourage them to rethink the very historicism they bring to bear on it.

It is a contention of this book, then, that Eliot and Benjamin present us with an understanding of history much richer and more varied than that of modernism's present-day critics. What I mean by this claim becomes clearer when we compare modernism to its historically minded readers on the matter of their shared historical inheritance. The latter does not describe a mere consciousness of the past (in the pleonastic sense that history is what we inherit and every inheritance is historical) but something closer to what Flaubert had in mind when he wrote to Edmond and Jules de Goncourt in 1860 that "the historical sense dates from yesterday. And it is perhaps the best thing about the nineteenth century" (23). Flaubert's approval of the nineteenth century's "historical sense" was not necessarily shared by his contemporaries, who were as likely to worry over the threat that this new recollection of the past might pose to "la mémoire du présent." Regardless, what Flaubert is describing—even as he is living through the final phase of its development—is the shift from a worldview based on static relations of identity and difference to one focused on temporal becoming, a shift that Michel Foucault would describe a century later as the "mutation of Order into History" (*The Order of Things* 220).[1] The names associated with this mutation are more or less well known—Kant, Herder, and Hegel, and then Niebuhr, Humboldt, and Ranke—and the changes wrought by it affected all of the traditional humanistic disciplines as well as the newly minted romantic theory of literature. So Friedrich Schlegel, one of the founders of Jena romanticism, could write to his brother August that "I am revolted by any theory that is not historical" (qtd. in Schaeffer 108), a remark that would have been impossible a generation earlier. To inherit history in this sense is to inherit a developmental model of the world, one in which the present makes up a meaningful whole, the truth of the present is contained in the events of the past, and the continuity of past, present, and future can be taken for granted.

At issue in the remarks of Schlegel and Flaubert, as well as in the works of Hegel and Ranke, is the codification of history both as an academic discipline—a method of analysis and a body of knowledge to be studied alongside theology, law, medicine, and so on—and as an increasingly hegemonic worldview. This all occurs in the nineteenth century, in the wake of the French Revolution and roughly concurrent with the birth of romanticism in the arts. Hayden White describes the creation of an autonomous discipline of history in the following terms:

> Chairs of history were founded at the University of Berlin in 1810 and at the Sorbonne in 1812. Societies for the editing and publication of historical documents were established soon after: the society for the *Monumenta Germaniae Historica* in 1819, the *École des Charles* in 1821. Government subsidies of these societies—inspired by the nationalist sympathies of the time—were forthcoming in due course, in the 1830s. After mid-century, the great national journals of historical studies were set up: the *Historische Zeitschrift* in 1859, the *Revue historique* in 1876, the *Rivista storica italiana* in 1884, and the *English Historical Review* in 1886. The profession became progressively academicized. (136)

Both modernism and its readers inherit a historical worldview, a worldview of which the institutional transformations that White observes are only the most visible manifestations. They inherit, that is, the belief that a thing's truth is to be found in the unified temporal process by which it came to be.

And this worldview has proved tenacious. For contemporary historicist critics, this means implicitly or explicitly assuming the same methods of analysis developed by nineteenth-century historians or philosophers of history. So these critics cleave to a Rankean empiricism when they delve into the archives in search of a neglected fact about twentieth-century life, or to a Hegelian Marxism when they insist on a fact's sociohistorical mediation. In any case, they complete their labors in a field of thought that was delimited in the nineteenth century, one that they remain incapable of seeing beyond. In Benjamin's characteristically cutting terms, they fall prey to that century's "narcotic historicism" (*AP* K1a,6). By this, Benjamin does not necessarily mean that the history to which they succumb is illusory—though, as I will argue later, there are moments when his attacks on the historiography of the day necessitate his claiming as much. Rather, he warns against a historicist dogmatism that would naturalize a certain way of viewing the relationship between past, present, and future. This dogmatism underlies figures of history as progress and as decline—it is operative in some varieties of Marxism as well as in the pessimistic histories of Spengler—but it is no less vital to every vision of events that attempts to depict the past—to cite again the words of Ranke—"as it really was." In other words, it determines every attempt to "do history" without first inquiring into history's assumptions, its interests, its epistemological, political, and (somewhat paradoxically) *historical* conditions of possibility.

Benjamin's own express goal—nothing less than a "Copernican revolution" in historiography (*AP* K1,2)—has its precursors in the early years of European modernism. One of the earliest, most direct, and best known of these challenges to historicism is found in Nietzsche's meditation *On the Advantage and Disadvantage of History for Life* (1874), in which readers are warned that "there is a degree of insomnia, of rumination, of historical sense which injures every living thing and finally destroys it, be it a man, a people, or a culture" (10). Since the beginning of the nineteenth century, Nietzsche complains, the European mind has been determined by an overwhelming awareness of what came before; and the results have been disastrous, as the past has slowly choked out the present. Nonetheless, Nietzsche does not conclude that history ought to be jettisoned—for, he notes, "the unhistorical and the historical are equally necessary for the health of an individual, a people, and a culture"—but argues instead that history must be put in the service of "life," which would entail "history being transformed into a work of art" (39). What this transformation of history into art might look like will be my focus in the chapters to follow. For now, it is worth stressing that the choice faced by modernists after Nietzsche is not between historicism and a naïve presentism—the presentism of Nietzsche's happily unhistorical cows, for example—but one between an uncritical acceptance of existing models of history and a newly imagined history, one more amenable to modernism's diverse artistic and political goals.

Since what is at stake is a challenge to history, I should pause to distinguish more carefully the argument of *Impossible Modernism* from the arguments of those critics who read in the texts of certain modernist authors—always the futurists and often Benjamin himself, Georges Bataille, Wyndham Lewis (at least during his vorticist period), Carl Schmitt, and Georges Sorel—a somewhat simplistic rejection of history in favor of what Fredric Jameson has described as "a succession of explosive and self-sufficient present moments of violence" ("End" 712). Here, Jameson targets the champions of those political and artistic "messianisms" who would attempt to "make it new" by "stepping, for an instant, outside of history." The "moment" has its present-day enthusiasts—above all Karl Heinz Bohrer, who describes the *Augenblick* as a "central theme of modernist literature" ("Instants" 113), but also contemporary theorists of the event such as Alain Badiou (whom Jameson does not mention) and Gilles Deleuze (whom he does, but perhaps should not). The danger of this fetishization of the "moment without duration" (Bohrer, "Instants" 113), Jameson suggests, is that it entails the displacement of politics (which must unfold historically) by metaphysics, where the latter privileges whatever can be said to exist outside of time: the pure act, the moment of crisis, or the irreducible physicality of the body. A couple of decades earlier, we find Franco Moretti using similar language in an attack on the "tragic worldview" of so much twentieth-century political thought: "no tragic yearning for catastrophe as the well-spring of truth, then: no metaphysical contempt for 'consequences,' no Baroque delight in 'exception'" ("Moment" 47). Moretti's target, like Jameson's, is the "unhealthy complicity of melodrama and emptiness" present in the uncritical celebration of revolutionary violence. As should be clear from his choice of terms ("tragedy," "melodrama," the "Baroque"), however, Moretti differs from Jameson in that he associates this celebration of violence with modes of representation that are, properly speaking, literary. The salient opposition is not only between the moment and history but also between modern tragedy and the novel. Moretti thus makes explicit what is less clear in Jameson's analysis: the manner in which the writing of literary (as well as of political) history tends to be controlled by the very generic terms that it ought to explain.

No doubt the fantasy of an absolute break with the past, of simply awakening from the nightmare of history, was a temptation for modernism; and in my discussions of Eliot and Benjamin, I explain how powerful this temptation could be. If history manifests itself as a litany of catastrophes, it also seems to invite a properly catastrophic break, and both Jameson and Moretti are right to be wary. Nonetheless, in what follows, I reject—as, I argue, Eliot and Benjamin rejected, so long as it was possible—their either/or: *either* the "narcotic historicism" of the nineteenth century, which Moretti associates with the novelistic mode, *or* the "tragic" disavowal of history *tout court*. Perhaps in spite of himself, Moretti, at least, helps us see beyond the limiting frame that he sets up when he suggests that the generic conflict between the novel and modern tragedy can be translated into a choice between two modes of representing history: one for which history is a lived process of continuous development, the other for which history is nothing but the crises that disarticulate it. Moretti's argument about the superiority of the former to the latter necessitates his establishing a position from which to evaluate—historically—these two modes of historical emplotment. His own historical analysis must, therefore, remain external to this generic conflict, and this is precisely what is at stake in the framing device with which his essay begins. Here, Moretti notes that the importance of tragedy as opposed to the novel in the modern German context (as well as the reverse in England and France) results from geopolitical factors: "The Europe of the novel is a well-differentiated system of self-enclosed nation states. . . . The Europe of modern tragedy for its part is the Europe of war: a far more abstract and homogeneous oppositional field, of which Germany is not so much the core as the 'no-man's-land' where universal dramas can be acted out" (41). As the essay progresses, though, Moretti is more and more willing to avail himself of the "tragic" structure he ostensibly mistrusts. Thus he admits that the opposition of the novel to tragedy is itself a "tragic rendering" of this conflict (43); and he goes on to describe the latter in terms of a "Darwinian history of literature, where forms fight one another, are selected by their context, evolve and disappear like natural species" (43–44). Are we so far from the naturalism of Ibsen ("the key figure of modern tragedy") or the early Strindberg (39)? Rather than securing a neutral vantage from which to adjudicate the opposition of genres or historical emplotments, Moretti succeeds in developing a version of literary history that is at times novelistic and at times tragic.

What occurs behind the back, so to speak, of Moretti's essay is not so different from what Nietzsche calls for explicitly in 1874, namely, history transformed into a work of art, and Eliot in 1923, when he writes with reference to Joyce's *Ulysses* that the novel is "a form which will no longer serve" to orient us amidst "the immense panorama of futility and anarchy which is contemporary history" (*SP* 177). What occurs, then, is a shift away from history understood only as the realistic—or perhaps better, the neutral—description of sequential events, and toward history conceived as the object of a distinctly literary labor. This is a notion of history as a literary-conceptual scheme, one that is not itself given historically—which is to say that it does not itself appear among the empirical events of history but is nonetheless effective in these events as their ordering principle. Keeping this distinction between event and scheme in mind allows us to understand why the attempt to determine the originality of modernist forms through even the most laborious archival research is likely to prove inconclusive, and why the complicated relationship between modernism and history does not disappear simply because we assert that modernism's alleged break with tradition was not so great after all, that "modernism in literature has not passed; rather, it has been exposed as never having been there" (Bloom, *Map of Misreading* 28). The way we answer the question of modernism's continuation of an earlier romanticism or symbolism or whatever depends on how we understand the shape of history, how we understand the relative continuity or discontinuity between historical moments and the efficacy of causal relations in the artistic sphere. By itself, no amount of fact-gathering can lift us out of the realm of the merely empirical. The notion of the original object or event only becomes meaningful under the aegis of particular historical schemes.

If these schemes are not already present in historical occurrences, they must be constructed. This construction, I argue, is essentially a literary one, carried out (however unsystematically) through the mobilization of literary devices (and here Paul de Man's late reflections on the relationship between literary form and historical event have had a greater effect on my thinking than my scattered references to his project might suggest[2]). We see the effects of this construction not only in more traditional works of history—as Hayden White and, more recently, Frank Ankersmit have demonstrated—but also in many of the great modernist engagements with the past, in the works of Eliot and Benjamin, for example, which instruct us, if we are willing to learn, in strategies for thinking history otherwise.

My argument in the chapters to follow unfolds as a series of readings: first, in the Introduction, of three moments from the history of philosophy or criticism that shed light on the coupling of literary and historical form: Aristotle's *Poetics* (especially book 9, with its famous elevation of poetic form over historical nonform), Marx's *Eighteenth Brumaire* (with its opposition of the poetry of the past to the poetry—or the *prose*—of the future), and the early writings of Friedrich Nietzsche (and most of all, the aforementioned *On the Advantage and Disadvantage of History for Life*). Here my aim is not to produce a stand-alone piece of intellectual history, to trace (even schematically) the interweaving of poetic and historical form from the ancients to the near present; rather, I want to establish the coordinates of the problem that informs modernism's poetico-historical project and so to establish a context in which Eliot's and Benjamin's specifically literary struggles with history can begin to make sense. The six chapters that follow focus on Eliot's and Benjamin's major works—Eliot's poetic experiments from "The Love Song of J. Alfred Prufrock" to *The Waste Land* and Benjamin's critical writings from "On the Program of the Coming Philosophy" to *The Arcades Project*—not in order to point out isolated moments of similarity, that is, not to compare Eliot to Benjamin (the chapters on Eliot address Eliot, while those on Benjamin address Benjamin) but to present Eliot's and Benjamin's writings as parallel responses to the same problem: the problem of historical representation as it was felt acutely during the early decades of the twentieth century.

The first chapter addresses Eliot's struggle with history as this struggle unfolds between 1910 and 1920, between the composition of "The Love Song of J. Alfred Prufrock" and the publication of "Gerontion." Challenging readings of Eliot's project as, from its inception, conciliatory—the terminus of a certain narrative of literary modernism, the moment when modernism became reconciled to its institutional status—I reveal in Eliot's lyric practice an opposed tendency. During the 1910s, I argue, Eliot characterizes the poetic ordering of literary history not only as a synthesis of diverse works but also as a practice whose success depends on a series of divisions, divisions inscribed in the consciousness or the life of the "mature poet" and duplicated in the poet's literary creations. Thus, in his composition of "Prufrock," Eliot stages a kind of poetic suicide (*sui-caedere*, self-cutting) by invoking in the poem, then excising, the authorial voice; in "Tradition and the Individual Talent," he splits the mind of the poet between its roles as active catalyst and passive container; and in "Gerontion," he finds a way both to recall and to reject "Prufrock," cutting himself free from his own poetic past. In each case, Eliot locates history under the sign of *crisis*.

How can the strategy outlined in Chapter 1—the strategy of managing literary history through recurring acts of self-division—be extended beyond the limited form of the lyric to the modernist long poem? In Chapter 2, I examine the formal role played by satire in the drafts of *The Waste Land*, focusing in particular on Eliot's parody of Alexander Pope's *Rape of the Lock* in an early version of "The Fire Sermon." In Eliot's hands, satire becomes a means of responding to a specifically modernist crisis in aesthetic judgment: the seeming impossibility of distinguishing, after the collapse of traditional standards of beauty, popular charlatans from individuals of real talent. By placing *The Waste Land* under the sign of satire, Eliot attempts to distinguish his long poem from the wasteland of literary history that it recollects. The excising of satire from the final version of *The Waste Land* following the editorial suggestions of Pound and Eliot's replacement of his earlier satirical method by the so-called mythical method—my topic in the next chapter—reflect satire's failure to accomplish its task.

Eliot's description of the "mythical method" in his 1923 essay "*Ulysses, Order, and Myth*" has been read as a defense, after the fact, of his own method of composition in *The Waste Land*. Like Joyce, Eliot is said to be concerned with "manipulating a continuous parallel between contemporaneity and antiquity," a project that also allows him to plumb the deepest depths of the literary tradition and extend the reach of his long poem beyond its own Western context. Chapter 3 of this book develops an opposed analysis of Eliot's turn to myth, one more in keeping with Eliot's strategy of creation through division and better able to grasp *The Waste Land* as a crisis poem. Examining the delimitation in *The Waste Land* of the history of verse as it develops from Chaucer to Whitman, I argue that Eliot turns to myth not to forge connections with something temporally or spatially other but to cut his poem free from its literary-historical past. Broken off from the unending historical cycles that provide *The Waste Land* with its subject matter, Eliot attempts—with mixed results—to place the poet's creative act within the realm of myth.

The three chapters that make up Part 2 of *Impossible Modernism* focus on the writings of Walter Benjamin, and specifically on Benjamin's attempt to complete what he describes in *The Arcades Project* as a "Copernican Revolution in historical perception." In the fourth chapter, I read some of Benjamin's earliest programmatic writings—"On Perception" and "On the Program of the Coming Philosophy"—in light of early twentieth-century debates over the legacy of Kantianism. And I treat in particular Benjamin's attempt to replace Kant's transcendental philosophy—Kant's ostensibly complete description of the conditions of human cognition—with what Benjamin refers to as a "doctrine of orders" (*Lehre von den Ordnungen*), a system of interlinked but non-identical structures of knowledge derived from linguistics, theology, aesthetics, and other domains. Benjamin's early project, I maintain, ought to be read not only as a revision of Kantianism but also as a deepening of Kantianism. It finds Benjamin taking seriously Kant's claim that human experience is constitutively finite and expanding this notion of constitutive finitude to include the Kantian transcendental itself, leaving the latter open to transformation through its encounters with a material, historical outside. Although references to Kant are rare in Benjamin's later writings, a modified version of Kant's philosophy—this is the claim of the chapter—is the foundation for Benjamin's later critique of historicism.

In Convolute S of *The Arcades Project*, a section of his unfinished master-work dedicated to "Painting, Jugendstil, Novelty," Benjamin opposes to the strictures of official history the "street insurgence" of the anecdote. The latter, he goes on, confronts historical time with "a standard adequate and comprehensible to human life." In Chapter 5, I ask how anecdote came to appear to Benjamin to provide a *critical* model of historical perception, critical in the sense that it eludes the failings of both the rationalist approach to the past (which Benjamin associates with Hegel) and the empiricist approach to the past (which Benjamin associates with Ranke). I argue, finally, that the critical, anecdotal model of historical perception is concretized in Benjamin's late "physiognomies," that is, in his examinations of the gambler, the flâneur, the melancholic, and other modern historical types. These figures and their diverse forms of life provide historical time with the "standard" that Benjamin seeks.

Chapter 6 concerns the role of allegory in Benjamin's writings. Nearly every critic of Benjaminian allegory has begun with the assumption that allegory is, for Benjamin, a fundamentally temporal form. Two possible readings thus present themselves: on the one hand, a finitist reading in which allegory insists on the implacable decay of all life against the organicism of the symbol; on the other, an infinitist reading in which allegory becomes the privileged figure for history's dialectical unfolding. Though each position has resulted in a number of powerful interpretations, neither has addressed the most radical feature of Benjaminian allegory: its challenge to time as the latter manifests itself by ordering human history. Benjamin develops his allegorical challenge to time in *The Origin of German Tragic Drama*, his studies of Baudelaire, and most profoundly, the ninth thesis of "On the Concept of History." In the last of these texts, Benjamin's allegorical presentation of the "new angel" depicts a vision of history without time, a vision in which events occur absent any temporal continuity. In this impossible vision, I argue, the critical force of what Benjamin calls the "allegorical intention" emerges.

"Lyric," "Satire," and "Myth"; "Order," "Anecdote," and "Allegory": these are the headings under which Eliot and Benjamin attempt a critique of historical reason; and so they are the headings that organize *Impossible Modernism*. Until this book's Conclusion—which is, though brief, both summative and speculative—I hold Eliot's and Benjamin's projects apart. My aim, again, is not to catalog their similarities and differences but to read them as two responses to the same problem (though here I am reminded of Benjamin's somewhat cryptic remark that the absence of "continuity" is the condition of two moments "touching" [*AP* N7,7]). The problem of historical representation, and of what it means for the desire to manage or to escape the past, is larger than Eliot or Benjamin; indeed, it is larger than modernism or any particular literary-historical designation (since this problem does, after all, concern the very possibility of periodization). But this problem appears, nonetheless, with a particular urgency at a certain moment, namely, the early twentieth century, in the wake of the transformations of history that occurred in the nineteenth, and, at this moment, in two projects—Eliot's and Benjamin's. Thus the focus of this book and some of the methodological problems it necessarily courts: what follows is a rational (if I am successful) examination of a historically specific struggle over historical reason.

Before looking at Eliot's and Benjamin's own projects, however, it will be useful to locate this struggle in a broader context. Let us turn, then, to a few dense moments from the long history of the contest between historical and literary form.

# ABBREVIATIONS

**Benjamin**

| | |
|---|---|
| *AP* | *The Arcades Project* |
| *C* | *The Correspondence of Walter Benjamin, 1910–1940* |
| *GB* | *Gesammelte Briefe* |
| *GS* | *Gesammelte Schriften* |
| *OG* | *The Origin of German Tragic Drama* |
| *SW* | *Selected Writings* |

**Eliot**

| | |
|---|---|
| *ASG* | *After Strange Gods: A Primer of Modern Heresy* |
| *CC* | *To Criticize the Critic and Other Writings* |
| *CP* | *Collected Poems 1909–1962* |
| *IMH* | *Inventions of the March Hare: Poems 1909–1917* |
| *Intro* | Introduction to Ezra Pound, *New Selected Poems and Translations* |
| *L* | *The Letters of T. S. Eliot*, vols. 1–3 |
| LL | "London Letter" |
| *SP* | *Selected Prose of T. S. Eliot* |
| *SW* | *The Sacred Wood: Essays on Poetry and Criticism* |
| T | "Tarr" |

| | |
|---|---|
| *TAWL* | *The Annotated Waste Land with Eliot's Contemporary Prose* |
| *UP* | *The Use of Poetry and the Use of Criticism: Studies in the Relation of Criticism to Poetry In England* |
| *WLF* | *The Waste Land: A Facsimile and Transcript of the Original Drafts Including the Annotations of Ezra Pound* |
| *WPF* | *"War-Paint and Feathers"* |

## Hegel

| | |
|---|---|
| *DFS* | *The Difference between Fichte's and Schelling's Systems of Philosophy* |
| *EL* | *The Encyclopaedia Logic, with the Zusätze* |
| *LFA* | *Aesthetics: Lectures on Fine Art* |
| *PN* | *The Philosophy of Nature* |
| *PS* | *Phenomenology of Spirit* |
| *SL* | *Hegel's "Science of Logic"* |

## Kant

| | |
|---|---|
| *CJ* | *Critique of the Power of Judgment* |
| *CPR* | *Critique of Pure Reason* |

## Nietzsche

| | |
|---|---|
| *AD* | *On the Advantage and Disadvantage of History for Life* |
| *BT* | *The Birth of Tragedy and the Case of Wagner* |
| *GM* | *On the Genealogy of Morality: A Polemic* |
| *GS* | *The Gay Science* |
| TL | "On Truth and Lying in a Non-Moral Sense" |

## Pound

| | |
|---|---|
| *LE* | *Literary Essays of Ezra Pound* |

# IMPOSSIBLE MODERNISM

# THE POETRY AND THE PROSE OF THE FUTURE

**THE ENTANGLEMENT OF POETRY AND HISTORY** has been with us for a long time. The poetic emplotment or embellishment of historical facts endemic to the epic tradition developed for centuries before Plato provided it with its first philosophical challenge. In the seventeenth century, Giambattista Vico—whose first writings were poems—argued that "all the histories of the gentile nations have had fabulous beginnings" (109); and by transforming Homer into the imaginative spirit of the Greek people, he positioned poetic wisdom at the origin of the Western tradition. More recently, Martin Heidegger has made the work of art, and the poem in particular, the locus of "a people's historical existence," or the "distinctive way in which truth . . . becomes historical" (*Off the Beaten Track* 75). These blendings of poetry and history are not all equivalent, but blendings they are. They speak to the fact that our thinking about history and our thinking about poetry have progressed together.

Today, reflection on the relationship between poetry and history is more likely to be motivated by ethical concerns. The question of whether or not a given aesthetic form is adequate to historical events—as we find in Adorno's query as to the possibility of poetry after Auschwitz, or in Lyotard's aesthetics of the sublime[1]—still assumes that the domains of poetry and history overlap, that poetry's task is at least in part to address the same events or experiences that worry more sober forms of historical reflection. But the relationship between poetry and history has changed, such that a gain in status for one has come to appear as a loss for the other. Those who doubt the continued relevance of poetry, or of art in general, might do so on the grounds of its "pastness," of its superannuation by the accelerated prose of the twenty-four-hour news cycle. So, when Joseph Epstein writes of "poor poetry" that it is "the Darfur of twenty-first century literature," he succeeds in showing not only that, like Darfur at the time of his writing, "everyone wants to do something about [poetry], but nobody quite knows what is to be done," but also, through the chasm separating the humanitarian crisis unfolding on every television screen from the chapbook on the coffee table, a possible explanation for poetry's misery. Conversely, when the continuous movement of history can no longer be taken for granted, when the very idea of progress appears as something fabulous or fictive, evidence of history's borrowings from poetry rises to the surface and suspicion sets in.

Poetry has been left behind by the events of history. History has promised us truth and given us only poems. Between these two assertions, the relationship between poetry and history has been determined as essentially crisis-ridden. Modernism inherits this crisis and brings it to a point of high tension, but it does not necessarily produce it. My aim in this chapter is to address this crisis as it exists prior to the period of literary modernism, and to do so by examining three moments that shed a particular light on what is at stake in the coupling of poetry and history. The first occurs in the fourth century B.C. in Aristotle's *Poetics*, the earliest attempt to provide a systematic definition of the structure and effects of poetry and, consequently, the origin of all later *crises de vers*. The second appears in Marx's *Eighteenth Brumaire*, a text that offers a complicated poetic response to a moment of crisis in Marx's own historical method. The third appears in the early writings of Friedrich Nietzsche, where, against the onset of the nineteenth-century science of history, the demand to see history become poetry is made explicit. Limiting myself to these three moments and to these three authors, I do not hope to present anything like a thorough treatment of the issue at hand. What follows will move freely between fourth-century Greece and nineteenth-century Germany, romantic poetry and radical politics; and while it will be organized chronologically, its structure is perhaps better understood as a relative of the historical-collage forms favored by Eliot and Benjamin (while its failure to do more to cleave to these forms should be attributed to my own limitations as a stylist). In any event, by examining the particular coordinates I have chosen, I aim to provide some of the necessary intellectual-historical context for my subsequent analyses of Eliot's and Benjamin's poetico-historical projects, and to show why, for Eliot and Benjamin, the problem of historical representation might seem to invite a specifically literary solution. Guiding these analyses will be the suspicion—already anticipated in the writings of Aristotle—that both poetry and history are centrally concerned with the relationship between universal and particular, and with the way that universal structures do or do not allow the singularity of events to appear.

## I. A More Serious Thing

> [P]hilosophy is not meant to be a narration of happenings but a cognition
> of what is true in them, and further, on the basis of this cognition, to
> comprehend that which, in the narrative, appears as a mere happening.
> —G. W. F. Hegel, *Science of Logic*

In a well-known passage from *Poetics* 9, in the midst of characterizing the nature of poetic emplotment, Aristotle pauses to distinguish poetry (*poiēsis*) from history (*historia*), and to celebrate the former at the latter's expense. Poetry, he writes, "is a more philosophical (*philosophōteron*) and more serious (*spoudaioteron*) thing than history" (1451b5–8). Aristotle does not base his distinction between poetry and history on the fact that the former is composed in verse—for, he notes, "the writings of Herodotus could be put into verse but they would be no less a sort of history in verse than they are without verses"— but on the fact that "poetry tends to speak of universals, history of particulars" (1451b1–10). And as Aristotle elsewhere reminds us, only the former, the universal, is the proper object of philosophical knowledge (*Metaphysics* 981a15–30).

Most immediately, this elevation of poetry might be read as a challenge to arguments developed by Plato, for whom the failure of poetry and of the mimetic arts in general is precisely their distance from the universality of the ideas. Because the poet imitates things that are themselves copies of eternal forms, Plato observes, the poet is "third in the descent . . . from the truth" (*Republic* 597e); as such, he provides no assistance to the philosopher and he threatens to mislead the public. Understood thus, poetry (the discourse of illusion) and philosophy (the discourse of ideas) are separated by a gulf as great as empirical reality itself. As the few surviving fragments of the dialogue *On Poets* evince, Aristotle rejected his teacher's criticisms of poetry, going so far as to note that the "form of [Plato's own] dialogues is between poetry and prose" (*Poetics* 56). Before the force of Aristotle's challenge to Plato's criticisms can be measured, however, the meaning of what Aristotle calls poetry's "universality" needs to be unpacked.

Aristotle provides a straightforward definition of universal and particular in his work *On Interpretation*: "By the term 'universal,' I mean that which is of such a nature as to be predicated of many subjects, by 'particular' that which is not thus predicated. Thus 'Man' is a universal, 'Callias' a particular" (17a40). Clear enough. Particulars are those things that we intuit in our everyday experience—*this* man, *that* horse, and so on—as opposed to the universal categories through which we come to describe these things. But the question persists: what is the universal about which poetry tends to speak? Should we say that poetry deals with "man" in general, though it may appear to be dealing with Oedipus or Achilles? Does poetry deal with universal values—justice, love, bravery, and the like—while seeming to describe particular events? Aristotle clarifies his claim: "[I]t is the function of a poet to relate not things that have happened, but things that may happen, i.e. that are possible in accordance with probability or necessity" (1451a39–b1). At first this remark is not particularly helpful. Its murkiness results from what seems to be its basing of the opposition of poetry to history on the opposition of future ("things that may happen") to past ("things that have happened"). And yet Aristotle cannot be arguing that the poet must avoid treating past events—as, for example, his readers would have understood the Trojan War—in favor of purely fictive scenarios, for, he goes on, "even if it turns out that he is representing things that happened, [an individual] is no less a poet; for there is nothing to prevent some of the things that have happened from being the sort of thing that may happen according to probability" (1451b29–33). Though the poet is not constrained by the "traditional stories" that myth or history provides, neither is he prevented from drawing on these traditional stories, as we tend to find in the cases of the great tragedies and epics. When the poet incorporates historical events into his art, however, he transforms them into something that goes beyond their particularity as history, something that may be grasped according to modal categories such as probability and necessity.

Aristotle sheds more light on the universality of poetry, as well as on the association of this universality with probability and necessity, in *Poetics* 23. While prescribing the norms of epic poetry, he writes that the poet "should construct plots that are dramatic (i.e., [plots] about a single whole action that is complete, with a beginning, middle, and end), so that [the poem] will produce the pleasure particular to it as a single whole animal does" (1459a18–22). In addition to offering an early formulation of the organicist model of the literary work—a poem should be akin to a "single, whole animal"[2]—Aristotle here clarifies the nature of poetry's universality. Poetry—tragic, comic, or epic—is not universal because it presents universal themes through its particular characters and events but because it provides events with a universal structure, one that includes, most basically, a beginning, a middle, and an end. In so doing, it presents these events as "a single action, and a whole one at that," such that "when some part is transposed or removed, the whole is disrupted and disturbed" (1451a31–34). "Probability" and "necessity" describe how, in a poem, one event probably or necessarily follows from another according to the laws of poetic emplotment, how all things begin and tend toward a specific end. They describe, therefore, something of the causal order of human events. Again, poetry must be distinguished from history in this regard, for in history "it is necessary to produce a description not of a single action but of a single time, with all that happened during it to one or more people; each [event] relates to the others at random" (1459a22–25). History is defined negatively, by its lacking access to the universal, causal structure of poetry. Consequently, it is essentially incomplete (since an infinite number of events are always occurring at a "single time") and random (since historical events do not tend toward any rational end).

*Epistēmē*, scientific or philosophical knowledge, is not achieved through a simple perception of events, Aristotle writes, "for perception must be of a particular, whereas scientific knowledge involves the recognition of a commensurate universal" (87b38–39). Poetry is more philosophical than history because it passes beyond mere perception so as to express something universal: the universality of dramatic action, of plot. As such, it resists Plato's attempt to locate it "third in the descent" from the ideality of universal knowledge. It does not do so, however, by attempting to depict the hypostasized forms of things—a project that Aristotle, contra Plato, elsewhere rejects. Rather, it expresses a causal order immanent to the events it describes. Again, these events need not be the same as those given to the mere perception of the historian, but they can be. When they are, we can judge most easily the difference between history and poetry: whereas "[historical] perception must be of a particular . . . , [poetic emplotment] involves the [expression] of a commensurate universal." Poetry provides the universal commensurate to historical particularity. So, in addition to being near to philosophy, poetry, insofar as it "tends to speak of universals," is also a way for particular events to gain purchase on philosophical universality. More succinctly, poetry is the locus of historical events' becoming philosophical.

By elevating poetry over history and by basing his determination on the distinction between universal categories—the proper objects of philosophical knowledge—and particular events, Aristotle unintentionally traces the path that history would have to follow to constitute itself as a science. It would have to become more like poetry, so long as the latter is defined neither by the verse form nor by fictionality as such but by the composition of plots. And this is not so far from the path that history would take in its struggles for and eventual attainment of philosophical respectability. Thus, reflecting on the birth of history in its modern sense, that is, on history's assumption of its place among the human sciences, Ernst Cassirer can write the following: "[The eighteenth century tried] to grasp the meaning of history by endeavoring to gain a clear and distinct concept of it, to ascertain the relation between the general and the particular, between idea and reality, and between laws and facts, and to establish the exact boundaries between these terms" (*Philosophy of the Enlightenment* 197). Not only particular realities or brute facts but universal structures: insofar as history possesses them it enjoys scientific validity. But for Aristotle, these structures—which do not themselves occur historically—are precisely what history lacks and what distinguish it from poetry.

In any case, history would finally achieve its place among the sciences in the nineteenth century, with chairs of history appearing almost simultaneously at the University of Berlin (1810) and the Sorbonne (1812), and historical societies such as the *Monumenta Germaniae Historica* (1819) and the *École des Chartres* (1821) following a few years later (White 136). The impetus behind these developments is no secret. Following the unprecedented occurrence of the French Revolution, all of Europe demanded to know "Could it happen again?" or "Could it happen here?" At its origin, institutional history came into being to answer these questions, and thus to complete the Enlightenment project by subsuming under laws of "probability or necessity" that last space of contingency, history itself. Under the eyes of the great nineteenth-century historians—Leopold von Ranke, Jules Michelet, Jacob Burckhardt, and others—the relation of past, present, and future became, if not wholly predictable, at least rational, open to the knowledge of the historian or the philosopher.

And yet, in this most historical of centuries and in the most historically minded of countries, the most historical of philosophers—G. W. F. Hegel—seems to reopen the question of the relationship between poetry, history, and philosophy, and in terms that echo Aristotle's own: "The representations of art," Hegel writes, "cannot be called a deceptive appearance in comparison with the truer representations of historiography. For the latter . . . remains burdened with the entire contingency of ordinary life and its events, complications, and individualities, whereas the work of art brings before us the eternal powers that govern history without this appendage of the immediate sensuous present and its unstable appearance" (*LFA* 9). History, or rather "historiography"—the distinction will prove important—appears to have once again been demoted. It is again characterized by particularity ("individualities") and randomness ("the contingency of ordinary life," "unstable appearance"), while the work of art again tends to speak of universals, of "eternal powers."

We should not, however, be misled. Between Aristotle's *Poetics* and Hegel's *Aesthetics*, everything has changed. On the one hand, for Hegel, "historiography" remains bound to contingent facts, to the sensuous immediacy apprehended by an essentially prephilosophical consciousness. It fails to grasp the universal, categorial structures that are the true content of this apparent immediacy. In the language of the *Phenomenology of Spirit*, historiography can only point to things without really comprehending them.[3] The passage out of this immediate sensuous present is the passage into philosophy conceived as the realm of universals. Poetry, as a sensuous appearing of the idea, lies between historiography and philosophy. Laying claim to the universality of the idea, it is already beyond the former, which remains trapped in particularity. But poetry is also "not yet" philosophy, for though it raises the sensual up so as to mobilize it as a vessel for the absolute, it does not succeed in freeing itself entirely from the sensual and acceding to the realm of pure thought.[4] Thus Hegel can agree with Aristotle's claim that "poetry is a more philosophical . . . thing than history," while retaining the distinction between poetry and philosophy.

On the other hand, this movement from historiography to poetry, or from sensuous immediacy to the sensuous appearance of the idea, only takes place because history—as distinct, for Hegel, from "historiography"—has seized control of the whole plot. Everything happens within a historical time that is indissociable from the "eternal powers" that govern it. The distance of history from philosophy and the nearness of poetry to philosophy are utterly transformed. For Aristotle, history would have needed to become poetic to become philosophical. But for Aristotle, there is no possibility of this taking place. Poetry, philosophy, and history may have essential similarities, but their essences remain static. Neither poetry nor philosophy nor history is something historical. Hegel's innovation is to volatilize these discrete discourses, and to do so by giving them over to a historical emplotment that, at least for poetry, will eventually prove fatal. Already in the nineteenth century,

Hegel can famously write that "art, considered in its highest vocation, is and remains for us a thing of the past. Thereby it has lost for us genuine truth and life, and has rather been transferred into our *ideas* instead of maintaining its earlier necessity in reality and occupying its higher place" (11). In history, and having already escaped the realm of sensuous immediacy characteristic of historiography, art becomes philosophy by ridding itself of the last residue of the sensuous world. The form art takes at the moment of its self-overcoming is poetry, which has the merit of being the most conceptual of all the forms of art. Thus, Hegel continues, "at this highest stage, art now transcends itself, in that it forsakes the element of a reconciled embodiment of the spirit in sensuous form and passes over from the poetry of imagination to the prose of thought" (89).

History carries us from art to philosophy, or from poetry to prose. Hegel does not, however, necessarily close the book on poetry. In the years after his own form of historical idealism had fallen out of favor, a generation of philosophers began to wonder if the "eternal powers" governing Hegel's history were not in some sense poetic. The most famous example of these queries appears in Josiah Royce's 1906 *Lectures on Modern Idealism*, in the suggestion that the *Phenomenology of Spirit*, and possibly Hegel's entire system, might be read as the "biography" of the *Weltgeist*, a bildungsroman akin to Goethe's *Wilhelm Meister* or Carlyle's *Sartor Resartus* (151).[5] Royce does not describe the affinities between the eternal powers of Hegel's historical dialectic and the conventions of poetic emplotment with the intention of damning the former (though more empirically minded philosophers and historians would); he merely notes that "this consideration has been singularly overlooked by most of those who have given an account of the work" (147). For our purposes, however, it is enough to note that the question of whether history is the ruse of poetry or poetry the ruse of history is once again in doubt.

## II. Poetry's Future

The social revolution of the nineteenth century cannot take its poetry [*Poesie*] from the past but only from the future. It cannot begin with itself before it has stripped away all superstition about the past. The former revolutions required recollections of past world history in order to smother their own content. The revolution of the nineteenth century must let the dead bury their dead in order to arrive at its own content. There the phrase went beyond the content—here the content goes beyond the phrase [*Dort ging die Phrase über den Inhalt. Hier geht der Inhalt über die Phrase hinaus*]. (Marx and Engels 11:106)

Those readers who forget the wider context of these remarks (the aftermath of the failed 1848 revolutions), the text in which they appear (*The Eighteenth Brumaire of Louis Bonaparte*), or even their author (Karl Marx, age thirty-three) are still likely to recall the suggestive notion of a "poetry of the future." In varied forms, and with or without reference to Marx, this phrase is repeated in the writings of Walt Whitman, Arthur Rimbaud, Leon Trotsky, Richard Aldington, and the members of L'Internationale situationniste.[6] The content behind this phrase is at times truly poetry, a literature appropriate to a new nation (Whitman) or to the more general experience of modernity (Aldington); and at times it is the more expansive Greek sense of *poiēsis*, of an ends-oriented production that can be political as well as literary.

The latter is emphatically the case for Marx, for whom "the poetry of the future" signals the unprecedented arrival of a truly human revolution rather than a literary representation adequate to it. Indeed, Marx's invocation of the poetry of the future seems to draw its energy from the opposition of production to representation and from the privileging of the former over the latter. Poetic representation, in the form of tragic or farcical drama, has characterized every past revolution, Marx notes, as "Luther put on the mask of the Apostle Paul, the Revolution of 1789–1814 draped itself alternately in the guise of the Roman Republic and the Roman Empire, and the Revolution of 1848 knew nothing better to do than to parody, now 1789, now the revolutionary tradition of 1793–95" (Marx and Engels 11:104). And it would seem that this accretion of masks has made it impossible to distinguish reality from fiction, or original from copy. The evidence: France has pinned its hopes on Louis Bonaparte, Napoleon Bonaparte's nephew, "a caricature of the old Napoleon" (11:105) and "a serious buffoon" (11:150). Smothered, blindered, the social revolutionaries of the nineteenth century must dispense with masks; they must slough off the fictive phrase and let the revolutionary content shine forth. But does this entail their taking leave of poetry?

To answer in the affirmative is to locate Marx securely within the Hegelian line.[7] If the poetry of the future has no need for historical costumery, then it is not so different from the Hegelian "prose of thought"—which also "forsakes . . . sensuous form." Of course, for Hegel the emphasis is on poetry's sensuousness. The embodied, properly aesthetic character of poetry is what consigns it to the past. For Marx, the problem with poetry is just the opposite.

Poetic representation is mere representation, form or phrase without corporeal content, something immaterial. None of this is terribly surprising. Hegel is an idealist, while Marx is a materialist; their discussions of poetry's overcoming differ accordingly. Even so, the essential character of this overcoming remains more or less constant when we pass from the one to the other. For each thinker, it entails man's purging what is inessential—(sensuous) matter for Hegel, (ideological) form for Marx—and grasping his own history, arriving at his own content, beginning with himself.

And yet, as so many readers of *The Eighteenth Brumaire* have noted, Marx has a peculiarly difficult time letting poetic representation go. Thus, in the passage with which this section began, he punctuates his rejection of the "superstition" of historical allusion by alluding to a verse from the Gospels: "Jesus said unto him, Let the dead bury their dead: but go thou and preach the kingdom of God" (Luke 9:60); and he presents his refusal of rhetorical excess, of the excess of poetic phrase over prosaic content, through the rhetorical figure of chiasmus: "die Phrase über den Inhalt . . . der Inhalt über die Phrase" (Marx and Engels 11:106). These instances and others have inspired critics to read Marx against himself and to attend to the complicated knot that binds Marx's inability to exorcise poetry to the persistence of the literary or political past in the revolutionary present. In a text nicely titled "Homo Alludens," the contemporary critic Martin Harries writes that "if amnesia is the model for the revolutionary language that Marx imagines, allusion is the model for that language that can never be fully severed from its past" (59). Literature is the means by which the failure of the dead (or the living) to "bury the dead" asserts itself, the means by which revolutionary amnesia is reversed. Accordingly, it registers "the difficulty of even imagining any place stripped of superstition and the poetry of the past" (60). An earlier treatment of this same theme winds through Walter Benjamin's late writings, in which the future-oriented "soothsaying" characteristic of some varieties of historicism is forbidden (*SW* 4:397) and Marxism is reconfigured as a "philology" that draws revolutionary energy from what has been (*AP* N11,6).

Because they provide us with a version of historical materialism better attuned to history in general and to the complexities of cultural inheritance in particular, these revisionist readings have much to recommend them. By rejecting any future-oriented soothsaying, they pledge fealty to at least one spirit of Marx—to the Marx alleged to have stated that "whoever draws up a program for the future is a reactionary,"[8] and who took pains to distance himself from the utopian socialism of figures such as Saint-Simon, Charles Fourier, and Robert Owen. Moreover, they succeed in revealing the centrality of the aesthetic to the historical-materialist articulation of the past with the revolutionary present, a field of research that in the last couple of decades has proven especially fruitful.[9] And yet, as valuable as these readings have been, they do their work only through another practice of exclusion. Rather than follow Marx in urging his readers to forget the past, they forget the future. If the latter appears at all, it does so tarred with the brush of reactionary programs or superstitious prophecies—as something social revolutionaries would do well to forget. And this forgetting has implications for poetry as well. Cut off from the future, poetry is saved, but only so long as it remains the domain of allusion, tied to the past—to the past that persists, *pace* Hegel, but to the past nonetheless.

Preserving the past and forgetting the future need not be paired activities, however. Another relationship of past to future, and of each to poetry, is possible. We have already seen this relationship limned in Aristotle's writings, in which poetry is defined not by its specific content or by its presentation in verse but by the universal structure of its emplotment. If we follow Aristotle and treat poetry not only as a set of canonical texts drawn from the tradition but also as the means by which events achieve their universality, then the exclusive association of poetry with the past is unfounded. Past, present, and future might be thought poetically—which is to say that instead of securing the past against the future, poetry might serve to articulate them. In any case, this articulation is at least intimated in *The Eighteenth Brumaire*. Before looking more closely at this text's poeticization of history, though, we first need to isolate the future, so as to ask why this category—now denigrated for its links to program and prophecy—should appear in Marx's writings at all.

The future appears in *The Eighteenth Brumaire* because the future is in question; and the future is in question because historical progress is in question. Marx felt this problem acutely during the time of *The Eighteenth Brumaire*'s composition. Indeed, this text is the product of a crisis in Marx's historical method, one that would not be resolved (and even then, only temporarily) until the publication of the first volume of *Capital* in 1867.[10] The failure of the 1848 revolutions and Louis Bonaparte's election in December of the same year, as well as his coup in 1851, signaled to Marx that the dialectical opposition of the proletariat to the bourgeoisie could not by itself explain the movement of nineteenth-century history, and that he would have to account for "the emergence of a state that represented no one but itself and yet was able to count upon the support of an extraordinarily diverse constituency" (Stallybrass 79). These complications were exemplified in the odd figure of Bonaparte. The latter represented no one in particular, though he held the support of the "lumpenproletariat," a group that seemed to stand apart from the binarism of modern class antagonism and thus, no less than Bonaparte himself, outside of the historical order (81). As Étienne Balibar notes, "the extent of the theoretical upheavals this produced in Marx's thinking should not be underestimated. It meant abandoning the idea of 'permanent revolution,' which precisely expressed the idea of an imminent transition from class to classless society" (8). The events that occurred from 1848 through 1851 called into question the very possibility of a science of history—dialectical or other—and risked returning history to what it was for Aristotle: a disordered span of time in which "each [event] relates to the others at random."

Here it is worth pausing to note how incompatible models of history proliferate in *The Eighteenth Brumaire*, as if Marx were reaching for something that could make sense of the apparently senseless events that had unfolded since 1848. Following the breakdown of the historical dialectic, Marx notes, "society now seems to have fallen back behind its point of departure" (Marx and Engels 11:106). Indeed, if the French Revolution "moved along an ascending line"—a line of increasing radicalization, with the Constitutionalists overtaken by the Girondins, who were overtaken in turn by the Jacobins—the Revolution of 1848 is characterized by a "descending line," a "retrogressive motion" (11:124). In this model, history still moves, but it now moves backward. Or perhaps knowledge of historical progress must give way to mythical prophecies of a closed future. Discussing the failure of the constitution of the Republic, Marx writes that "Thetis, the sea goddess, prophesied to Achilles that he would die in the bloom of youth. The constitution, which, like Achilles, had its weak spot, also had, like Achilles, a presentiment that it must go to an early death" (11:117). Or history has become "a constant repetition of the same tensions and relaxations" (11:125); there is nothing new under the sun. Or history has simply lost all connection to the events that it purports to describe, such that we face a "history without events" (11:125), the dried husk of historical order.

And so on. No sooner does Marx present one of these models of history than he moves on to the next. Not one seems particularly promising as an alternative to the dialectical conception of history or provides a secure vantage from which to judge the post-1848 crises. Together, they speak to an overpowering awareness of historical disorder. In the midst of this disorder, we find Marx turning to poetry or demanding a poetry drawn from the future. But this demand only achieves its urgency because history now lacks the clear relationship to "probability or necessity" that would allow it to be characterized as poetic, which is to say that it has lost the universality that was poetry's hallmark for Aristotle and history's achievement for Hegel. This universality, secured in Marx's pre-1848 writings by the dialectical antagonism between the bourgeoisie and the proletariat, describes the orderliness of history. Additionally, it describes the fact that the future is "our" future, the effect of our past and present actions. Lost, it must be reestablished. As such, Marx's call for a poetry of the future must first be a call for a poeticization of the future, not because the future must be dressed up in the costumes of the past but because the continuity of history—past, present, and future—must be poetically reconstructed.

The questions we ought to pose, then, concern the effect of poetry on history in *The Eighteenth Brumaire*: How does poetry work against the sort of historical disorder diagnosed by Marx in the middle of the nineteenth century? How does it unite what recent events have torn asunder? How does it once again make the future ours? Again, our ability to ask these questions finds support in a tradition of critical thought on poetry and history that reaches back as far as Aristotle's *Poetics* and, more immediately, to the unstated borrowings from literary form that Royce discerned in Hegel's historical idealism. In this case, though, it proves more productive to compare Marx to one of his near contemporaries—to the romantic poet Percy Bysshe Shelley, whose 1821 "A Defence of Poetry" provides a model for thinking about a poetic future very much in line with that of Marx.

In "A Defence of Poetry," Shelley seeks to save poetry from the half-joking dismissal it received in "The Four Ages of Poetry" (1820), an essay written by his erstwhile friend Thomas Peacock. In his own essay, Peacock denigrates poetry for its failings as an instrument of social good, and he predicts that the "progress of useful art and science, and of moral and political knowledge, will continue more and more to withdraw attention from frivolous and unconducive, to solid and conducive studies." Modern poetry, he avers, will be a casualty of these transformations, as "the poetical audience will not only continually diminish in the proportion of its number to that of the rest of the reading public, but will also sink lower and lower in the comparison of intellectual acquirement" (Peacock 328). Shelley thus presents his "Defence" not only as an aesthetic justification of poetry's value but also as a social justification. As such, his radical political views are never far from the surface. Celebrating his art in words that anticipate Marx's own in their contempt for historical repetition, Shelley writes that the poet "creates anew the universe after it has been annihilated in our minds by the recurrence of impressions blunted by re-iteration. It justifies that bold and true word of Tasso: *Non merita nome di creatore, se non Iddio ed il Poeta*" (533). The poet intervenes in history *qua* repetition through his coupling of production and prediction, through something akin—but only akin—to the omnipotence and omniscience of the divine creator. And here it is worth quoting Shelley at length:

> Poets, according to the circumstances of the age and nation in which they appeared, were called, in the earlier epochs of the world, legislators, or prophets: a poet essentially comprises and unites both these characters. For he not only beholds intensely the present as it is, and discovers those laws according to which present things ought to be ordered, but he beholds the future in the present, and his thoughts are the germs of the flower and the fruit of latest time. Not that I assert poets to be prophets in the gross sense of the word, or that they can foretell the form as surely as they foreknow the spirit of events: such is the pretence of superstition, which would make poetry an attribute of prophecy, rather than prophecy an attribute of poetry. (513)

Like Marx, the avowedly atheist Shelley eschews "superstition." It is not the case, he argues, that the poet knows the actual form of future events, though "he beholds intensely the present as it is, and discovers those laws according to which present things ought to be ordered." In so doing, he achieves a knowledge of the "spirit of events" that can be transposed from present to future.

How is this possible without recourse to soothsaying, to prophecy "in the gross sense of the word"? The answer is to be found in Shelley's claim that the poet "comprises and unites" his roles as prophet and legislator. Two and a half centuries earlier, in his own "Defense of Poetry" (1579, 1595), Philip Sidney had already noted of poetry that "both Roman and Greek gave divine names unto it, the one of 'prophesying,' the other of 'making'" (100). Poetry is a "making"—again, in the Greek sense of *poiēsis*—and the poet is a *vates*, a prophet or diviner. When Shelley describes the poet as uniting the roles of legislator and prophet, he does little more than modernize Sidney's earlier observation. "A poet," Shelley notes, "participates in the divine nature as regards providence no less than as regards creation" (514). As to the latter, the poet does not create out of nothing, but his thoughts are still the "germs of the flower and the fruit of latest time" (517). As the "fruit of latest time," poetry is engendered by the seeds of what preceded it; and as "the germs of the flower," it is the source of future forms. These forms are poetry, certainly, but more generally they are "those laws according to which present things ought to be ordered"—and future things as well. The poet "comprises and unites" the roles of prophet and legislator because he produces the order, the laws, of present and future history. In the tradition of Vico's *verum et factum convertuntur*, then, his knowledge is a "maker's knowledge." The poet knows the spirit of events because he produces this spirit out of himself.

Marx, "who understood the poets as well as he understood the philosophers and economists" and who once said of Shelley that "he was essentially a revolutionist, and . . . would always have been one of the advanced guard of socialism," was almost certainly familiar with Shelley's "Defence" (qtd. in Warren 130). And Marx was not alone in his endorsement of Shelley's radical credentials. In the 1840s, Friedrich Engels entertained plans to publish a German edition of Shelley's collected writings—a project that was interrupted by the historical crises addressed above—and in *The Condition of the Working Class in England* (1845) he praises Shelley as "the genius, the prophet" (Marx and Engels 4:538).[11] We can note here the proximity of Engels's language to Shelley's own: the poet is once again a "prophet"; and as a "genius"—from the Latin *gignere*—the poet is also one who *engenders*, who produces. Additionally, in the nineteenth-century German context, Engels's use of "genius" cannot help but allude to Immanuel Kant's well-known definition—foundational for the romanticism that Shelley himself inherited—of the genius as he who prescribes the rule or "law" (*Regel*) to art (*CJ* 309). The genius legislates.

Regardless of whether Shelley exerted any actual influence on Marx's understanding of the relationship between poetry and history at the time of *The Eighteenth Brumaire*'s composition, Shelley's "Defence" does help us to see what the "poetry of the future" might entail in Marx's writings. Most basically, it points to the coordination of production and knowledge, of "legislation" and "prophecy." Encountering the lawlessness of historical events, the social revolutionaries of the nineteenth century act as *poets*—in Shelley's as well as in Marx's expansive sense. That is to say, they undertake the poetic labor of engendering a world open to historical knowledge; in doing so, they come to know the order of the history that they produce—they "arrive at their own content." As a linguistic artifact, *The Eighteenth Brumaire* itself reflects this poeticization of history in the only way it can: through its interpolation into the historical events it recounts of rhetorical figures and literary allusions.

I am not certain that this binding of history to poetry, or this transformation of the revolutionary into the poet, persists in Marx's writings; it is, at least, much more difficult to argue that it survives in *Capital*. My point is only that it appears in Marx's texts at the very moment when the dialectical ordering of history is called into question. At the moment when history seems most in danger of an irremediable dispersal, Marx charges poetry with what was poetry's original task: to lend disordered events the universality at which poetry, as well as history in the modern sense, aims. In this coupling of poetry and history, poetry puts history in the service of the revolutionary future.

Marx does not choose poetry over history. He makes use of poetry while keeping his eye fixed on the reality of historical events. Minimally, this attention to what is actually the case is the condition of materialist historiography. When Marx turns to poetry in a moment of crisis, however, he registers a tension that would only intensify as the nineteenth century progressed. This tension is between, on the one hand, a history that could only present the world as it is or was and, on the other hand, the demand for a transformation of this world. This demand goes beyond the insistence that history order events according to probability or necessity, that it exhibit some rational order. Though the historical confusion of post-1848 Europe certainly demanded order, this order had to be one in which revolutionary activity was possible. The need that *The Eighteenth Brumaire* registers, then, is for a history that would serve not only the past but also the future. As in Shelley's understanding of poetry, this would be a history in which one could come to know the world that he or she produced; but it would also be a history in which the production of a new world would be conceivable in the first place.

### III. *Zukunftsphilologie!*

In 1872, Friedrich Nietzsche published his first book, *The Birth of Tragedy out of the Spirit of Music*, a study of the rise of tragedy from Dionysian ritual to the dramas of Aeschylus, its double betrayal by Euripides and Socrates, and its rebirth in the music of Richard Wagner. Soon after its publication, the young German philologist Ulrich von Wilamowitz-Moellendorff composed a scathing response, "Philology of the Future!" ("Zukunftsphilologie!"; 1872). Wilamowitz-Moellendorff's choice of titles for his polemical pamphlet was most likely a play on the title of Wagner's 1861 "Music of the Future" ("Zukunfts-musik")—itself Wagner's echoing of his own 1849 "The Artwork of the Future" ("Das Kunstwerk der Zukunft")—and so a mocking reference to Nietzsche's then membership in the Wagner cult. Wilamowitz-Moellendorff's target was not the company Nietzsche kept, however, but the sloppiness of his philological method, his choosing of metaphysical speculation over historical research, his dreaming of the future rather than attending to the past. Since he apparently has no interest in the science of philology, Wilamowitz-Moellendorff averred, Nietzsche ought to "step down from the lectern" at the University of Basel:

> He may gather tigers and panthers around his knees but not Germany's philo-
> logically interested youth who are supposed to learn—in the asceticism of self-
> denying work—to look everywhere for nothing but the truth, to free their judg-
> ment through deliberate devotion, so that classical antiquity will provide them
> with the unique and eternal insight that only the favor of the muses promises,
> and that only classical antiquity can guarantee in its abundance and purity. (24)

In 1879, Nietzsche would step down from his post at Basel, though not as a result of Wilamowitz-Moellendorff's challenge.[12] And in 1886, he would publish his own critique of *The Birth of Tragedy*, though his characterization of the work as "ponderous, embarrassing, image-mad and image-confused, sentimental" would bear little relation to Wilamowitz-Moellendorff's more sober and scholarly dismissal (*BT* 18). In the years following the dispute, Wilamowitz-Moellendorff would become one of the most respected philologists in Germany. Nietzsche would become *Nietzsche*. And this is where the story ought to end.

The story persists, though, and it persists because Wilamowitz-Moellendorff's insult—*Zukunftsphilologie*—can be taken as a cipher for its target's future projects. After the publication of *The Birth of Tragedy*, and however unconsciously, Nietzsche would struggle to make himself equal to the letter if not the spirit of Wilamowitz-Moellendorff's charge. He would insist on locating his work under the sign of the untimely (*Unzeitgemäße*) and would carry out his philological or "genealogical" forays into the past with an eye toward the future. So, in one of the few places where he pauses to reflect on the significance of his philological training, the second of his *Untimely Meditations* (1874), Nietzsche writes the following:

> Only so far as I am the nursling of more ancient times, especially the Greek,
> could I come to have such untimely experiences about myself as a child of the
> present age. That much I must be allowed to grant myself on the grounds of my

profession as a classical philologist. For I do not know what meaning classical philology would have for our age if not to have an untimely effect within it, that is, to act against the age and so have an effect on the age to the advantage, it is to be hoped, of a coming age. (*AD* 8)

Philology here is already in the service of the future, but only insofar as it disrupts the present, producing within the latter "an untimely effect" to the benefit "of a coming age."

It is the desire to produce this untimely effect—from the past, in the present, and for the future—that puts Nietzsche and his philology of the future in dialogue with what I have described in the preceding section of this Introduction as the poetry of the future. In both cases, what is at stake is a kind of literary-linguistic labor carried out on history, one that ought to bring history in line with radically innovative artistic or political goals. In this sense, the second of Nietzsche's *Untimely Meditations*, focusing as it does "On the Advantage and Disadvantage of History for Life," is a good place to look for this future philology's unfolding. By examining the relationship of history to life, this text also addresses the relationship of history to art. The latter, for Nietzsche, presents man with his "highest metaphysical" task and is, thus, finally synonymous with will and with life. Before turning to this text, though, it will be worthwhile to examine more closely Nietzsche's own understanding of the critical role of his philology.

Wilamowitz-Moellendorff's point in "Zukunftsphilologie!" is not that Nietzsche is doing a different sort of philology but that he is failing to do philology at all, that he has betrayed philology for the sake of unmoored speculation. In response, Nietzsche might lay claim to Vico's earlier and more capacious definition—"By philology, I mean the science of everything that depends on human volition" (Vico 6)—and so resist the argument that philology is only or even essentially the science of written texts.[13] Whatever Nietzsche understands by philology, he clearly has no desire to limit himself to making claims about the texts of classical antiquity. Even in *The Birth of Tragedy*, which, despite Wilamowitz-Moellendorff's indictments, is the closest he ever came to writing a proper work of classical scholarship, Nietzsche moves freely between an analysis of classical texts and a symptomatology of the present.

Despite his faith in the broad reach of philology, however, and despite his occasional impatience with the sort of scholarly diligence that Wilamowitz-Moellendorff prescribes, Nietzsche does retain in his own philological practice an attention to the specifically linguistic character of his objects. Indeed, it is this attention that lets his philology function as a critical tool, for he detects in modern culture a layering of linguistic determinations. Turning to these de-terminations, he affirms the grand scope of the Viconian notion of philology while maintaining that "everything that depends on human volition" might be submitted to an analysis informed by linguistic scholarship. The most familiar example of this approach in action is the discussion of "*Schuld*"—the German term for "guilt" as well as for "debt"—that Nietzsche develops in *On the Geneal-ogy of Morality* (1887). A more programmatic treatment of the critical potential of philology occurs earlier, however, in a short essay written a year after *The Birth of Tragedy* but unpublished during Nietzsche's lifetime, "On Truth and Lying in a Non-Moral Sense."

In "On Truth and Lying," the linguistic basis of human experience is made explicit. "What," Nietzsche asks, "is truth?" His answer:

> A mobile army of metaphors, metonymies, anthropomorphisms, in short, a sum of human relations which have been subjected to poetic and rhetorical inten-sification, translation, and decoration, and which, after they have been in use for a long time, strike a people as firmly established, canonical, and binding; truths are illusions of which we have forgotten that they are illusions, metaphors which have become worn by frequent use and have lost all sensuous vigour, coins which, having lost their stamp, are now regarded as metal and no longer as coins. (TL 146)

What appear to us as concepts with some legitimate purchase on the real world—on the "thing-in-itself" (144)—are in fact the products of "artistic translations" (147). These translations occur, Nietzsche explains, when sensory data pass from the world to the mind of the observer and are then transformed into the stuff of verbal expression: "[T]he stimulation of a nerve is translated into an image: first metaphor! The image is then imitated by a sound: second metaphor!" (144). Translation is necessary because the stimulation of a nerve in no way resembles the image that it engenders, just as the image bears no neces-sary relationship to the word that expresses it. This movement from world to word, that is, the process of concept formation or translation, only occurs as a series of catachrestic—or as Nietzsche writes, "metaphorical"—leaps. The result is the presence of "truths" that bear only the most tenuous relationship to any mind- or language-independent reality.

Nietzsche's understanding of the process of concept formation maintains a philosophical basis in modern, Kantian epistemology—and specifically in Kant's claim that our concepts are produced through the spontaneous activity of the understanding rather than being found ready-made in the world.[14] Nietzsche diverges from Kant, however, by likening the creative aspect of this process to the activity of the poet. Rather than produce concepts, the spontaneous subject produces "metaphors," which only become concepts once their origins in artistic creation have been forgotten. Whereas for Kant and his progeny the work of empirical concept formation is effected according to a complicated set of law-governed cognitive processes, processes shared by all finite, rational creatures, Nietzsche, by describing the "middle sphere" between subject and object as the purview of poetry (TL 148), cannot help but inject into these processes an element of caprice.

The problems that this rewriting of epistemology invites are easy to discern. For example, the "empirical realism" with which Kant balanced his own transcendental idealism (*CPR* A375) cannot be maintained absent any necessary relationship between the subject's cognitive-linguistic activities and the stuff of the object world. The gap between subject and object, like the gap between different subjects' experiences, turns out to be unbridgeable, and skepticism seems the only possible response. Nietzsche notes, however, that we do not under normal circumstances experience the world as the product of individual acts of artistic creation; indeed, he writes,

> only by forgetting this primitive world of metaphor, only by virtue of the fact that a mass of images, which originally flowed in a hot, liquid stream from the primal power of the human imagination, has become hard and rigid, only because of the invisible faith that *this* sun, *this* window, *this* table is a truth in itself—in short only because man forgets himself as a subject, and indeed as an artistically creative subject—does man live with some degree of peace, security, and consistency; if he could escape for just a moment from the prison walls of this faith, it would mean the end of his "consciousness of self" [*Selbstbewußtsein*]. (TL 148)

The implication of the last claim—that man would lose his "consciousness of self" if he were to remember his own artistic-creative role in concept formation—is that the ego is itself the result of one of the "anthropomorphisms" that serve in Nietzsche's "mobile army" of rhetorical figures. We can say "we" or "I" only insofar as this anthropomorphism is securely in place, and so only insofar as the artistic sources of our concepts and of our selves are forgotten.

We will return to this issue in a moment. First, though, let us pause here to note why, given this vision of the workings of human knowledge, philology should appear to Nietzsche as such a powerful tool of critique. Our concepts

and even our selves are the products of artistic—and specifically, rhetorical—
operations, operations that have, over time, become sedimented, in the very
same sense in which Emerson, in a text Nietzsche must have known well, could
describe our conceptual language as a "fossil poetry" (190). To do philology,
then, to exhume the primitive sources of our conceptual language, is already to
do epistemology, the kind of critical epistemology practiced by Kant when he
set out to determine the conditions of possible experience. And Nietzsche's philology ought to go further than Kant's own epistemology, for the latter takes as
natural the sedimented concept and so leaves unremarked the essentially artistic
operations that lie behind it. Nietzsche does not stop at the concept; he does
not even stop at the metaphor. Instead, he follows our concepts, our metaphors,
back to the primordial "drive to form metaphors, that fundamental human drive,
which cannot be left out of consideration for even a second without also leaving
out human beings themselves" (TL 151). This drive will go by a number of names
in Nietzsche's writings until in 1883 he settles on the term "will to power."[15]

And yet the "truth" that philology reveals—the truth of creativity, art, and
will—is not a truth that humanity can hope to embrace, for it would put an
end to humanity's "peace, security, and consistency," and finally to its "sense of
self." The individual may be essentially a poet—the original source of "metaphors, metonymies, anthropomorphisms"—but he lives in the world only by
forgetting this fact. The knowledge that Nietzsche's philology reveals, then, the
knowledge of our poetic being-in-the-world, proves incompatible with life.
And so, at this moment in Nietzsche's writings, and despite its considerable
critical force, Nietzsche's philology is still a philology of the past. By this I mean
that his philology reveals to humanity the origins of its knowledge in something
that exceeds both rational knowledge and the human subject, but it cannot help
humanity to mobilize this revelation for any future-directed project. Humanity
cannot coexist with the knowledge that philology provides. Somewhat paradoxically, then, one lives only by forgetting the forces that are the source of life.

Less than a year after completing "On Truth and Lying," Nietzsche turns again
to knowledge and forgetting in the second of his *Untimely Meditations*, "On the
Advantage and Disadvantage of History for Life." He presents this study as a
critical rejoinder to the historical consciousness dominating nineteenth-century
Germany. It is, however, no less an attempt to understand how any historical
practice—including his own philological method—might be put in the service
of life, and so in the service of the future, how it might resist what he diagnoses
as "a kind of closing out of the accounts of life for humankind" (14). Now, at least

on the surface, the threat posed by history to life is altogether different from the threat posed to life by Nietzsche's own philology. Where philology finally reduces the individual to unknowable forces, history overburdens the individual with objective facts. The effects of these two practices are, however, essentially the same: "[T]he individual becomes timid and unsure and may no longer believe in himself: he sinks into himself, into his own inner being, which here only means: into the heaped up chaos of knowledge which fails to have an external effect, of teaching which does not become life" (29).

In the second *Meditation*, Nietzsche toys with a response to the weight of historical knowledge comparable to the forgetfulness prescribed in "On Truth and Lying." This response is modeled in the "blissful blindness" of the child who "[plays] between the fences of past and future" and so lives "unhistorically" (9), or in the undivided existence of the animal that "goes into the present like a number without leaving a curious fraction" (9). Nietzsche rejects, however, the extreme alternative of "unhistorical" existence; or, more exactly, he opposes to the latter's wholesale negation another relationship to history: "Only if history can bear being transformed into a work of art," Nietzsche writes, "may it perhaps preserve instincts or even rouse them" (39). Only as art does history serve life.

Nietzsche describes the perspective for which history becomes art as "superhistorical," a third term that interrupts the dyad "historical-unhistorical." "By the word 'unhistorical,'" Nietzsche writes, "I denote the art and the strength of being able to *forget* and enclose oneself in a limited *horizon*; 'superhistorical' I call the powers which guide the eye away from becoming and toward that which gives existence an eternal and stable character, toward *art* and *religion*" (62). The unhistorical serves life by resisting—by forgetting—those aspects of the past that prevent the new from appearing. Conversely, the superhistorical raises the becoming of the past or the present to the level of eternal being by reimagining it as art or as something like the art-religion of the ancient Greeks. It describes, therefore, an operation of selection, one that must be at work in every instance of (historical) remembering as well as in every instance of (unhistorical) forgetting, if these acts are to issue in anything but an overwhelming assemblage of historical facts or the oblivion of an animalistic existence.[16] This power of selection, this ability to lift and preserve an event that would otherwise be lost to the flow of time, raises superhistorical recollection over a historical recollection that too often reveals only the "false, crude, inhuman, absurd, [and] violent" (39).

Nietzsche remains silent on the specifics of this superhistorical transformation of history into art; nonetheless, we are in a good position to make some inferences about the form that it must take, as well as about its desired effects. First, all historical knowledge—the historical knowledge produced by a Ranke or a Hegel no less than the superhistorical knowledge that Nietzsche prescribes—is the outcome of the same poetic processes laid bare in "On Truth and Lying." The so-called "laws of history" (*AD* 55), like all "laws of truth," exist only through the "legislation of language" (*Gesetzgebung der Sprache*; TL 143). The "poetic elaboration" of history that Nietzsche deems superhistorical (*AD* 36) differs, however, from other forms of historical representation insofar as it recognizes itself as poetic. This recognition is likely to produce pain in the great majority of humanity—it is, after all, essentially the same unendurable knowledge of the real source of conceptual truths described in "On Truth and Lying"—and Nietzsche reserves it for humanity's "highest specimens" (53).[17] These are the individuals capable of returning historical truth to the terrain of "metaphors, metonymies, anthropomorphisms" and so rewriting history as poetry.

Second, the poetic presentation of history is not merely (aesthetically) preferable to the "scientific" or "objective" one. The stuff of history is not transformed through a superhistorical practice into a work of art for the sole reason of someone's wanting to witness something beautiful or lasting. It is transformed in the name of the creative instincts. Poetic history is not to be written from the point of view of the spectator, then, who would judge it to be beautiful or ugly; rather, it is to be written from the point of view of the artist.[18] Or perhaps more exactly, it is to be written from a notion of art in which the assertion "this is beautiful" refers to the ability of a work to quicken the artist's vital impulses and encourage the production of new works. The success of superhistorical history can be decided only on the basis of its ability to present to the artist a historical environment in which the production of new art is possible.

And this is the task of the philologist of the future: to produce, poetically, a history in which poetic production—including his own historical-poetic production—is possible. Insofar as he accepts this task, he accepts at the same time his role as the poet of the future. And so, through the intermediary of history, he enables poetry to rejoin itself. Poetry as a means of ordering history, or as the articulation of knowing and making, prophecy and legislation, history and life, establishes itself as its own condition of possibility. History becomes the detour through which poetry begets poetry.

## Conclusion

I began this Introduction with some remarks on the entanglement of poetry with history. In Nietzsche's writings, this entanglement seems to achieve a kind of self-consciousness, a self-consciousness that appears as well among the next generation of artists and philosophers. By drawing a relatively short line from Nietzsche to Eliot or to Benjamin, then, or by drawing a longer line from Aristotle to Marx or to Nietzsche, we perhaps make explicit the persistence of a problem—the problem of composing the poetry or the prose of the future—a problem that exceeds the limits of any particular (literary-)historical period, and pertains (how could it not?) to the very question of periodization. In examining this problem, in trying to trace its historical development, we can hardly avoid suggesting other problems. The problem of filiation (that is, of influence or of one's debt to the past); the related problem of the tradition (not only of what it would mean to lay claim to the tradition but also of what it would mean to interrupt or redirect it); the more general (and probably unsolvable) problem of historical causality or directionality (which will, of course, haunt Nietzsche's later thought and which continues to worry Western Marxism)—these are precisely the problems at stake in Eliot's and Benjamin's writings. It is premature to say that Eliot or Benjamin or European modernism more generally inherits from any particular literary or critical or philosophical tradition a notion of the contest between historical and poetic form. Matters of tradition or inheritance are, again, at issue. But do we have better terms? For now, let us just say that Eliot and Benjamin enter the fray at a critical moment.

# GATHERING DUST, T. S. ELIOT

# LYRIC

**ON 30 SEPTEMBER 1914**, Ezra Pound wrote to Harriet Monroe, the founding editor of *Poetry: A Magazine of Verse*, the following lines about his new discovery:

> I was jolly well right about Eliot. He has sent in the best poem I have yet had or seen from an American. PRAY GOD IT BE NOT A SINGLE AND UNIQUE SUCCESS. . . . He has taken it back to get it ready for the press and you shall have it in a few days. He is the only American I know of who has made what I can call adequate preparation for writing. He has actually trained himself *and* modernized himself *on his own*. The rest of the promising young have done one or the other but never both (most of the swine have done neither). It is such a comfort to meet a man and not have to tell him to wash his face, wipe his feet, and remember the date (1914) on the calendar. (Letters 80)

T. S. Eliot had completed "the best poem yet seen from an American"—"The Love Song of J. Alfred Prufrock"—in 1911, roughly a year before Pound declared the birth of imagism. "Prufrock" would finally appear in *Poetry*'s June 1915 issue, then a few months later in Pound's *Catholic Anthology 1914–1915* (1915), and then again as the first poem in Eliot's *Prufrock and Other Observations* (1917).[1] Pound's letter to Monroe is noteworthy not only because it attests to Pound's ear for talent, nor because it initiates the productive relationship between Pound and Eliot that would culminate in *The Waste Land*, but because it augurs, in the figure of Eliot that Pound sketches, a shift in the character of literary modernism. As Pound presents him to Monroe, Eliot appears as the poet of "both/and." He has both "trained himself" in the tradition—mastered the poetry of the past—and "modernized himself." He has both learned his manners, which bind him to what was, and recognized the "date on the calendar," the present moment, which makes its own demands on the poet. For Pound, who in 1914 still felt himself pulled between his roles as translator of past forms and as avant-gardist in the style of his friends Wyndham Lewis and Henri Gaudier-Brzeska,[2] Eliot, in his articulation of history and poetry, represented a position that Pound himself might occupy—and that modernism might occupy as well. Already in 1914, then, Pound could glimpse in Eliot's individual talent a map of modernism's trajectory from rupture to historical reconciliation.

Much has been written on this trajectory, and on the importance of Eliot's poetics within it. Three-quarters of a century after Pound announced Eliot's arrival, Michael Levenson would conclude his *Genealogy of Modernism* with a discussion of the conciliatory role that Eliot had played during the period. Unlike much of the London avant-garde, Levenson notes, "Eliot himself had not joined the attack on tradition. He had not chanted with the Vorticists that 'Life is the Past and the Future. The Present is Art.' He thus entered the debate at an opportune moment to assert the need for the regenerating example of past forms" (158). Eliot arrived slightly late to the London scene, missing by a couple years the "futurist moment" that had marked the poetry and the person of Pound; but Eliot arrived with the benefit of a historical perspective, and this allowed him to correct the overweening ambitions of his contemporaries. With Eliot, then, literary modernism became sadder but wiser. It became historical.

Historians of modernism, whether they celebrate Eliot for his renewal of a movement that appeared destined for exhaustion or decry the deadening effects of his conservatism, at least agree on his success in uniting modern poetry and history. In these readings, the stress tends to fall less on the specific themes or formal characteristics of Eliot's writings than on the way his writings—and most typically, his critical writings—were taken up by the next generation of literary scholars, by the American New Critics and, most essentially, by F. R. Leavis. In what follows, my approach to Eliot's writings shall be somewhat different. I do not intend to challenge the claim that Eliot turned poetry toward history and so returned modernism to the great tradition of Western literature from which the former had seemingly sought to escape. For better or worse, this is Eliot's legacy. I do, however, want to resist the tendency to conflate this legacy with Eliot's actual project, at least as this project unfolded in the writings up to and including *The Waste Land*. I want to resist, then, the tendency to read Eliot's turn to the past as an essentially restorative gesture, as a traditionalist's attempt to smooth over the cracks in cultural history that had been spreading since the second half of the nineteenth century. My feeling is that this rendering of Eliot's project errs insofar as it treats as a solution what was, for Eliot, a—and perhaps *the*—problem: history. If Eliot turned to the past, to history, where so many of his contemporaries remained focused on the present, he did so not because history could be counted on to recontain the troubling fact of rupture; rather, he did so to ask what model of history could make his own poetic practice possible. And this entailed a thoroughgoing critique of a historicism that was, no less than romanticism, an essential part of the nineteenth century's legacy. This critique reached its zenith in 1922, with the publication of *The Waste Land*. Eliot's so-called "traditionalism" is only its popular face.

My hope is that by separating Eliot's alleged traditionalism from Eliot's critique of historical form, I will be able to lay the groundwork for two complementary projects. The first concerns Eliot's poetic production during his early London years. Against those readers who treat Eliot's turn to history during this period as the first stirrings of the classicism, royalism, and Anglo-Catholicism that would become synonymous with his work following his 1927 conversion, I want to shift the focus to what Eliot did to history. To anticipate the argument to follow: Eliot did not go to history for the "regenerating example of past forms," at least not at first; rather, he turned to history out of an awareness of the limits that it sets to poetic accomplishment and to attempt a poetic reimagining of history, one that might allow him to exceed these limits. Eliot's lyrical, satirical, and mythical articulations of literary history are where we find this reimagining carried out. The second project is of a piece with the broader concerns of this book. I want to make the case for including Eliot in a larger tradition of poetic thinking about history, a tradition that I sketched in the preceding chapter and that includes the works of—among others—Marx, Nietzsche, and (the subject of this book's second half) Walter Benjamin.

This chapter will address Eliot's struggle with history as it unfolded between, roughly, 1910 and 1920, between the composition of "Prufrock" and the publication of "Gerontion." The decade is a significant one in Eliot's career not only because it saw considerable development in Eliot's poetic technique—from the early emulation of Laforgue's symbolism to a more austere style that was, as Wyndham Lewis remarked, formally "school of Ezra" (*Blasting and*

*Bombardiering* 286)[3]—but also because it found Eliot articulating the theory of tradition that would inform his critical and creative mobilizations of literary history. With the publication in 1920 of *The Sacred Wood*, a collection of essays that includes the now canonical "Tradition and the Individual Talent" (1919), as well as more specific studies of Dante, Jonson, Blake, Swinburne, and others, Eliot secured his position as a poet-critic, making good on his own claim in "The Perfect Critic" that "the critic and the creative artist should frequently be the same person" (*SW* 9). This ideal unity of critic and artist is only the first of many synthetic horizons associated with Eliot's project. It anticipates and supports the synthesis of literary history ostensibly attempted in *The Waste Land* as well as (more mediately) the synthesis of European culture endorsed in Eliot's last writings.

Insofar as he tries to produce something like what Pound would come to call "a poem including history," Eliot does participate in a synthetic project. Nonetheless, I am less interested in those moments in Eliot's writings of personal or historical synthesis than in the moments of division that serve as their enabling condition. Throughout the 1910s, Eliot tends to characterize the poetic ordering of literary history not only as a synthesis of diverse works but also as a practice whose success depends on its being preceded by a division, a division that is inscribed in the consciousness or the life of the "mature poet" and that is reduplicated in the poet's own literary creations.[4] At this early stage in his career, Eliot associates this division of the poetic consciousness with the form of the lyric in particular. In the next chapter, I shall examine the limitations of this form as a means of managing literary history and the way that an awareness of these limitations forced Eliot to shift from a lyrical to a satirical mode. For now, I want to provide something like a genealogy of the theory of lyrical division elaborated in Eliot's early critical writings and exemplified in "The Love Song of J. Alfred Prufrock" and "Gerontion."

Now, understanding the importance of lyrical division to the problem of historical representation will necessitate my asking the question of how history became a problem for Eliot in the first place. Answering this question will require my looking into Eliot's own personal history. My reason for doing so is not that I believe that Eliot's biography's provides the ultimate key to his writings. Rather, I hope to show that Eliot treated his own person as an occasion for literary experimentation and thus that his much-remarked anxieties, for example, might themselves be taken as what the Russian Formalists used to call a "motivation of the device."[5]

## I. Prufrock and His Problems

Pound's exhortation to Monroe regarding "Prufrock"—"PRAY GOD IT BE NOT A SINGLE AND UNIQUE SUCCESS"—is pure hyperbole, designed to signal to a potential sponsor the importance of Eliot's accomplishment. Nonetheless, before his poem was even published, Eliot was himself doing a bit of praying, struggling to match the achievement that Pound would herald. In a letter to his friend Conrad Aiken from September of 1914, he laments the fact that "I have done nothing good since J. A[lfred] P[rufrock] and writhe in impotence" (*L* 1:63). Two years later, and only a few months after "Prufrock" had finally appeared in print, Eliot confesses to his older brother Henry that "I often feel that 'J.A.P.' is a swan song, but I never mention the fact because Vivienne is so exceedingly anxious that I shall equal it, and would be bitterly disappointed if I do not" (1:165–166). And in a letter to Mary Hutchinson, this one dated July 1917, Eliot expresses his dismay that, with another republication on the way, "Prufrock" is likely to appear to his friends as *"réchauffé"*—"they are tired of waiting for something better from me" (1:209). Eliot was not yet twenty-eight years old when he sent this last letter to Hutchinson, hardly aged for a poet. Nonetheless six years had passed since he had completed his first mature lyric, and though it would not be entirely accurate to call this period a "dry spell," Eliot's correspondences leave little doubt that he experienced it as such. References to his literary struggles intermingle with descriptions of ailments both physical—"My teeth are falling to pieces, I have to wear spectacles to read, and from time to time I am contorted with rheumatism" (1:211)—and psychological—"I have been going through one of those nervous sexual attacks which I suffer from when alone in a city" (1:82). Though some of these complaints betray Eliot's youthful attempts to depict himself as a doomed pessimist in the mold of Rimbaud or Laforgue, evidence from Eliot's later life confirms that the psychological ailments, at least, were real—as was the fear that, almost before his career had begun, he had completed his "swan song."

Over the years, Eliot's social and sexual anxieties have received considerable attention from critics (and, admittedly, it is hard to ignore Eliot's description of his writer's block as the experience of "writhing in impotence" or his fear that his inability to perform poetically will disappoint his wife).[6] There is something to be said, however, for refusing to reduce literary struggle too quickly to psychosexual conflict and for taking Eliot at his word when he maintains that his real fear is that he will be unable to equal "Prufrock." Doing so helps us to see how, for Eliot at this early stage in his career, two senses of the past—the literary and the personal—become entangled. How does this occur? Some years back, Walter Jackson Bate wrote of "the remorseless deepening of self-consciousness, before the rich and intimidating legacy of the past" as one of the defining marks of modern literature (4). Here, Bate had in mind the anxiety that results when the poet stands before the masterworks of the literary tradition. In his letters to his family and his friends, Eliot describes a similarly "remorseless deepening of self-consciousness." In this case, however, the source of his anxiety—the "rich and intimidating legacy" with which he must contend—is found closer to home. It is not the demand that he become the equal of Dante or of Shakespeare that causes Eliot to writhe; rather, it is the demand that he become the equal of the man he was only a few years ago, the man who completed the best poem Ezra Pound had yet seen from an American. In sum, Eliot has watched his own accomplishment, "Prufrock," mutate into an expectation or a demand—"Do it again! Do it better!" And so, before he can hope to struggle with the greater literary past, he must find a way to manage his own past as poet.

An acute awareness of this problem informs what must appear in hindsight as one of Eliot's earliest reflections on poetic impersonality. In the same letter to Aiken in which he regrets his "impotence," Eliot waxes philosophical on the nature of his troubles and suggests a possible solution:

> Does anything kill as petty worries do? And in America we worry all the time. That, in fact, is I think the great use of suffering, if it's *tragic* suffering—it takes you away from yourself—and petty suffering does exactly the reverse, and kills your inspiration. I think now that all my good stuff was done before I had begun to worry—three years ago. I sometimes think that it would be better just to be a clerk in a post office with nothing to worry about—but the consciousness of having made a failure of one's life. Or a millionaire, ditto. The thing is to be able to look at one's life as though it were somebody's else—(I much prefer to say somebody else's). That is difficult in England, almost impossible in America. . . . Anyway, it's interesting to cut yourself to pieces once in a while, and wait to see if the fragments will sprout. (*L* 1:63)

Again, Eliot dates the beginning of his "petty worries" to 1911, three years before he composed these lines and so almost from the moment that he completed "Prufrock."[7] As a remedy for these worries, which "kill inspiration," he prescribes raising his "petty suffering" up to the level of tragedy or smothering it with the distractions of everyday life. Each approach "takes you away from yourself" and so suppresses what Eliot would later call "the man who suffers" for the good of "the mind which creates" (*SW* 31). Eliot figures this process as a self-division, relying on a metaphor—"it's interesting to cut yourself to pieces once in a while, and wait to see if the fragments will sprout"—that would return nearly a decade later in the first section of *The Waste Land*: "That corpse you planted last year in your garden, / Has it begun to sprout?" (71–72). In its earlier form, however, this image of fecundity through fragmentation seems designed to explain why Eliot had to cut himself off from the land of his birth, America, where the ability "to look at one's life as though it were . . . somebody else's" proves "almost impossible." He had to cut himself free, then, from "T. Stearns Eliot," the American poet who wrote "The Love Song of J. Alfred Prufrock."

Eliot describes in his letter to Aiken an operation to be performed not on his poetry but on his person—a "[cutting] into pieces" as a way of cutting himself free from his past and, fundamentally, from "Prufrock," which had come to weigh like a nightmare on his brain. He would try a number of techniques—in addition to leaving the United States, he would also experiment with writing in French (*L* 1:194). The operation would prove complicated, however, and not only because "Prufrock" was such a significant accomplishment, one that Eliot could hardly entirely desire to forget, but also because both the paralyzing anxieties that Eliot details and the solution of a therapeutic self-division that Eliot prescribes are prefigured, however obscurely, in the poem. Indeed, "Prufrock" can be read as a kind of dramatization *avant la lettre* of Eliot's struggle with his own personal history, "Prufrock" included. Thus Eliot's cutting himself free from "Prufrock" entails as well his cleaving to it, or at least to a certain conception of cutting free figured in the poem. To see how this is the case, we need to turn to the poem itself.

Most basically, "Prufrock" presents the fragmentary inner life of an individual incapable of passing from contemplation to action. The first stanza reads:

Let us go then, you and I,
When the evening is spread out against the sky
Like a patient etherized upon a table;
Let us go, through certain half-deserted streets,
The muttering retreats
Of restless nights in one-night cheap hotels
And sawdust restaurants with oyster-shells:
Streets that follow like a tedious argument
Of insidious intent

To lead you to an overwhelming question . . .

Oh, do not ask, "What is it?"

Let us go and make our visit. (1–12)

These lines are preceded by an epigraph taken from canto 27 of Dante's *Inferno*, which, in addition to framing the poem's modern setting as a realm of eternal torment, encourages us to take the "you and I" of the first line as the heirs of Virgil and Dante, set off on some great journey. The lines that follow, "through certain half-deserted streets," progress toward a kairotic moment, "an overwhelming question." But this question is neither posed—at least not explicitly—nor answered. And so the poem introduces what will be a recurring structure, one in which the eponymous speaker approaches what ought to be a critical juncture—"Should I . . . / Have the strength to force the moment to its crisis?" (79–80)—only to interrupt this movement, question its significance—"And would it have been worth it, after all . . . ?" (87)—and begin again.

In short, J. Alfred Prufrock suffers under the "spell of indecision." The phrase comes from Franco Moretti, who, in an essay of the same name, describes a typically modernist ideology in which "life as 'actuality' has become far less meaningful than that parallel form of life, life as 'possibility'" (31); and so modern literature is charged with mobilizing all of the techniques at its disposal to maintain itself in the realm of the possible, to ward off the moment of decision. As evidence, Moretti quotes without comment the following lines from "Prufrock" (which are, presumably, so plainly symptomatic of the modern malaise that they need no explication): "And indeed there will be time . . . And time yet for a hundred indecisions, / And for a hundred visions and revisions" (23, 31–32; qtd. in Moretti 31). Accepting that Prufrock's indecision is endemic to Western literary culture from the romantics forward, Moretti is particularly interested in how, as the nineteenth century passes over into the twentieth, the connection between possibility—the state of indecision that modern literature strives to maintain—and anxiety—the feeling of guilt over the failure to decide—breaks down. Here, he points to the figure of Leopold Bloom, whose daydreams allow him to maintain himself more or less comfortably in the realm of the possible; and he points more generally to the world that *Ulysses* embraces, in which "adultery has become a harmless pastime, and even the most extreme experiments of [*Ulysses*'] modernist imagination may well produce stupefaction but no longer evoke anything threatening" (31). While adultery reflects the belief that one need not decide between lovers, *Ulysses*' "most extreme experiments"—Moretti has in mind Joyce's use of stream of consciousness, which "deals not with consciousness but with what is usually called the preconscious, which contains the countless 'possible selves' of each individual: what he/she would like to be, or to have been, but, for whatever reason, is not" (31)—evince the penetration of this indecision into literary form itself.

In at least one way "Prufrock" fits well into Moretti's schema. The inability to decide—from the Latin *de-caedere*, meaning "to cut off" (*OED*)—is not only the source of the speaker's failures; it is also the source of the poem's existence, the conceit that allows it to keep going. So long as every decision can be hesitated over, can be revised and revised again, the speaker's desultory laments—and thus the poem itself—need never stop. The spell of indecision characterizes, then, not only Prufrock but also "Prufrock." And this goes some way toward explaining the form that the poem's conclusion must take. Developing according to a mechanism through which it can prolong itself indefinitely, the poem can only wrap up the "visions and revisions" that it comprises through the introduction of a more or less arbitrary—but nonetheless unrevisable—cut. And this is exactly what it does: "We have lingered in the chambers of the sea / By sea-girls wreathed with seaweed red and brown / Till human voices wake us, and we drown" (129–131). The poem ends with the interruption of dreams, and so with a forced transition from the realm of the possible to that of the actual. This transition occurs, however, not as Prufrock's decision finally to act, "to murder and create" (28), which would, after all, falsify his character as it has developed up to this point; rather, it occurs as Prufrock's own death by water, the sort of caesura—from *caedere*, again—that Prufrock's potentially endless monologue exists to delay. So long as life is figured as possibility, possibility's other, actuality, can only be figured as death.

In a sense, then, the struggle to decide—and it is a struggle, a source of anxiety, *pace* Moretti—drives Prufrock toward death, even as the failure to decide defers it. And it is in this light that we can read the failed actualizations that Prufrock undergoes over the course of the poem, the failure to become Hamlet—"No! I am not Prince Hamlet" (111)—or to become John the Baptist—"Though I have seen my head (grown slightly bald) brought in upon a platter, / I am no prophet–and here's no great matter" (82–83). To become Hamlet, for example, would surely lend Prufrock's indecisiveness some tragic weight. But truly to be Hamlet—or truly to be anyone at all—would mean to exit the realm of the possible, of life, and so not to be. That is to say, if life is, in "Prufrock," possibility, hesitation, indecision, then to decide is to see life canceled, to answer Hamlet's own "overwhelming question" in the negative. Mutlu Blasing is correct, then, to find in the poem "impulses to dismemberment and suicide" (40), for a suicide—a self-cutting, *sui-caedere*—is precisely the form that Prufrock's deciding would have to take. And so the poem leaves us with a disconcerting alternative: indecision—which is the realm of the possible, of life, and, it would seem, of literature itself—or death. And here we can return to Eliot's letter to Aiken.

In his letter, let us remember, Eliot describes the poetic impotence from which he has suffered since he completed "Prufrock," such that the queries Prufrock voices in the poem—"Do I dare / Disturb the Universe?" (45–46), "And how should I begin?" (69)—have become Eliot's own. Prufrock's laments come to an end only when he is decided on. Eliot, however, can expect no such assistance. Rather, he must decide for and on himself. And so, he writes to Aiken, a self-cutting will be necessary: "Anyway, it's interesting to cut yourself to pieces once in a while, and wait to see if the fragments will sprout." That this self-cutting has to be a kind of suicide is figured in the image of the sprouting fragments that Eliot proffers, an image that, we can now see, looks back to Dante's *Inferno* as surely as it looks forward to *The Waste Land*. For in the *Inferno*, in the seventh circle of Hell, it is the suicides who "sprout" as plants. One of the condemned, Pietro della Vigna, explains:

> "Whenever the violent soul forsakes the flesh
> From which it tore itself by its own roots,
> Minos assigns it to the seventh pit.
>
> "It plummets to the wood—no place is picked—
> But wherever fortune happens to have hurled it,
> There it sprouts up like a grain of spelt;
>
> "It springs into a sapling and wild tree." (13.94–100)

Having treated their bodies as objects on Earth, and having sprouted as trees in Hell, the suicides are fated at the day of judgment to gaze on their own mangled corpses as though they were somebody else's:

> "Like others we shall go to our shed bodies,
> But not to dress ourselves in them once more,
> For it is wrong to own what you tossed off.
>
> "Here shall we haul them, and throughout the sad
> Wood forevermore shall our bodies hang,
> Each from the thornbush of its tortured shade." (13.103–108)

Though it may evoke his love song's Dantean framing, this self-cutting eludes Prufrock. For Eliot, however, it remains his best hope for overcoming his creative impotence. It can only be a question of what form his self-cutting will take. And here, "Prufrock"—or, more exactly, the complicated history of its composition—is revealing, as "Prufrock" becomes the location where Eliot's experiments with self-cutting are carried out.

In 1912, after "Prufrock" was ostensibly already completed, Eliot reopened the poem, inserting into it thirty-eight additional lines. Recalling the fate of these lines in a 1960 letter to the *TLS*, Aiken writes that "Mr. Eliot maintains to this day that on my suggestion a certain passage—now presumably lost— had been dropped from ['Prufrock']. I can only say that I have no recollection of this, but if so, what a pity!" (*IMH* 176). In his response, Eliot notes that he did "make some additions in 1912, and I am grateful to Mr. Aiken for having perceived at once that the additions were of inferior quality." The additions to which he refers are now available in the collection of Eliot's "lost" writings, *The Inventions of the March Hare*, as "Prufrock's Pervigilium." The "Pervigilium" describes Prufrock's continuing journey through a nightmarish urban space, "Where evil houses leaning all together / Pointed a ribald finger at me in the darkness / Whispering all together, chuckled at me in the darkness" (15–17). As the section progresses, Prufrock's anxieties intensify and tend toward a "madness" (29, 36), which, given voice, he hears singing and chattering before him. The "Pervigilium" was to have been located at the center of the poem, right after Prufrock asks "And should I then presume? / And how should I begin?" (68–69). All that remains of it in the published version are its first lines, which read "Shall I say, I have gone at dusk through narrow streets / And seen the smoke which rises from the pipes / Of lonely men in shirtsleeves, leaning out of windows" (1–3), as well as two lines from its penultimate stanza: "I should have been a pair of ragged claws / Scuttling across the floors of silent seas" (33–34).

Perhaps it is the emotional pitch of the "Pervigilium," coupled with its deletion from the final version of "Prufrock," that has encouraged critics to read it as particularly personal, as a symptom of its author's own psychosexual problems (Mayer 183). In an early review of *Inventions*, for example, Nicholas Jenkins wonders, "[C]an this idiom of nerves and madness be just a question, as [the editor] Mr. Ricks' notes tend to suggest, of masks and literary borrowings?" (15). The implication, of course, is that Eliot is here writing out of his own experience of "nerves and madness," and having recognized this fact, decided to eliminate this too-personal expression of his suffering. And Jenkins is not alone in treating this section as autobiographical. In her biography of Vivienne Eliot, Carole Seymour-Jones decides that the excised lines reveal that at some point Eliot sought out a prostitute, "but that the encounter was not a success" (51). Somewhat less speculatively, James Miller writes that "in the 'Pervigilium' passage, Eliot's authorial voice tends to dominate, while that of his Prufrock persona recedes" (155). And so the "Pervigilium" affords us a rare glimpse of the man behind the mask.

Despite the claims of Jenkins and others, I cannot see much of an argument for reading "Prufrock's Pervigilium" as any more a product of Eliot's biography than the published poem from which it was excised. And yet, the responses of these critics are still valuable insofar as they identify accurately in these lost lines a rising passion in their speaker's voice, and so a real shift in the poem's emotional pitch. It is this shift that makes the "Pervigilium"—and its excision—significant. Again, the shift is from a mood of anxiety to one of terror, as Prufrock describes his descent into madness, his having "writhed in fever" and "nausea" as "the world began to fall apart" (18, 26, 32). Rather than treat this shift as evidence of the replacement of Prufrock by Eliot, however—and thus of the interruption of the poem *qua* poem—we might treat it as an intraliterary effect. What the "Pervigilium" does—and does well, as its contemporary readers demonstrate—is suggest the presence in "Prufrock" of another voice, a more authentic voice, that can be heard over Prufrock's own laments. Heard over or overheard: if, as Mill famously claimed, "the peculiarity of poetry" is that it is essentially "overheard," and overheard as it "[confesses] itself to itself in moments of solitude" (348), then the "Pervigilium" is doubly poetic. It produces within a monologue that is already poetry the effect of a voice—an authorial voice—overheard. The failure of the critical accounts detailed above is not that they miss this additional voice. In fact, they all hear it quite clearly. Their failure, rather, is that they mistake what is in fact a poetic doubling for the absence of poetry. Whether or not the "Pervigilium" provides us with insight into Eliot's inner life, it promises us this insight by producing—poetically—the effect of the poet within the poem.

And it is this effect that, with Aiken's assistance, Eliot excises. Playing a kind of *fort-da* game with the most "personal" portion of "Prufrock," Eliot produces "himself"—or perhaps more accurately, the appearance of his authorial voice—within the poem only to cut himself away. Having accomplished this task, he leaves behind only a trace of the "Pervigilium": the three lines that were to have introduced it—and that are more or less consistent in tone with the lines that precede them—and the synechdochal "ragged claws" of a scavenging crab, torn free from their original context. As the residue of the portrait of the artist in the poem, the image of ragged claws is worthy of Nietzsche, who also compared the genius to "ein blinder Seekrebs" (a blind sea-crab; *Werke* 11:298), to a creature that grabs and shapes absent any conscious intention. Similarly, in the final version of "Prufrock," this image marks an absence—where the poet, the man who suffers, had seemingly appeared, we have only the trace of his having been cut away—as well as a presence, the presence of something impersonal, inhuman, but still active. After the "Pervigilium" is cut away, after "Eliot" is cut away from "Prufrock," all that remain are the tools of the creative process: blind claws that grab and shape.

What if Eliot survives this suicide? The personal, the anxious, worried young man, has been cut away. All that remains is a particularly pure figure of the poetic operation. It is only a matter of systematizing this operation, of putting it to work. Here, the pieces are in place for Eliot's theorization of the tradition, as well as for a model of the modern poet as "the ideal scavenger of the rubbish of our time" (*SW* 26). And here we can turn to Eliot's attempt to move from personal strategy to poetic program, to "Tradition and the Individual Talent."

## II. Amputation and Catalysis

"Tradition and the Individual Talent," first published in two installments in the September and December 1919 issues of *The Egoist*, is Eliot's most programmatic statement on the relationship of the poet to the enormous fact of literary history. Near the end of his life, and despite having undergone some significant modifications in both his personal outlook and his poetic technique, Eliot could still state that the essay describes accurately the theory that had informed his fifty years of poetic practice: "I do not repudiate 'Tradition and the Individual Talent'" (*UP* 10). To what extent we should take Eliot at his word here—to what extent, for example, the positions Eliot articulates in "Tradition" can actually make sense of the shift from a lyric to an epic mode signaled by *The Waste Land*—will be one of my concerns in the next chapter. For now, though, I want to focus on how "Tradition" works to systematize some of the solutions to the problem of personal history that we examined in Eliot's struggle with the legacy of "Prufrock"—that is, how it extends to the broader arena of literary history the strategy of self-cutting that we found in the earlier work. My approach to "Tradition and the Individual Talent" differs from established readings of the essay in at least two respects: first, it involves appreciating that literary history appears in "Tradition" as a problem, as an object of struggle and a source of real anxiety. And second, by shifting emphasis from synthesis to division as Eliot's solution to this problem, this approach to "Tradition" suggests a very different understanding of Eliot's debt to the idealist philosophies with which he was preoccupied during the 1910s. The problem—literary history—and the solution—self-division—are entirely entangled; nonetheless, I will attempt to separate them (temporarily), beginning with the problem of literary history.

At first, the suggestion that literary history has a problematic status in "Tradition" is likely to seem questionable. Is it not more accurate to say that, here, the problem that the poet faces is not history's presence but the threat of its absence, such that the poet should be willing to sacrifice everything to possess it? "Anyone who would continue to be a poet beyond his twenty-fifth year," Eliot notes, must labor to develop a "historical sense," a sense, precisely, of the living presence of the "whole of the literature of Europe" (*SW* 28). Only by doing so, only by opening himself to a communion with the "the dead poets, his ancestors," can the modern poet hope to gain a purchase on his ancestors' "immortality" (28). The latter does not come without a cost, and, Eliot goes on, the poet's "progress" as an artist will also be "a continual self-sacrifice, a continual extinction of personality," and "a continual surrender of himself as he is at the moment to something which is more valuable" (30). As was the case in his struggles with the legacy of "Prufrock," Eliot here binds the life of poetry to the symbolic self-destruction of the poet. Poetry becomes possible only when the "man who suffers," with all his petty worries, is excised so that the "mind which creates" can flourish (31). Between the self-cutting of "Prufrock" and the self-sacrifice of "Tradition," however, two things have changed. First, and most obviously, what in "Prufrock" was only Eliot's own strategy for surviving as a poet becomes in "Tradition" a program to which every poet must submit, at least if he would "continue to be a poet beyond his twenty-fifth year." Second, and more important for our purposes, is the claim in "Tradition" that this sacrifice of personality not only frees the poet from his own personal history but also promises to open him to another history, to a history that is more valuable because it comprises the "whole of the literature of Europe from Homer" (28). By sacrificing, by surrendering, the modern poet exchanges particular for universal. *Sit ius liceatque perire poetis.*

In exchanging personal history for literary history, particular for universal, the poet and his poetry prosper. Wherein lies the danger? Though he takes pains to minimize its seriousness, Eliot admits that the poet assumes a risk in surrendering himself to something that is more valuable. The poet who surrenders himself to history, Eliot writes, faces "great difficulties and responsibilities" (28). Specifically, the poet must accept that "he [will] be judged by the standards of the past" (28–29)—that is, that he will be judged by those standards implicit in the "whole of the literature of Europe." But this judgment, Eliot is quick to clarify, is not something to worry over, for it is in truth hardly a judgment at all. In fact, it is better understood as a kind of "comparison," one in which "two things"—the old and the new, the past and the present—"are measured by each other" (29). And so, Eliot writes, to be "judged" by the standards of the past is not to be "amputated" by them. What appears as judgment is really only a manifestation of a deeper symbiosis, a productive fusion of history and poetry. Nothing could be further from amputation.

Eliot's aim is to assuage the fears of the poet confronted with the demands of literary history; nonetheless, Eliot's paraliptic invocation of amputation ought to give us pause. As a figure for the threat posed to the modern poet by the past, amputation recalls the threat posed to Eliot by his own past as a poet, the threat of his being judged by the standards of the past and so cut off from his creative élan. But as a figure of cutting, amputation also recalls Eliot's response to this threat, the response of cutting himself into pieces. Indeed, amputation, derived from the Latin *putare*, "to prune" (*OED*), recalls us to the wood of suicides, and so joins with the figures of suicide, self-cutting, decision, excision, sacrifice, and surrender that collect in Eliot's writings over the course of the 1910s and that—I want to insist—condition his better-known theories of poetic synthesis. Eliot's dismissal of amputation in favor of "judgment" still remains within this same logic of cutting, for in addition to the fact that judgment can always result in a verdict of amputation—of a head, a hand, or some other member—"judgment" itself, as de-cision, as the German *Ur-teilung* that so fascinated Hölderlin,[8] or even as *putare*, which means "to judge" as well as "to prune," tends to contain a cutting within it. The problem that Eliot faces, then, is how to prevent the healthy and altogether necessary self-cutting carried out in "Prufrock" and prescribed in "Tradition," the self-cutting that frees the poet from his petty worries and opens him to literary history, from passing over into the stultifying cutting that history threatens to perform on the poet and that Eliot himself conjures up as "amputation."

More than just an indication of Eliot's difficulties in managing his language, the invocation of amputation points to a very different conception of the mature poet's relationship to literary history, one in which history wounds rather than enlivens. Because his aim is principally to deny the threat of amputation, however, Eliot offers little in the way of a positive characterization. To understand what amputation by history might look like, we need to turn briefly from "Tradition" to its companion piece, "The Perfect Critic."[9] In this essay, initially published half a year after "Tradition" and collected alongside it in *The Sacred Wood*, Eliot paints a darker picture of the effects of knowledge—and, specifically, of historical knowledge—on modern life:

> The vast accumulations of knowledge—or at least of information—deposited by the nineteenth century have been responsible for an equally vast ignorance. When there is so much to be known, when there are so many fields of knowledge in which the same words are used with different meanings, when everyone knows a little about a great many things, it becomes increasingly difficult for anyone to know whether he knows what he is talking about or not. (*SW* 6)

In this passage, Eliot ties the proliferation of information to the decay of real knowledge. He would partially echo this sentiment—and would entirely echo its anaphoric presentation—a few years later in yet another denunciation of cultural decay. Compare the last sentence of the above passage with the following sentence from Eliot's November 1922 "London Letter":

> When every theatre has been replaced by 100 cinemas, when every musical instrument has been replaced by 100 gramophones, when every horse has been replaced by 100 cheap motor cars, when electrical ingenuity has made it possible for every child to hear its bed-time stories through a wireless receiver attached to both ears, when applied science has done everything possible with the materials on this earth to make life as interesting as possible, it will not be surprising if the population of the entire civilized world rapidly follows the fate of the Melanesians. (663)

We will have the opportunity to look more closely at this later passage in the next chapter. For now, it helps us to see the complicated role that history plays in Eliot's writings at the end of the 1910s. Before he identifies technology or popular art forms—his targets in the "London Letter"—as sources of cultural degeneration, Eliot associates this threat with an excess of information. Significantly, he holds the nineteenth century responsible. It is this century, let us recall, that bestows on its progeny not only its own history, the record of its own events and discoveries and works, but also the "historical sense" itself, the demand that we preserve and learn from the past. As the century of history, then, it originates the movement that worries Eliot, the movement from the proliferation of information to the impoverishment of knowledge.

And this movement threatens to leave the modern individual amputated. In the face of an overwhelming accumulation of fragments of information, the individual loses the ability "to know whether he knows what he is talking about or not." He may persist in chattering "about a great many things"; he cannot, however, know with certainty that his discourse is meaningful, even to himself, for he can no longer distinguish his own ostensible knowledge from the degraded bits of information with which it intermingles. His situation is not so different, then, from the situation we characterized in the previous chapter in terms of a tension between historical knowledge and poetic life—a tension marked by Nietzsche's warning to his nineteenth-century contemporaries that "with a certain excess of history life crumbles and degenerates" (*AD* 14). In each case, the vast accumulation of historical knowledge deposited by the nineteenth century proves to be too much for the mind of the modern individual, and so the individual loses himself to history.

As I have suggested, one name that Eliot gives to this loss is "amputation": the individual who is overwhelmed by history is cut off from his ability to write, to think, to produce something lasting. Eliot may have had an experience of this sort himself during his years as an extension lecturer at Oxford and the University of London, a period in his life when the demand that he assimilate an overwhelming accumulation of literary history made time for writing especially hard to come by.[10] Another name for this loss, though, is "ordinary experience"—the experience that Eliot opposes to the experience of the poet:

> When a poet's mind is perfectly equipped for its work, it is constantly amalgamating disparate experience; the ordinary man's experience is chaotic, irregular, fragmentary. The latter falls in love, or reads Spinoza, and these two experiences have nothing to do with each other, or the noise of the typewriter or the smell of cooking; in the mind of the poet these experiences are always forming new wholes. (*SW* 124)

The mind of the poet is essentially a synthetic mind, a mind that orders the world rather than letting it remain, in the words of William James, "one great blooming, buzzing confusion" (462). The mind of the ordinary man, however, is not up to this task, and so the ordinary man's experience is "chaotic, irregular, fragmentary." This remark appears in Eliot's 1921 essay on "The Metaphysical Poets," postdating "Tradition" by two years. Eliot had, however, already made a similar point in a letter to Mary Hutchinson from July of 1919, a letter that includes a number of the same themes that would appear again a couple of months later in "Tradition." In this earlier letter, Eliot writes that the "ordinary mind," in contrast to the mind of the poet, is "completely unorganized," completely unable to transform experience into something coherent. As a result, "some people really read too much to be cultivated" (*L* 1:377–378). When they read, they add one experience, one bit of information, to another in a series that lacks any synthetic moment. The distinction that Eliot draws in his letter to Hutchinson, then, is not between the individual who opens himself to the past—to the "presence of the past"—and the individual who remains closed to it. Rather, the salient distinction is between two ways of experiencing the past: the experience characteristic of the poet, who is "always forming new wholes," and the experience characteristic of the ordinary man, who, always already amputated, becomes less cultivated the more he reads.

It is, of course, possible to read these remarks concerning the distinction of the poet from the ordinary man as signs of Eliot's burgeoning elitism, although if one were to do so, one would also need to acknowledge that, at least in his letter to Hutchinson, Eliot doubts (or plays at doubting) the powers of his own mind, writing of himself that he is, after all, "a *metic*—a foreigner" and perhaps a "savage" (1:379). We might linger over these remarks for another reason, though. By distinguishing the experience of the poet from the experience of the ordinary man, Eliot indeed underscores the synthetic powers of the poet's mind. This is clear enough. But it is also true that Eliot brings the poet's synthetic powers into relief chiefly by distinguishing the poet from the ordinary man. And this need to distinguish, to separate, pervades the letter to Hutchinson—in Eliot's separation of "two kinds of intelligence: the intellectual and the sensitive," for example—up to and including Eliot's treatment of the "historical sense" itself, which appears in this letter for the first time and which Eliot characterizes not as a synthetic grasp of the past but as "the ability to discriminate one's own passions from objective criticism" (1:378). Possessing the historical sense, then, the poet is separated from the ordinary man not only on the basis of his synthetic mind but also on the basis of his ability to separate—to separate what he feels from what he knows and therefore to separate one aspect of himself from another.

It is in light of the role played by separation in the above remarks that I want to return to "Tradition," and specifically to one of the essay's most famous and most perplexing passages, the protracted analogy of the catalyst included in the essay's second section. That the analogy is intended to explain the process of poetic creation that Eliot has been circling up to this point is evinced by its dramatic appearance in "Tradition," initially as a teaser in the essay's first installment and sans explanation: "I shall, therefore, invite you to consider, as a suggestive analogy, the action which takes place when a bit of finely filiated platinum is introduced into a chamber containing oxygen and sulphur dioxide" (30). The meaning of this "suggestive analogy" is not revealed until the next installment of the essay, published a few months later. Here, all is explained. "[T]he mind of the mature poet," Eliot writes,

> differs from that of the immature one not precisely in any valuation of "personality," not being necessarily more interesting, or having "more to say," but rather by being a more finely perfected medium in which special, or very varied, feelings are at liberty to enter into new combinations. The analogy was that of the catalyst. When the two gasses previously mentioned are mixed in the presence of a filament of platinum, they form sulphurous acid. This combination takes place only if the platinum is present; nevertheless the newly formed acid contains no trace of platinum, and the platinum itself is apparently unaffected; has remained inert, neutral, and unchanged. The mind of the poet is the shred of platinum. (30)

In the process of literary creation that Eliot analogizes, the experiences of the poet—the "numberless feelings, phrases, images" that exist in the poet's mind—are combined to form "the new (the really new) work of art" (28). What are these experiences? They are, Eliot makes clear, nothing personal, for the "mature poet" is not distinguished by his "personality" but by his role as a "medium," a "receptacle" (31). These experiences are, then, the very stuff of literary history to which the poet has surrendered. The mind of the poet is the receptacle in which literary history is catalyzed.

And yet, this characterization of the poet's mind as strictly a receptacle or a medium—as a principle of unity that stands apart from the "gasses" of literary history even as it synthesizes them—is not maintained. For the poet's mind, Eliot writes, is not only the receptacle in which the reaction occurs; it is also "the shred of platinum" that triggers the reaction, the catalyst that, though "inert, neutral," is nonetheless necessarily present. The poet's mind does not stand apart from the stuff of literary history, then; it intermingles with it. Eliot ends his analogy with the summary assertion that "the mind of the poet is the shred of platinum" and thus, presumably, settles on the characterization of the poet's mind as a catalyst. Nonetheless, when he returns to the analogy a couple of pages later, he claims again that the poet's mind is "only a medium" (32), and so, again, that the poet's mind is distinct from what it is tasked with synthesizing. In his oscillation, Eliot distributes the poet's mind between its roles as medium and catalyst, container and contained. Where we would expect to find an affirmation of unity—of the unity of literary history as it is secured by the unifying consciousness of the poet and expressed in the unified form of the poem—we find instead a doubling of the poet's mind, a doubling that has the effect of muddling the distinction between this mind and the world.

When critics have addressed this apparent equivocation, they have tended to see in it evidence that Eliot's analogy is itself "faulty" (Dean 56) or "deeply confused" (Smith 27), and perhaps also an indication that Eliot is unable to eliminate entirely the particular personality of the poet. In a recent article, Tim Dean has laid out the problem in the following terms: "Unable to decide whether a poet's mind should be understood as the receptacle that contains elements requiring catalysis or whether it represents the catalyst itself, Eliot also comes close to nullifying the distinction between a poet's mind and the medium of poetic practice" (56). In other words, by introducing the notion that the poet's mind is a catalyst as well as a medium, that the poet's mind is one more element in the amalgam of "feelings, phrases, images" that, nonetheless, interact within the poet's mind, Eliot confuses the distinction between inside and outside, poetic cerebration and literary history, mind and world, on which the analogy of the catalyst seems to rely. Eliot himself may have accepted the validity of this criticism, for in his 1934 collection *After Strange Gods* he writes of "Tradition" that, in the fifteen years since its initial publication, "I have discovered, or had brought to my attention, some unsatisfactory phrasing and at least one more than doubtful analogy" (15). Though the analogy of the catalyst is not the essay's only candidate for the title of "more than doubtful analogy,"[11] it does seem to be the obvious choice.

Rejecting Eliot's equivocation concerning the poet's mind and settling on the notion that it is merely a medium would certainly make for a more coherent analogy. But it would also have the effect of reducing the analogy to a probably unnecessary restatement of the straightforward claims concerning the importance of history to poetry, the synthetic character of literary creation, and so on that Eliot develops—without recourse to doubtful analogies—in the first section of "Tradition." Moreover, it would mean ignoring Eliot's own gloss on his aims in developing the analogy of the catalyst. What, for example, are we to make of Eliot's remark a couple of pages after the analogy's appearance that "the point of view which I am struggling to attack is perhaps related to the metaphysical theory of the substantial unity of the soul: for my meaning is that the poet has, not a 'personality' to express, but a particular medium, which is only a medium and not a personality, in which impressions and experiences combine in peculiar and unexpected ways" (32)? With this remark, Eliot re-affirms his conclusions about the mind of the poet—its mediumistic character, its impersonality—which he has already developed in a figurative register in the analogy of the catalyst. Now, however, he reframes these conclusions as an attack on the unity of the soul. By doing so, he suggests that what has been at stake in the analogy all along is not so much synthesis—though synthesis is certainly to be desired—or even impersonality—though impersonality does play a role—but division. And this latter can only be the division of the poet's mind that Eliot presents as the division between medium and catalyst, a divi-sion that describes not the lack of distinction between the poet's mind and the world but, rather, the division of the poet's mind from itself.

Again, Eliot explains this division as an attack on a point of view akin to "the metaphysical theory of the substantial unity of the soul." This language is significant, and Eliot's terms need to be unpacked. The classic question of the soul's substantial unity—the question, that is, of whether the soul unites within it both the rational and the appetitive faculties or whether multiple souls exist—has a long history, appearing in different forms in the writings of Plato, Aristotle, and the Church Fathers. Eliot would have encountered it in the context of his studies of ancient philosophy with the Oxford idealists Harold Joachim and John Alexander Smith. Both Joachim and Smith—the latter, the English translator of Aristotle's *De anima*, a text Eliot quotes at the conclusion of "Tradition"—were formidable scholars. In his correspondences, Eliot writes that Joachim, for example, is "really almost a genius, with respect to Aristo-tle" (*L* 1:91). But—and this is essential to the manner in which the unity of the soul appears as an object of criticism in Eliot's essay—both Joachim and Smith tempered their interest in the classics with a worldview shaped by nineteenth-century German thought, such that Eliot could note Joachim's "fatal disposition . . . toward Hegelianism" (1:91) and write of Smith that his lectures "represent the purest strain of old fashioned Hegelianism to be found in England" (1:73).

Though, in general, Eliot shows every indication of having tried to keep Hegel's idealism at arm's length,[12] his studies with or writings on Joachim, Smith, R. G. Collingwood, Josiah Royce, and, fundamentally, F. H. Bradley would have exposed him to a whole tradition of idealist thought from Leibniz through Hegel and onward.[13] Finding himself within this tradition, Eliot would have learned to think holistically, to say "as Mr. Bradley says, 'whatever you know, it is all one'" (*TAWL* 191). But he would have learned as well that, as Hegel says, "mind itself is an inherent division" (*EL* 79), and, more colorfully, the subject "wins its truth only when it finds itself in utter dismemberment (*in der absoluten Zerrissenheit*; *PS* 19). In other words, he would have learned from the idealist tradition that the subject, before it dismembers the world through the power of its analytic judgment, before it divides reality into subjects and predicates, dismembers itself. It splits itself between its empirical and formal characteristics—as occurs in Kant's inaugural gesture—or between its existence as a subject who knows and a subject who knows this knowing—as occurs in Hegel's own division of consciousness between what it is "in itself" and "for itself."

The result of this division is not the existence of two substantial entities—two "souls"—but a robust notion of self-consciousness, an ability to engage critically with one's own knowledge. Eliot would seem to have something similar in mind when he writes at the beginning of "Tradition" that "we might remind ourselves that criticism is as inevitable as breathing, and that we should be none the worse for articulating what passes in our minds when we read a book and feel an emotion about it, *for criticizing our own minds in their work of criticism*" (*SW* 27; my emphasis). Again, the salient distinction is between two moments of knowledge. The first occurs as knowledge of the world, knowledge that is very much in the world, immersed in the vast accumulations of historical information that the modern world provides. This knowledge is necessarily "chaotic, irregular, fragmentary," for it knows the world without knowing that it knows it, without bringing this first knowledge together into something unified. The second moment of knowledge, though, occurs as the knowledge of this first knowledge. It occurs as the ability to judge this first knowledge, to criticize it, and so to divide good knowledge from bad, true from false. It judges and it synthesizes. The mature poet is simply the figure who can maintain his mind in this state of division—which is, again, the division of catalyst from medium, of content from form, of knowledge from the knowledge of this knowledge. His capacity for literary-historical synthesis is greater than that of the ordinary man only insofar as his mind is more perfectly divided than the ordinary man's, more capable of standing apart from the "numberless feelings, phrases, images" with which it also, necessarily, intermingles.

The "mature poet"—and this is, I think, the key claim developed in "Tradition"—names the division of "the man who suffers" from the "the mind which creates," the catalyst from the medium, and thus the ordinary man from the poet. Only through this division—only after the poet finds himself in utter dismemberment—does literary-historical synthesis become possible. We can find examples, as well as thematizations, of this division and of the synthesis it enables in Eliot's contemporary lyric practice. In the last part of this chapter, I want to turn to one case of this practice, to the poem "Gerontion." This poem, in addition to being perhaps Eliot's most accomplished lyric—"the most important poem Eliot wrote between 'The Love Song of J. Alfred Prufrock' and *The Waste Land*" (Brooker 82)—allows us to describe the possibilities and the limitations of lyric as a form for managing literary history.

## III. From Nature to History

Eliot completed "Gerontion" in the summer of 1919, not long after the Treaty of Versailles definitively concluded the First World War. It was published in 1920 as the first poem in the collection *Ara Vos Prec* (the title of the English edition) or *Poems* (the title of the American edition), despite its being the most recent poem included therein. In its form—that is, as a lyric poem that develops as a series of lamentations—"Gerontion" looks back to "The Love Song of J. Alfred Prufrock," to which it is often compared.[14] And in its content—that is, in its more or less explicit thematization of the struggle with history—it both echoes the concerns of "Tradition and the Individual Talent" (albeit in a poetic register) and looks ahead to *The Waste Land*, to which it was to have served as a prelude before Pound advised Eliot to keep the two poems separate (*L* 1:629–630).[15] "Gerontion" thus stands not only on its own considerable merits as a poem but also on its ability to braid together its author's poetic past, present, and future— a somewhat ironic result, since this (fragmentary, pessimistic) poem seems to call into question the viability of just this sort of historical-synthetic project. In the pages to follow, I want to take seriously the paradoxical character of "Gerontion"—a learned poem that warns us not to waste our time with learned poems, a synthetic statement on the implausibility of synthesis—and to do so as a way of thinking through the effectiveness of the self-cutting that informs Eliot's poetic project in the 1910s and that has concerned us up to this point.

"Gerontion" is framed as a meditation on youth and old age, through its first lines—"Here I am, an old man in a dry month, / Being read to by a boy, waiting for rain" (1–2)—through its epigraph, a slightly modified passage from *Measure for Measure*—"Thou hast nor youth nor age / But as it were an after dinner sleep / Dreaming of both"[16]—and through its title, which roughly translates to "little old man." "Gerontion" was not Eliot's first choice for a title. The poem was initially to have been titled "Gerousia." The latter refers to the Spartan "Council of Elders" (*Gerontes*), the twenty-eight males over the age of sixty—the age at which Spartan military service was terminated—who governed Sparta alongside its kings. The typically wealthy individuals who served on the council were chosen by lot; those who received the loudest cheers from the populace came to govern. In his *Politics*, Aristotle calls this electoral practice "childish" (1270b), and Eliot likely encountered the *Gerousia* in his studies of Aristotle. Consequently, the poem's original title should evoke not only rule by the elderly but also the possibility that this rule is illegitimate, the result of a practice more suited to children. By rejecting "Gerousia" in favor of "Gerontion," Eliot does not signal a change in his conception of the poem so much as a clarification of his aims. "Gerousia" retains connotations of privilege and power (however ill-gotten), while "Gerontion," a disrespectful diminutive, does not. Accordingly, the poem will find little in old age worthy of respect.

The choice of "Gerontion" over "Gerousia" as a title is significant for another reason, though. "Gerousia" describes a gerontocracy that, while possibly illegitimate or corrupt, still holds power over youth. And this power is never more visible than in periods of military conflict. The poem's speaker admits that "I was neither at the hot gates / Nor fought in the warm rain / Nor knee deep in the salt marsh, heaving a cutlass, / Bitten by flies, fought" (3–6). This may be true, but if the speaker indeed serves on the *Gerousia*, then he enjoys the right to send others into battle, to send young men to fight and die at Thermopylae (the "hot gates")—or Ypres, or Verdun, or anywhere else he chooses. Having lost his friends Jean Verdenal (2 May 1915), Karl Henry Culpin (15 May 1917), and T. E. Hulme (28 September 1917) in a war fought by the young for the old—for a civilization that Pound described in *Hugh Selwyn Mauberley* (1920) as "an old bitch gone in the teeth"—Eliot would have felt acutely the dislocation between the decisions made by the old and the consequences suffered by the young. When "Gerousia" becomes "Gerontion," however, this connection to the Great War all but vanishes. If the speaker is not in a position to have sent someone else to fight and die in his stead at Thermopylae, if he is, rather, just a

little old man with no particular political influence, then the poem cannot really be taken to register a protest against the aged in power. Perhaps old age still
rules over youth, but this is less because the latter is conscripted by the former
than because the former is the latter's destiny (at least if one is luckier than
Verdenal, Culpin, and Hulme).

By changing the title of his poem from "Gerousia" to "Gerontion," Eliot cuts
one of the threads linking the poem to its wartime context, and as a result, to
its (and to Eliot's own) history. But he does so only to find for history another
place in the poem. Lines 34–47 read:

> History has many cunning passages, contrived corridors
> And issues, deceives with whispering ambitions,
> Guides us by vanities. Think now
> She gives when our attention is distracted
> And what she gives, gives with such supple confusions
> That the giving famishes the craving. Gives too late
> What's not believed in, or if still believed,
> In memory only, reconsidered passion. Gives too soon
> Into weak hands, what's thought can be dispensed with
> Till the refusal propagates a fear. Think
> Neither fear nor courage saves us. Unnatural vices
> Are fathered by our heroism. Virtues
> Are forced upon us by our impudent crimes.
> These tears are shaken from the wrath-bearing tree.

These lines are some of the poem's most famous—they seem to provide
"Gerontion" with its thesis, or as Hugh Kenner described them, with its
"method." It is worth bearing in mind, then, that history was not the subject
of these lines in earlier drafts of the poem. It was, rather, "Nature" that possessed "many cunning passages" (*IMH* 34–35). Eliot's substitution of "History"
for "Nature" in the published version of the poem—probably the most significant emendation carried out between the later drafts and the final version—
is roughly contemporary with his substitution of "Gerontion" for "Gerousia."
Again, history is not removed from "Gerontion" so much as it is relocated. In its
being relocated, however, history is also transformed. At issue is no longer—or
not only—this or that recent tragedy; at issue, rather, is historical knowledge itself, the question of whether history is ever anything but the ruse of real knowledge. In this light, we might read Eliot's shift from "Gerousia" to "Gerontion,"

and concurrent shift from "Nature" to "History," as registering an awareness that, before this or that historical event can be considered—as meaningful or as meaningless—the status of historical knowledge must be decided.

B. C. Southam has suggested that the choice of "History" over "Nature" in the final version of "Gerontion" was perhaps motivated by Eliot's encounter with the "Nestor" episode of James Joyce's *Ulysses*, which Eliot read for *The Egoist* before it was published in the magazine's January–February 1919 issue (75). The episode includes Stephen Dedalus's oft-quoted remark to the school headmaster Mr. Deasy that "[h]istory . . . is a nightmare from which I am trying to awake" (28).[17] The speaker of "Gerontion" presents his own judgment of history more circuitously; nonetheless, he arrives at the same verdict. History is not, as Deasy wants to claim, a movement "towards one great goal, the manifestation of God." It is, rather, a collection of ruses—cunning, contrived, deceptive, and, we might add, nightmarish. Eliot's reading of "Nestor" may be relevant to the composition of "Gerontion" for another reason, though. In the "Nestor" episode, Joyce presents Stephen's dealing with Deasy as a struggle in which the older man tries to position the younger as a pupil, and the younger man resists. If Stephen were to yield, this would mean submitting not only to Deasy's claims about history, which are as inaccurate as they are sanguine, but also to Deasy's attempts to see him as the man he was—a student/apprentice—rather than as the man he is—a teacher/artist. At stake in the episode, then, is Stephen's relationship to his own history, as well as to historical knowledge more generally. Now if we pull back a bit, we can see that the presence of these themes in "Nestor" establishes a continuity between the first episodes of *Ulysses*—of which "Nestor" is the second—and the text of Joyce's that preceded them, *A Portrait of the Artist as a Young Man*. The earlier text focuses on Stephen—principally as a student—insofar as he suffers from the claims made on him by his Irish, Catholic past. *Ulysses* "awakens" from this history when it passes from its early episodes to its later episodes, when it becomes Bloom's book rather than Stephen's. But this awakening only occurs through its recollecting and incorporating into its own substance Stephen's book, *Portrait*.

It is probably risky to push these claims about the structure of *Ulysses* vis-à-vis *Portrait* too far, at least without doing the necessary hermeneutic work to make these claims stick. In any case, one discovers that a settling of accounts with the past comparable to the one outlined above occurs in "Gerontion," and that this settling of accounts is absolutely central to the way that history comes to be taken up as a theme in the poem. Just as *Ulysses* recollects *Portrait*,

"Gerontion" recollects its own past. Fundamentally, it recollects "The Love Song of J. Alfred Prufrock," the very text from which Eliot had tried to cut himself free nearly a decade earlier. This is not to say, as some readers have said, that the two poems in fact present the same speaker in his youth and then in his old age.[18] It is, however, to recognize that the later poem thematizes as well as accomplishes an act of literary-historical recollection, and that the content of this recollection includes fragments of "Prufrock."

The contention that there is at least a connection between "Prufrock" and "Gerontion" is unlikely to be controversial. Both poems are dramatic monologues whose overeducated speakers—Denis Donoghue notes these speakers' "unmoored eloquence" (81)—lament their indecisiveness. The "I am not Prince Hamlet" of "Prufrock" becomes the "I was [not] at the hot gates" of "Gerontion." The "hundred visions and revisions" of the first becomes the "thousand small deliberations" of the second. What distinguishes the two poems is that the former presents its speaker's indecisions as they are lived—such that Prufrock can ask directly "Do I dare . . . ?"—while in the latter the speaker's indecisions are merely recollected. Indeed, recollection provides the speaker with his only real content. He exists only as the memory of where he was not—the hot gates, the salt marsh—and what he did not do—heave a cutlass, fight. And yet, his not having done is the flipside of another sort of life. If the speaker of "Gerontion" can refer with unearned familiarity to the "hot gates" or "the salt marsh," or if he can allude to Dante's "backward devils" or to Lancelot Andrewes's commentary on the Gospels, it is because, instead of living and fighting, he has read and ruminated. A truly hopeless romantic, he has chosen literature over life. As such, the content of his monologue is not merely a litany of his failures; it is also a collection of literary-historical allusions. And among these allusions is "Prufrock," its melancholy voice and its presentations of indecisiveness. In the gloomy consciousness of the gerontion, allusions to Eliot—by way of "Prufrock"—intermingle with those to Herodotus, Dante, Andrewes, and others.

"Gerontion" recollects "Prufrock"; it contains the earlier work within it as old age contains within it the youth that it was. Eliot has given us a model for thinking about this sort of literary-historical recollection in "Tradition," writing that "the difference between the present and the past is that the conscious present is an awareness of the past in a way and to an extent which the past's awareness of itself cannot show" (SW 29). The movement from past to present is also a movement from a partial knowledge to a more complete knowledge, or from knowledge to knowledge of this knowledge. Eliot is here thinking of literary history more generally, not of the relationship of one particular work to another and certainly not of the relationship between the works of a single author; nonetheless, there is no reason why the same characterization should not hold, ceteris paribus, for each of these forms. The movement from "Prufrock" to "Gerontion" should, therefore, also present an increase in knowledge, an awareness of the earlier poem to which the earlier poem was not itself privy. In other words, what we should find is—on a considerably diminished scale—something akin to the ideally synthetic progress of the "mind of Europe . . . which abandons nothing *en route*, which does not superannuate either Shakespeare, or Homer, or the rock drawing of the Magdalenian draughtsmen" (29).

That "Gerontion" seems to deny this development is, therefore, worthy of attention. When we read from "Prufrock" to "Gerontion," what we encounter is not a narrative of expanding knowledge but one of an ever-worsening disarticulation of consciousness. "Gerontion," through its speaker, separates literature from life, such that, in the poem, the very scholarly labor that Eliot prescribes to burgeoning poets in "Tradition" is located at the furthest remove from any creative activity. As it progresses, however, the poem also calls into question the very possibility of recollection. By the poem's penultimate stanza, the speaker's monologue has become a broken current of images:

> These with a thousand small deliberations
> Protract the profit of their chilled delirium,
> Excite the membrane, when the sense has cooled,
> With pungent sauces, multiply variety
> In a wilderness of mirrors. What will the spider do,
> Suspend its operations, will the weevil
> Delay? De Bailhache, Fresca, Mrs. Cammel, whirled
> Beyond the circuit of the shuddering Bear
> In fractured atoms. Gull against the wind, in the windy straits
> Of Belle Isle, or running on the Horn,
> White feathers in the snow, the Gulf claims,
> And an old man driven by the Trades
> To a sleepy corner. (61–73)

In these lines, which are as difficult as any Eliot had penned up to this point, images of confusion or disorder—"a wilderness of mirrors," "fractured atoms"—set the tone. Heretofore unfamiliar characters—De Bailhache, Fresca, Mrs. Cammel—are whirled into the poem only to be spun beyond any worldly context, while the scene itself pulses between the impossibly small—again, "fractured atoms"—and the impossibly great—the Mallarméan "shuddering Bear," perhaps one of the Ursa constellations, which we are, in any case, whirled beyond. And within this scene appears the "old man" himself, apparently having tumbled down into the chaosmos of his own scattered thoughts. The poem thus passes from a recollection of failure to a failure of recollection—not so much a failure to bring to mind the particular moments of one's life as a failure to collect any moments together in an orderly whole. Eliot has, of course, named this disarticulation of experience "amputation," and so long as we remain within the speaker's "dry brain," the term seems apt. We encounter him as the doomed modern man—the most ordinary man—who, unable to pass from information to knowledge or from literature to life, has lost himself in the passages of history or the passages of his books, the two having become indistinguishable.

When we read from "Prufrock" to "Gerontion," then, we face a narrative of increasing disorder, a breakdown of the very faculties that should allow the latter to recollect the former. And yet, despite the chaos regnant within the world of "Gerontion," the borders of this world are very carefully maintained. The poem marks these borders by its first lines—"Here I am, an old man in a dry month, / Being read to by a boy, waiting for rain"—and by its last lines—"Tenants of the house / Thoughts of a dry brain in a dry season." Everything that occurs within the poem—the wilderness of mirrors, the explosion of atoms, the shuddering bear, Dante, Shakespeare, and Eliot himself—occurs within a single consciousness, or as the effect of a single voice. As a lyric poem, "Gerontion" maintains its speaker, however minimally, as the locus of his own laments. By doing so, however, it produces as well a position distinct from these laments, a position from which they might be observed and evaluated. "Gerontion" thus effects a self-division comparable to the division that Eliot himself undergoes during his composition of "Prufrock," as well as to the self-division that Eliot recommends to aspiring poets in his critical writings. In "Gerontion," the division is between an inside—the disordered contents of the speaker's consciousness—and an outside that, lacking any content of its own, is simply a position from which the poem can be grasped as a single, unified whole.

This operation, as well as its essential connection to the form of the lyric, were elaborated with particular lucidity in the deconstructive criticism of the 1980s under the heading of "blockage." The latter, a term employed by Neil Hertz, describes the way in which "an indefinite and disarrayed sequence is resolved . . . into a one-to-one confrontation, when numerical excess can be converted into that supererogatory identification with the blocking agent that is the guarantor of the self's own integrity as an agent" (53).[19] In other words, blockage is the means by which an apparently anarchic collection of data is brought together as a single figure, or concept, or name. Once minimally ordered in this fashion, what appeared formerly as an unmanageable excess becomes a single obstacle to which a "self" can see itself opposed. And it is this opposition that ensures the self's identity, its ability to say "I" and "it." The speaker of "Gerontion" is unable to effect this blockage for himself. He is, however, its operator within the poem. The very fact that he laments his inability to weave together diverse moments of history or to move from history to action provides the content for a poem that does both, a poem that translates literary history into poetry.

Who or what occupies the position outside of the poem—the position from which the disordered contents of the gerontion's dry brain have become an "it" and so a poem—is hard to determine. I am not certain that the most obvious answer—that it is Eliot himself, the poet rather than his dramatic persona—is satisfactory. The problem with this answer is that it fails to account for the fact that Eliot is no less inside the poem—whirled along with De Bailhache, with Fresca (who will be whirled right out of "Gerontion," into the drafts of *The Waste Land*, and so into my next chapter), and with Mrs. Cammel—than he is outside it in his role as the poem's author. The line that divides "Gerontion" divides Eliot as well. It cuts across Eliot's own personal history, dividing "Prufrock" from "Gerontion" and so dividing Eliot from himself. It is, however, this division that allows Eliot to take possession of literary history, his own literary history as well as that of the whole of Europe. Why, then, locate himself on one side of the division or the other?

It seems to me better to conclude that what lies outside of "Gerontion," what occurs in the position of the "I" in Hertz's description of blockage, is merely the place from which history can be grasped and managed. If it is tempting to identify this place with the person of the author, perhaps it is because the structure under consideration so closely resembles the structure of self-consciousness itself, whether this structure appears as the knowledge of one's own knowledge, or as the poetic apprehension of (literary) history, or simply as the production of poetry—which, as Eliot insists, is finally inseparable from the mature poet's recollection of the past. Regardless of what occupies the place of the "outside" effected by the division, then, the division remains the very possibility of the synthesis of the critical and the creative that has become the hallmark of Eliot's poetic project. And so it remains as well the very possibility of the movement of literary history as Eliot has described it.

"The Love Song of J. Alfred Prufrock" and "Gerontion" stand on either side of Eliot's development in the decade leading up to his composition of *The Waste Land*. In these early poems, the lyric form supports a critical engagement with literary (as well as personal) history, a means of managing a potentially hazardous excess of the past. Lyric succeeds in the task that Eliot sets for it, though, only insofar as it is bound to a certain model of consciousness, one for which consciousness can divide itself from, so as to reflect critically on, itself. When Eliot passes from a lyric to an epic mode, however, when he passes from "Gerontion" to *The Waste Land*, he breaks with this model. The question posed by *The Waste Land*, then—and this is really the question at stake in all of the debates over whether the poem is finally spoken by one voice or by many—is how a poem might order history in the absence of a (lyric) consciousness. How does poetry reflect on itself when its form is not that of a speaking individual but literary history itself?

## CHAPTER 2

# SATIRE

**OVER THE LAST COUPLE OF DECADES,** several books and articles have appeared focusing on T. S. Eliot's complicated relationship to popular culture.[1] Spurred on by the publication of Eliot's earliest—and coarsest—poetic sketches in *Inventions of the March Hare* (1997), these studies share a distrust of the one-dimensional image of Eliot as a prematurely aged conservative and tireless foe of the average man. In its place, they present an Eliot who devoured detective novels, laughed at slapstick, enjoyed the London music halls, and most importantly, incorporated these experiences into his poetry. In the most authoritative of these studies, *T. S. Eliot and the Cultural Divide* (2003), David Chinitz locates his own revisionist reading of Eliot's project within the changing history of Eliot scholarship. If the postwar critics presented Eliot as a standard-bearer for the "cultural-political consensus," Chinitz observes, and the critics of the 1960s gave us Eliot the "bogeyman," the embodiment of a "hierarchical, elitist tradition," now is the time for a "messy, intractable Eliot who unsettles, rather than confirms, the received notions of literature, culture, and modernism," an Eliot who "helps us to recover the anarchic shock that modernist literature delivered in its original moment" (16–17). To find putatively low forms at work in Eliot's exceedingly high modernism, then, is to find a place where the division between low and high, the division that Eliot's writing is supposed to secure, threatens to become "messy," perhaps even to collapse. In making his argument, Chinitz notes the "complex case" of *The Waste Land* and specifically the form of the poem as it existed before Ezra Pound's editorial intervention. As we know thanks to the availability of the pre-publication drafts, Eliot's early conception of *The Waste Land* borrowed at least as much from the lyrics of popular songs, the rhythms of working-class speech, and the atmosphere of public houses as it did from fire sermons and grail quests. Pound made *The Waste Land* more compact, more fragmentary, and more modern; but he also removed from the poem most of its references to popular forms. Without Pound's intervention, then—this is Chinitz's claim—"*The Waste Land* would have openly established popular culture as a major intertext of modernist poetry" ("T. S. Eliot and the Cultural Divide" 241–242). Eliot's masterpiece would have resisted rather than exacerbated the "cultural divide" that has become synonymous with the modernist project.

I have a hard time quarreling with the aim of revisionist readings such as the one that Chinitz sets forth: to find in Eliot's poetry—and so in the version of modernism that Eliot's poetry represents—something more than high-art snobbery.[2] The upshot is, or ought to be, an avant-garde Eliot, one who, like the affiliates of the historical avant-gardes and unlike the high-modernist mandarins, turned to popular forms both out of a real sense of enjoyment and "to displace and estrange the deadening givens of accepted practice" (Crow 4). Still, I have my doubts about the ability of these readings to make sense of what Eliot was attempting in *The Waste Land*. There are really two issues here. The first— and, I think, the less interesting of the two—concerns Eliot's predilection for popular forms. Eliot did enjoy popular forms—vaudeville and minstrel shows, detective novels and dirty jokes. But he also took pains to distinguish the "mind which creates" from "the man who suffers" (*SW* 31)—and, presumably, from the man who enjoys as well. We need not take him at his word, of course; but we should at least concede that even the man who suffers and enjoys is often himself divided, and so the pleasure or pain felt by Eliot in the presence of popular entertainments is likely a complex matter. No less a critic of "kitsch" than Clement Greenberg admitted in an interview near the end of his life to having as a youth dreamed of painting like Norman Rockwell (de Duve 39).[3] This admission should not be terribly surprising. If there is one thing that a study of twentieth-century culture teaches, it is that aesthetic pleasure in the twentieth century is rarely simple and not always pleasurable. This is, after all, the century that gave us "good bad books."[4]

I do not want to spend time trying to ascertain which, if any, of Eliot's pleasures were guilty. I hope, though, that we can agree that Eliot's pleasure in the popular need not have been the same pleasure he felt before Dante or

Dryden, that Eliot need not have experienced his enjoyment of the low and the high in quite the same way. And if the commingling of the low and the high in Eliot's consciousness was perhaps complicated, why should we assume that this commingling in Eliot's poetry is any less so? This brings me to the second issue, the more interesting one. It concerns not the fact that low forms appear alongside high in the drafts of *The Waste Land* (and in the final version of the poem as well, though their presence is diminished); it concerns, rather the way the poem manages these forms. I assume here something like the philosopher W. V. O. Quine's distinction between "mention" and "use."[5] Eliot mentions all sorts of things in his poetry; the question the critic must ask, though, is how he uses them. Eliot himself employs a version of this distinction in "*Ulysses*, Order, and Myth," an essay from the same period as *The Waste Land* in which he defends Joyce's novel—though the adequacy of this term, Eliot suggests, is doubtful—against his friend Richard Aldington's charge that Joyce opens the door to Dadaist formlessness.[6] Here is the relevant passage:

> It is much easier to be a classicist in literary criticism than in creative art— because in criticism you are responsible only for what you want, and in creation you are responsible for what you can do with material which you must simply accept. . . . The question, then, about Mr. Joyce, is: how much living material does he deal with, and how does he deal with it: deal with, not as a legislator or exhorter, but as an artist? (*SP* 177)

Unlike the critic, the creative artist "must simply accept" the material that he encounters. Eliot himself accepts Dante, Shakespeare, and Dryden; and he accepts—perhaps he must simply accept—popular forms as well. All appear together in *The Waste Land*. But this alone tells us nothing about how Eliot uses his material, how he deals with it, not as an exhorter of popular forms but as a poet.

In what follows, I want to address Eliot's attempts in the drafts of *The Waste Land* to deal with the living material of culture, both high and low, as a poet. And this means attending to how Eliot works on his material, how he subordinates one bit of cultural detritus to another, how he draws (and resists drawing) equivalences. And so it means attending to how—to quote again from Eliot's defense of *Ulysses*—he struggles to give "a shape and a significance to the immense panorama of futility and anarchy that is contemporary history" (*SP* 177). More particularly, my claim is that during the period when he was drafting *The Waste Land*, Eliot was thinking of nothing more than providing the living material of his culture with "shape and significance," and that, to accomplish this task, he turned to satire. It is satire that promised for a time to allow Eliot to extend beyond the limited form of the lyric the strategy I outlined in the previous chapter: the strategy of managing literary history through recurring acts of self-division. For what is satire if not a machine for producing divisions—between self and other, for example, or between what deserves respect and what calls for ridicule? Accordingly, the disappearance of satire from the final version of Eliot's poem following the editorial suggestions of Pound, and Eliot's replacement of his earlier satirical method by the so-called mythical method—my topic in the next chapter—reflects satire's failure to accomplish the task that Eliot set for it.

Before turning specifically to Eliot's experiments with satire, however, we need to look more closely at Eliot's early conception of *The Waste Land*, and at his struggle to provide his poem with "shape and significance." This should help to lead us into the problem for which satire appeared to Eliot, however temporarily, as the solution.

## I. A Long Poem

On 18 December 1919, in a letter conveying his holiday greetings to his "Dearest Mother," Eliot notes that his New Year's resolution for 1920 is the following: "to write a long poem I have had on my mind for a long time and to prepare a small prose book from my lectures on poetry" (*L* 1:424). As for the latter, *The Sacred Wood* would be published by Methuen in November of 1920. The former, however—the "long poem" that had long been on Eliot's mind—would not be ready for public consumption for another two and a half years. *The Waste Land* would eventually appear almost simultaneously in the October 1922 issue of *The Criterion* and the November 1922 issue of *The Dial*, before being published as a book in the United States by Boni and Liveright (December 1922) and in England by Hogarth Press (September 1923). From conception to completion, the poem followed a circuitous route, and determining when, exactly, the poem's various sections and subsections were written has kept critics busy since Valerie Eliot's facsimile edition of the manuscripts became available in 1971. Grover Smith, Hugh Kenner, Helen Gardner, Lyndall Gordon, and most recently Lawrence Rainey have all set themselves the task of dating *The Waste Land*.[7] As a result of their labors, we know that Eliot did much of his work on the poem in 1921, during a stretch of time marked by challenges both professional—the demands of his job at Lloyds Bank, for example—and personal—his wife's recurrent bouts of nervous illness and his own breakdown. But *The Waste Land* includes as well much earlier material, fragments of verse written nearly a decade earlier while Eliot was still a student at Harvard. If we locate the origin of *The Waste Land* in these early poetic experiments, then it is indeed true that, in the last days of 1919, *The Waste Land* had already been on Eliot's mind (in one form or another) for a very long time. And so it is no great surprise that only a couple of weeks after the poem's publication, Eliot would be ready to put *The Waste Land* behind him. On 15 November 1922, he would write to Richard Aldington that *The Waste Land* had already become for him "a thing of the past" (*L* 1:786–787).

But let us return to Eliot's New Year's resolution. At the end of 1919, and before he knew much of anything else about *The Waste Land*, Eliot knew that it would be "a long poem." He knew that it would comprise more material—historical, cultural—than anything he had written up to that point. Much of this material is still present in the final version of *The Waste Land*, but much is not, owing to the editorial work of Pound and (to a lesser degree) Vivienne Eliot, as well as to Eliot's own willingness to murder his darlings. In the drafts handed over to Pound in January 1922, the poem commences not with the now familiar invocation of cruel April, but with a lengthy description of a pub crawl in Boston. The doomed voyage of Phlebas the Phoenician—only eight lines in the published version of "Death by Water"—includes an additional eighty-three lines. "The Fire Sermon" features a much longer treatment of the carbuncular young man's seduction of the typist and begins with a parody of Pope's *Rape of the Lock* (1714). On balance, the draft version of the poem contains a good deal more modern material—Kenner described it as "an urban panorama refracted through Augustan styles," noting the importance of Dryden's *Annus Mirabilis* (1667) as a precursor ("Urban Apocalypse" 46)—while the poem's archaic dimension is less pronounced. The "wasteland" of the poem's title (though this was not yet the poem's title) is not the blighted landscape of Arthurian legend but Boston, Paris, Munich, and especially London as they appeared in Eliot's own present.

In the drafts of *The Waste Land* and in the dense, allusive style that he had been developing over the last decade, Eliot depicts a world very close to the world that he knows best. He "accepts" this world, to echo again the language of "*Ulysses*, Order and Myth." Indeed, in the first section of the poem he reproduces his own itinerary. The poem begins in America, in a pub in the northeastern United States where we meet the author's namesake—"First we had a couple of feelers down at Tom's place / There was old Tom, boiled to the eyes, blind" (*WLF* 1–2)—before progressing to Europe. The latter is marked by a babel of English, French, and German voices, as well as by an intermingling of the (literary) past and the (urban) present, of high culture and low. In the world Eliot describes, the writings of Ovid find their place next to the typewriter, while one's recollection of *The Tempest* is interrupted by "O O O O that Shakespeherian Rag" (53). London remains London, though superimposed upon it is Dante's vision of Hell. Pound is present—conspicuous in his Stetson hat—as is Eliot himself, both as the "Old Tom" of the poem's first lines and in the fragments he shores of his own earlier verse experiments, variants of lines from "After the Turning" (1913), "So Through the Evening" (1913), and "Death of St. Narcissus" (1914–1915) now incorporated into the body of *The Waste Land*.

With *The Waste Land*, Eliot continues the project initiated in his earlier lyrics, recollecting histories literary as well as personal. He breaks from the relative minimalism of these earlier verse experiments, however, to embrace the maximalism of a form that we may as well call "epic." Why he chooses to do so is not entirely clear. James Longenbach offers an explanation as convincing as we are likely to find when he locates Eliot within "a generation of studiously diminished lyric poets . . . confronted with an epic subject, one that seemed to cry out for the power and scope of the kind of poetry that Wordsworth wrote in the wake of the French Revolution" (108). "The results," Longenbach goes on, "were *The Cantos*, *The Waste Land*, *Spring and All*, *Observations*, and *The Tower*: all the most ambitious work of the modern poets, coming in the twenties, was at least in part the result of the social and aesthetic challenge of the war" (109). I do not think that Longenbach expects us to accept that the content of these diverse works was in each case prescribed by the war, but to recognize that the world after 1914 was sufficiently different from the prewar world to recommend a different sort of poetry, a poetry of greater scope. Additionally, Eliot had before him the example of Pound's *Hugh Selwyn Mauberley* (1920), which he would have been aware of while Pound was developing the poem in late 1919. And as he began serious work on *The Waste Land*, Eliot was very much aware of Joyce's *Ulysses*, the latter serialized from 1918 to 1920 in *The Egoist* and *The Little Review* until its publication was halted for reasons of obscenity. The "Oxen of the Sun" episode in particular, with its inventory of literary styles, likely encouraged Eliot to multiply voices in *The Waste Land*—a desire underscored in the poem's working title, "He Do the Police in Different Voices."

Eliot, however, provides his own justification for his long poem near the end of a short essay on the metaphysical poets occasioned by the publication of Herbert J. C. Grierson's edited collection *Metaphysical Lyrics and Poems of the Seventeenth Century: Donne to Butler* (1921). Shifting his focus from the seventeenth century to the twentieth, he describes the task of the modern poet in the following terms:

> It is not a permanent necessity that poets should be interested in philosophy, or in any other subject. We can only say that it appears likely that poets in our civilization, as it exists at present, must be *difficult*. Our civilization comprehends great variety and complexity, and this variety and complexity, playing upon a refined sensibility, must produce various and complex results. The poet must become more and more comprehensive, more allusive, more indirect, in order to force, to dislocate if necessary, language into his meaning. (*SW* 128)

Modern poetry must be difficult because the modern world is difficult. The latter's "variety and complexity . . . must produce various and complex results." Presenting Eliot with the Nobel Prize for Literature in 1948, the Swedish poet Anders Österling cited Eliot's remarks on the necessity of poetic difficulty as a way of framing Eliot's entire project: "[A]gainst the background of such a pronouncement, we may test [Eliot's] results and learn to understand the importance of his contribution" (50). Österling's point is that Eliot succeeded in what he set out to do—he responded to a difficult world with difficult poetry. To reject the latter for its difficulty is to misunderstand its relationship to the former, and so to misunderstand the nature of Eliot's achievement.

Something is missing, though, from Eliot's defense of difficulty as well as from Österling's defense of Eliot: an explanation of how, exactly, the variety and complexity of the modern world is taken up in the modern long poem. It is wrong, I believe, to assume that when Eliot describes modern poetry and the modern world in the same terms—both are "various," both are "complex"—he means that they are various and complex in the same way, that a modern poem must map as nearly as possible its modern territory. It is wrong to assume, then, that in its own variety and complexity *The Waste Land* simply reproduces the difficulty of the world that it poetically represents.[8] The modern world is difficult because it is disordered, chaotic. Modern poetry responds to this chaotic content, but it responds with formal order, for only through this order can poetry hope "to force, to dislocate if necessary" its materials into something meaningful. Eliot's goal in his composition of *The Waste Land* is to use one sort of difficulty—the difficulty of a rigorously complex form—to manage another—the difficulty of a disordered world. Between these two senses of "difficulty" lies the chasm that *The Waste Land* must bridge.

Eliot describes the particular difficulty of the modern world in detail in his "London Letters," the brief essays he published in the pages of *The Dial* beginning in the spring of 1921. In the last of these "Letters," completed after *The Waste Land* had already appeared but very much in keeping with the poem's representation of postwar London life, Eliot provides the modern world with a prognosis. I cited these lines in the previous chapter; here they are again:

> In a most interesting essay in the recent volume of *Essays on the Depopulation of Melanesia* the great psychologist W. H. R. Rivers adduces evidence which has led him to believe that the natives of that unfortunate archipelago are dying out principally for the reason that the "Civilization" forced upon them has deprived them of all interest in life. They are dying from pure boredom. When every theatre has been replaced by 100 cinemas, when every musical instrument has been replaced by 100 gramophones, when every horse has been replaced by 100 cheap motor cars, when electrical ingenuity has made it possible for every child to hear its bed-time stories through a wireless receiver attached to both ears, when applied science has done everything possible with the materials on this earth to make life as interesting as possible, it will not be surprising if the population of the entire civilized world rapidly follows the fate of the Melanesians. (663)

Eliot presents these quasi-ethnographic remarks as part of an obituary for the music hall performer Marie Lloyd, who had died 7 October 1922. In them, he laments the transformation of a truly popular culture—the culture, Eliot argues, that Lloyd exemplified—into an impersonal and degraded mass culture, a transformation that presages our extinction. The transformation occurs not only through the replacement of the theater by the cinema, the musical instrument by the gramophone, the better by the worse. It occurs as well through the replacement of one by one hundred—*one hundred* cinemas replace each theater, *one hundred* gramophones each instrument, and so on. What is at stake in Eliot's "Letter," then, is both degeneration—all of society, he writes, seems doomed to "drop into the same state of amorphous protoplasm as the bourgeoisie"—and proliferation. The technologies that Eliot lists proliferate: just as cars clog the street, gramophones and radios are now found in every home. And many of these technologies are themselves agents of proliferation, multiplying images and multiplying sounds.

The modern world is various and complex. It is also cluttered and degenerate. Insofar as he must map this modern world, the modern poet must take up the world's variety and complexity as well as its metastasizing excesses. And this taking up is a problem—*the* problem—for the modern poet; for it involves him in an activity of literary-historical retrieval that can be hard to distinguish from the proliferation and degeneration to which this activity ought to be opposed. We find an especially good example of what this taking up looks like as well as the problem it presents in the central stanza of the second section of *The Waste Land*, "A Game of Chess" (initially titled "In the Cage"). Following a long stanza in blank verse that commences with an echo of Shakespeare's *Anthony and Cleopatra*—"The Chair she sat in, like a burnished throne / glowed on the marble . . ." (*WLF* 1–2)—the meter of the poem becomes irregular as it opens onto the following fragmented exchange. In the draft version of the poem, it reads as follows:

> "My nerves are bad to-night. Yes, bad. Stay with me.
> "Speak to me. Why do you never speak. Speak.
> "What are you thinking of? What thinking? Think. What?
> "I never know what you are thinking. Think."
>
> I think we met first in rats' alley
> Where the dead men lost their bones.
>
> "What is that noise?"
> > The wind under the door.
>
> "What is that noise now? What is the wind doing?"
> > Carrying
> Away the little light dead people.
>
> "Do you know nothing? Do you see nothing? Do you remember
> "Nothing?"
>
> > I remember
> The hyacinth garden. Those are pearls that were his eyes, yes!
>
> "Are you alive, or not? Is there nothing in your head?"
> > But
>
> O O O O that Shakespeherian Rag—
> It's so elegant—
> So intelligent— (36–55)

These lines remain relatively unchanged between the drafts of the poem and the published version. In each, they take the form of a fractured dialogue between (it is usually assumed) a neurasthenic woman and her disaffected spouse. With their reference to the "hyacinth garden" (which appears exclusively in the drafts) as well as their invocation of the failures of speech, sight, vitality, and knowledge, they recall a moment from the first section of *The Waste Land*, "The Burial of the Dead": "Yet when we came back, late, from the Hyacinth garden, / Your arms full, and your hair wet, I could not / Speak, and my eyes failed, I was neither / Living nor dead, and I knew nothing" (37–40).[9] Indeed, when in the draft of "A Game of Chess" the speaker states "I remember / The hyacinth garden," the poem effectively re-members itself, bringing together two moments that might otherwise have seemed disconnected.

In the lines cited above, the question "Do you remember / Nothing?" receives two answers, however. The first, "the hyacinth garden," Eliot cut from the published version of the poem (though he allowed the other echoes of "The Burial of the Dead" to stand). The second, "those are pearls that were his eyes," a fragment of Ariel's song from *The Tempest*, Eliot retained. In the context of the fragmented exchange, the recitation of this line demonstrates that the speaker does remember something, that he retains a connection to his own—or at least to a larger cultural—past. In the wider context of "A Game of Chess," the allusion to *The Tempest* recalls the allusion to *Anthony and Cleopatra* with which the section began. And in the still wider context of *The Waste Land*, the content of Ariel's song recalls the drowned sailor of "The Burial of the Dead" and anticipates the drowned father of "The Fire Sermon" (the poem's third section), as well as the drowned sailor of "Death by Water" (the poem's fourth).

The art historian T. J. Clark has written that form is, finally, only a "controlled repetition" (7)—a repetition of marks, tones, phrases, themes, it is "endlessness without malignancy" (5). Accepting Clark's claim, we might say that Ariel's song provides *The Waste Land* with (some) form, helps to order it with echoes and anticipations—or, in the language of *The Waste Land*, with "memory and desire." But Ariel's song does something else as well. Almost as soon as it appears in the poem, it is transformed, passing over into a song that Eliot might have heard playing on "100 gramophones": "But / O O O O that Shakespeherian Rag— / It's so elegant— / So intelligent—." "That Shakespearian Rag," a 1912 ragtime hit and one of the few mentions of mass culture in *The Waste Land* to elude Pound's pen, suggests the leveling of culture that, in Eliot's "London Letter," points to the Melanesians' and our own ruin. Indeed, other lyrics of the "Rag" (which Eliot does not quote) seem to poke fun at the ease with which the high becomes the low or at the impossibility of distinguishing the one from the other: "Bill Shakespeare never knew / of ragtime in his days, / But the high browed rhymes, / Of his syncopated lines, / You'll admit, surely fit / any song that's now a hit" (Buck and Ruby 52).

And herein lies the problem. As we saw in the previous chapter, Eliot characterizes poetic creation as depending on "a process of depersonalization": again, "the progress of an artist is a continual self-sacrifice, a continual extinction of personality" (*SW* 30). The mature poet empties himself of his own personality, all the better to open himself to literary history, to the "mind of Europe," a mind that in its development "does not superannuate either Shakespeare, or Homer, or the rock drawing of the Magdalenian draughtsmen" (29). The mature poet becomes, finally, a "receptacle" in which literary history is "catalyzed" (30–31). This is the position that Eliot lays out in "Tradition and the Individual Talent," and it is one that Eliot never repudiates. But is this position not exemplified as well by the speaker of "A Game of Chess"? Challenged by his anxious interlocutor to express a personal truth, the speaker responds instead with literary history: "Those are pearls that were his eyes." And so he responds as a poet, for as a poet he should have nothing in his head but lines from Shakespeare (from Homer, from Dante, from Dryden, and so on). In his response, in his recollection, the speaker produces something new: he recalls Shakespeare, and he transforms Shakespeare. Formally, then, his activity has everything in common with the critical anamnesis that Eliot prescribes; the speaker is a model of the mature poet. And yet his activity is not something that Eliot could possibly endorse. When the speaker recalls William Shakespeare, he transforms the bard into Bill. He produces, then, not real novelty but waste. As a result, his act of poetic recollection proves complicit with and perhaps indistinguishable from the processes of cultural degeneration that, *qua* poetic, it ought to combat.

In "A Game of Chess," we are left with a lack of distinction between high and low, poet and gramophone, William and Bill. How, then, does Eliot distinguish his own poem—itself built through acts of creative anamnesis—from the degenerate recollections thematized therein? The problem is not so different from the problem we encountered in "Gerontion," a poem in which what is "kept" (or recollected) is "adulterated." In the earlier lyric, recall, we meet a speaker who has lost himself in the passages of history and the passages of his books, a speaker whose ever-worsening disarticulation of consciousness threatens the poem in which he appears with formlessness. "Gerontion," however, resists this disorder, managing its own diverse materials by setting up a division between an inside—what occurs as the chaos of history within the poem's speaker's "dry brain"—and an outside—the perspective from which this chaos can be recognized as the possession of a single consciousness, the content of a single lyric. I characterized this operation as the poem's strategy of "blockage," its resolution of its own "fractured atoms" into a single obstacle to which a more enlightened position could be opposed.

In a late moment in the composition of *The Waste Land*, Eliot considered a strategy for managing his long poem's varied and complex materials similar to the strategy he employed in "Gerontion." Or rather, he considered employing "Gerontion" *as* a strategy. In a January 1922 letter to Pound in which he thanks his friend for his criticisms of the drafts of *The Waste Land*—"accepted so far as understood"—Eliot begins a numbered list of questions by asking, "Do you advise printing Gerontion as prelude in book or pamphlet form?" (*L* 1:629) The question is not so odd, given the formal and thematic similarities of the two poems—each prefers the allusive to the direct, and each presents history as something nightmarish. The poems do fit together. More importantly, though, to print "Gerontion" as a prelude to *The Waste Land* would be a way of using the former to manage the disorder of the latter. Once in place as a frame, "Gerontion" would suggest that the different voices comprised by *The Waste Land* all echo within the head of the same old man. It would thus collect together the high and the low, all of the proliferation and decay characteristic of a formless age. And so it would force in *The Waste Land* the same totalizing moment of blockage at work in the earlier poem. If, as Pound proclaimed in "Date Line," "an epic is a poem including history," "Gerontion" would become a lyric containing epic.

Pound's reply to Eliot's query arrived a few days later: "I do not advise printing 'Gerontion' as preface. One don't miss it at all as the thing now stands. To be more lucid still, let me say that I advise you NOT to print 'Gerontion' as prelude" (*L* 1:630). Pound does not elaborate on why including "Gerontion" as preface or prelude would be such a mistake; he simply advises against it, twice. We can, however, conjecture. By prefacing *The Waste Land* with "Gerontion," Eliot would have provided his long poem with a principle of order, but only insofar as he sacrificed his desire to make *The Waste Land* a long poem. The effect of including the earlier lyric, though it would have increased the length of *The Waste Land* by some seventy-five lines (and so, perhaps, have eliminated the need for

Eliot's explanatory notes),[10] would have been—significantly, if paradoxically—
to make *The Waste Land* smaller. It would have reduced the long poem to the
mechanisms of a single consciousness and so have canceled the poem's claim to
map the variety and complexity of its modern historical moment. Unlike "Prufrock," "Gerontion," or any other lyric, then, *The Waste Land* cannot rely on a
metaphor of consciousness as a source of unity, at least not while still making
good on its author's epic ambitions. And so the strategy of blockage available to
Eliot in the earlier lyrics cannot function in the same way in Eliot's long poem.
Perhaps Eliot did not see this as clearly as Pound. Pound had, after all, spent
more time than had Eliot thinking about long poems—he had completed work
on *Hugh Selwyn Mauberley*, and he was at work on the *Cantos*. Or perhaps Eliot
was simply frustrated, prepared to give up on his own epic aims and to accept
his role as a writer of (admittedly very long) short poems.

Here I want to interrupt my preliminary treatment of the composition of
*The Waste Land* in the hopes that I have at least succeeded in sketching the
problem that Eliot faced and the fact that the solution to this problem could not
be the same solution effected in the earlier lyrics—at least not without betray-
ing the ambitions of *The Waste Land*. Coming as it does in January 1922, Eliot's
suggestion to Pound regarding "Gerontion" reveals that, even at this late stage
in the poem's composition, Eliot's conception of *The Waste Land* remained un-
settled. His willingness to reimagine *The Waste Land*—for this would have been
the effect of including "Gerontion" as a preface—attests to some prior disap-
pointments, to unsuccessful struggles to make his long poem cohere. I want to
turn to what was probably the most significant episode in these struggles: Eliot's
experimentation with satire. For satire—this will be my claim in what follows—
promised to order the proliferations and degenerations characteristic of our
disordered age, and so to shepherd *The Waste Land* from formlessness to form.

## II. Falling, Laughing

In his "Reflections on *Vers Libre*," published in the *New Statesman* in March
of 1917, Eliot concludes his discussion of the most modern tendencies in verse
with a nod to a moment from the literary past that, he argues, might determine
the literary future: "We only need the coming of a Satirist—no man of genius is
rarer—to prove that the heroic couplet has lost none of its edge since Dryden
and Pope laid it down" (*SP* 36). With this remark, Eliot isolates an especially
rigid and seemingly exhausted poetic form—the heroic couplet—so as to insist

on the possibility of its contemporary resuscitation and so on the possibility of a return to "formal, rhymed verse." He targets the proponents of so-called free verse. The latter, in extolling the virtues of freedom from pattern, meter, and rhyme, assume that literary history progresses through the elimination of formal constraints. Eliot turns this assumption on its head. If the heroic couplet has "lost none of its edge" since the age of Dryden and Pope, then the present cannot be said to overtake the past. And if "the man of genius" whose coming Eliot anticipates is not the man who has outgrown pattern, meter, and rhyme—if he is, on the contrary, the man who demonstrates their continued vitality—then the familiar opposition of historically sedimented form to creative élan must ring false. The "decay of intricate formal patterns" that we see around us, Eliot concludes, does not reflect the necessary ascent of free verse; rather, this decay is to be expected at those moments when a "closely-knit and homogeneous society, where many men are at work on the same problems" is lacking. Europe in the early twentieth century is quite simply not "such a society as those which produced the Greek chorus, the Elizabethan lyric, and the Troubadour canzone" (36). But under the right conditions, and perhaps compelled by a man of genius, these forms might live again.

"Reflections on *Vers Libre*" is one of Eliot's earliest critical essays, appearing in print a couple of months before *Prufrock and Other Observations* (1917). And yet, despite its relatively early date of publication, the essay anticipates concerns that would dominate Eliot's critical writings over the next decade and, indeed, for the remainder of his career. Already we find Eliot bringing together, on the one hand, a description of modern society as dispersed, as lacking the integral order characteristic of fifth-century Athens or Elizabethan London; and, on the other, an apology for historical knowledge and formal stringency. Between the one and the other, however, between cultural confusion and literary form, Eliot introduces not the poet *cum* catalyst but the satirist, "no man of genius is rarer." The satirist, Eliot suggests, should he arrive, will secure our difficult passage from formlessness to form. He will prove that even so antiquated a technique as the heroic couplet "has lost none of its edge since Dryden and Pope laid it down."

For a time, Eliot seemed to believe that satire carried the hopes of literary modernism—that it might help to reverse the "decay of formal patterns," certainly, but also that it might serve as a bulwark against what he would describe a few years later in a letter to the writer Max Bodenheim as the "putrescence of English literature and journalism" (*L* 1:531). And Eliot was not unique among the "Men of 1914" in his high estimation of satire. "Satire" was the term Ezra Pound chose to describe his own early vorticist experiments (Hofer 463); and Pound remained attached to this term, so that on receiving *Poetry* magazine's Harriet Monroe Memorial Prize in 1962, he could describe himself (albeit with a bit of false modesty) as only a "minor satirist" (qtd. in Kenner, *Pound Era* 556). Satire was still more essential to Wyndham Lewis, the figure with perhaps the best claim to being the satirical "man of genius" whose coming Eliot foretold. Though he composed no couplets, Lewis completed the greatest work of modernist satire, *The Apes of God* (1930), a brutal attack on the mores of the 1920s London literati. More than a decade before *The Apes of God* was published, Eliot had already celebrated Lewis's comic acumen in an early review of Lewis's *Tarr* (1918), singling out for praise the novel's distinctively English humor (T 105). And Eliot would reaffirm his judgment of Lewis—this time with reference to Lewis's paintings rather than to his fiction—in his "London Letter" of May 1921, writing of Lewis's "Tyros" series that "I have always thought [Lewis's] design at its greatest when it approached the border of satire and caricature" (*TAWL* 169).

From the heroic couplets of Dryden and Pope to the caricatures of Lewis—it is easy to lose the thread that connects the diverse instances of satire that proliferate in and around Eliot's writings during the 1910s and 1920s. In a 1921 study of Dryden, Eliot himself acknowledges that satire is indeed hard to pin down, and he warns against "letting our familiarity with the word blind us to differences and refinements; we must not assume that satire is a fixed type" (*SW* 114). Eliot's caveat is important, for it prevents satire's being fixed at any particular historical moment—the eighteenth century, for example—or tied to any particular verse form—the heroic couplet, for example; and it allows for the possibility of satire's mutating in response to the needs of its (modern) practitioners. Nonetheless, and bearing Eliot's warning in mind, we can still indicate some qualities of satire in general, qualities that might help us to understand why Eliot found satire so promising.

Here, let me cite a remark that appears in Richard Aldington's 1915 "Reflections on Ernest Dowson," an essay in which Aldington anticipates many of the sentiments expressed in Eliot's own "London Letters"—"popular art was all right so long as it was the art of the people, but now that it has become the possession of the middle classes it is hopeless"—and presents, perhaps in spite of himself, the problem that satire would be tasked with solving. "The arts," Aldington writes, "are now divided between popular charlatans and men of talent, who, of necessity, write, think and paint only for each other, since there is no one else to understand them" (37). Aldington's remark exhibits a high-modernist confidence—the division between "popular charlatans and men of talent," Aldington suggests, is secure—and we find similar claims in the writings of Aldington's contemporaries. So, Pound in a letter to William Carlos Williams: "As for the 'eyes of a too ruthless public': damn their eyes. No art ever yet grew by looking into the eyes of the public, ruthless or otherwise" (4). But Aldington's remark exhibits as well, I think, a high-modernist anxiety. As Aldington admits, modernist art faces a public that is not just uninterested but uncomprehending as well, and so it must seek validation from a coterie composed solely of the artists who produce it. But how is the validity of this coterie's judgment determined? Who has decided that its artists are themselves truly "men of talent"? The answer that they are men of talent because they have produced good art would have to be circular. And so Aldington's assertion is just that, an assertion.

In trying to answer the question "How can fraudulent art be exposed?" Stanley Cavell brings the anxiety implicit in Aldington's assertion into focus:

> There is no one feature, or definite set of features, which may be described in technical handbooks, and no specific tests by which [an artwork's] fraudulence can be detected and exposed. Other frauds and impostors, like forgers and counterfeiters, admit clear outcomes, conclude in dramatic discoveries—the impostor is unmasked at the ball, you find the counterfeiters working over their press, the forger is caught signing another man's name, or he confesses. There are no such proofs possible for the assertion that the art accepted by a public is fraudulent; the artist himself may not know. (190)

This problem of fraudulence, Cavell wants to claim, belongs to art in general. For art's quality is decided by a judgment of taste, a judgment that, in the last instance, cannot be explained by pointing to any discernible qualities of the artwork itself, as one could to reveal a forgery, for example. And this problem is exacerbated in the situation of modernism. Modernism eschews classical standards of beauty—Cavell points to transformations in music from Schöenberg to Cage, but he could as easily have pointed to transformations in painting from Manet to Rauschenberg, or in the novel from Flaubert to Beckett—and modernism relies on an audience that simply cannot be trusted: "[T]he philistine audience cannot afford to admit the new; the *avant-garde* audience cannot afford not to. This bankruptcy means that both are at the mercy of their tastes

or fears and that no artist can test his work either by its rejection or its acceptance" (206). The coterie on which Aldington's division between "popular
charlatans and men of talent" depends is precisely the audience that cannot
afford not to admit the new, that cannot risk itself by dividing the fraud from
the genuine article. And so Aldington's artist, like Cavell's artist, finds himself
in a state of uncertainty, unable to decide whether his talent is real or fraudulent. For there exists no legible criterion—neither rules of composition, nor the
response of the audience, nor the conviction of the artist himself—by which the
authenticity or the fraudulence of the modernist work can be decided.

It is within this situation—a situation marked not by the clear division of
charlatans from men of talent, impostors from the genuine article, but by the
inability to separate the one from the other and so by bare assertions, ongoing
struggle, and the constant threat of fraudulence—that satire appears so promising. And this because satire offers to secure the very divisions that art, and,
a fortiori, modernist art, leaves insecure. Here, I draw on the theory of satire
developed by Fredric Bogel. Bogel is himself particularly interested in the Augustan context; indeed, the authors and works he discusses are often the same
works discussed by Eliot in the latter's numerous essays on the luminaries of
the eighteenth century; but the conception of satire that Bogel puts forward is
especially relevant to the situation of modernism as I have described it:

> The "first" satiric gesture is not to expose the satiric object in all its alien differ-
> ence but to *define* it as different, as other: to make a difference by setting up a
> textual machine or mechanism for producing difference. The mechanism does
> more than that, but we should begin here: not with the recognition of difference
> but with anxiety about proximity or sameness or identification and with the
> consequent production of difference. (42)

Satire is mistakenly construed as a rejection of what is so plainly alien as to
invite easy mockery; but "if a thing were at a safe distance it wouldn't seem
pressingly odious." We would do better to say that satire appears as a value only
in situations of troubling proximity, situations in which the distance between
the satirist and the object of ridicule threatens to collapse. Lewis does a nice job
in one of his autobiographies of characterizing a situation of this sort, writing
that "we are all in the melting pot. I resist the process of melting so have a very
lively time of it. I know that if I let myself melt I should get mixed up with all
sorts of people I would sooner be dead than mixed into" (*Blasting* 15).[11] Satire—
and this is really the source for Lewis of its appeal—is a way to combat the

threat of melting. It does so, in Lewis's words again, with a "laugh like a bomb" (Lewis et al., *Blast I* 31). The violent laughter that attends satire is all the proof needed that the division on which satire insists has been recognized, has been accepted as real. Just as this laughter marks in the eighteenth century the division of Pope and Swift from their Grub Street contemporaries, from "dunces" and "scribblers," it should mark in the twentieth the division of "men of talent" from "popular charlatans" and "frauds."

Eliot provides no detailed treatment in his critical writings of satire's power to divide. He does, however, endorse a theorization of the comic that, read alongside his scattered remarks on satire, helps us to understand better satire's importance to his poetics. In *Eliot's Dark Angel*, Ronald Schuchard describes the young Eliot's "immersing himself in the savage and violent tradition of English comedy, from Christopher Marlowe and Ben Jonson to Charles Dickens, thence to the most contemporary manifestation of the ferocious comic in England—his bawdy friend Wyndham Lewis" (89). And Eliot immersed himself as well in philosophical reflections on humor, paying particular attention to Charles Baudelaire's 1855 *On the Essence of Laughter* and Henri Bergson's 1900 *Laughter*. Especially important is Eliot's encounter with the earlier Baudelaire essay—"*qui vaut bien celui de Bergson*," Eliot writes (*TAWL* 169)—because it is in this essay that Baudelaire associates laughter with a power of division in general and self-division in particular.

Baudelaire himself describes "On the Essence of Laughter" as "purely an artist's and a philosopher's article." He locates the basis of laughter in the "Satanic" idea of one's own superiority. The latter is revealed by the joy one feels at "the sight of a man falling on the ice or in the street" (*Painter of Modern Life* 152). Laughter thus signals a difference—"I am not my fellow man"—and a hierarchy—"because I am better than him, because I would not have fallen." This difference separates a man from the world, from his fallen contemporaries, but it can also separate a man from himself, at least if he is a certain sort of man: "The man who trips would be the last to laugh at his own fall," Baudelaire notes, "unless he happened to be a philosopher, one who had acquired by habit a power of rapid self-division and thus of assisting as a disinterested spectator at the phenomena of his own ego. But such cases are rare" (154). The philosopher is the man who can separate himself from himself to reflect critically on his own consciousness. He shares this power of self-division with an unusual cast of characters, with Maturin's Melmoth and with the Pierrot of the English pantomimes. Of the former, Baudelaire writes that he is a "living contradiction," that he has "parted company with the fundamental conditions of life; his bodily organs can no longer sustain his thought" (153). And of the latter, he recalls a scene played at the Théâtre des Variétés in which the trunk of the decapitated Pierrot "jumped to its feet, triumphantly lifted its own head as though it was a ham or a bottle of wine, and, with far more circumspection than the great St. Denis, proceeded to stuff it into its pocket!" (161).

Laughter, as Baudelaire describes it, marks the division between "us" and "them" that satire is supposed to secure. But it marks as well, at least potentially, another division, a division within the self of the individual who laughs. I want to underscore this second division—not of the man of talent from the popular charlatan, for example, but of the man of talent from himself—for it is this division in particular that proves central to Eliot's mobilization of satire in *The Waste Land*. For in *The Waste Land*, Eliot presents poetry itself as a potential source of degeneration and so tasks satire with separating the poet from himself, from his own degraded double. I discussed in some detail in the previous chapter the young Eliot's strategy of self-division, of self-cutting. This strategy, I claimed, is characteristic of Eliot's relationship to personal as well as literary history in the early lyrics. With satirical self-division, then, we find ourselves on familiar ground. What has changed, though, is the scope of Eliot's project. Having moved beyond the form of the lyric, Eliot has moved as well beyond the metaphors of consciousness that the lyric entails. And so by turning to satire, he turns from psychological categories to generic ones, from the lyrical self to the satirical operation.

### III. Digestion and Division

As I noted above, the importance of satire to the construction of *The Waste Land* appears most vividly in the drafts, completed in Switzerland in late 1921 while Eliot was convalescing following a nervous disorder and delivered to Pound for editorial corrections in January 1922. In these drafts, Eliot finally attempts to make good on his suggestion that "we only need the coming of a Satirist . . . to prove that the heroic couplet has lost none of its edge since Dryden and Pope laid it down." In the draft of "The Fire Sermon," the first stanza reads:

> Admonished by the sun's inclining ray,
> And swift approaches of the thievish day,
> The white-armed Fresca blinks, and yawns, and gapes,
> Aroused from dreams of love and pleasant rapes.

> Electric summons of the busy bell
> Brings brisk Amanda to destroy the spell;
> With coarsened hand, and hard plebian tread,
> Who draws the curtain round the lacquered bed,
> Depositing thereby a polished tray
> Of soothing chocolate, or stimulating tea. (*WLF* 1–10)

The poem continues in heroic couplets for sixty-two more lines. Eliot alludes to Pope, and specifically to Pope's own satirical *Rape of the Lock*, signaling his indebtedness to the eighteenth century's "master of hatred" (*SW* 102) through the stanza's form (heroic couplets) and content (a scene of awakening), as well as by the more heavy-handed mention of "pleasant rapes." "Fresca" stands in for Pope's "Belinda," but she also serves to recollect Eliot's own poetic past: she has, recall, already made a brief appearance in "Gerontion," where she was whirled together with "De Bailhache" and "Mrs. Cammel" (67). In the earlier poem, Fresca was just a name. In the drafts of "The Fire Sermon," however, she is quite literally fleshed out, initially defined solely in terms of her bodily functions—sleeping and awakening, then drinking, eating, and defecating. Awakened from sexual dreams, she begins her day with chocolate or tea, retreats to the bathroom, returns to bed, eats an egg, and relaxes in a bath.

As the stanza progresses, Fresca reveals herself as a consumer not just of chocolate, tea, and eggs, but of culture as well, an avid reader with eclectic tastes. On the toilet, ". . . the pathetic tale of Richardson / Eases her labor till the deed is done" (*WLF* 13–14); she "explores a page of Gibbon as she eats" (16); and while she lies in a bath, we learn that "Fresca was baptized in a soapy sea / of Symonds—Walter Pater—Vernon Lee. / The Scandinavians bemused her wits / the Russians thrilled her to hysteric fits" (56–59). In these lines, the distinction between physical consumption and intellectual consumption proves rather confused. Fresca does not read the letters that she receives; rather, she "devours" them (19). On the other hand, she "sinks in reverie" while contemplating the "well-rounded dome" of a hard-boiled egg (17–18). In short, she fails to distinguish high literature not only from mass forms but also from any other consumable object. She enacts a largely mindless ingestion of culture (an action that positions her more or less comfortably on one side of the binary that opposes male production to female consumption).

But Fresca's activities prove more complicated. Like the speaker of "Gerontion," the poem in which she originates, she lives a vicarious life, a life of "unreal emotions, and real appetite" (53). That is, while her bodily desires

persist, her emotional experiences come secondhand from the texts she consumes. But unlike the speaker of "Gerontion," who cannot pass from literary-
historical reminiscence to present action, Fresca does create something: "She
scribbles verse of such a gloomy tone / That cautious critics say her style is
quite her own" (65–66). And here I think that we can recognize the threat that
Fresca embodies, the threat that makes her, for Eliot, such an ideal satirical
target. Fresca embodies not the threat of indecision or creative sterility that we
encountered in "Prufrock" or "Gerontion," but the threat of unchecked poetic
(re)production. Fresca moves all too easily from the consumption of Gibbon,
Richardson, and Pater to the generation of her own gloomy verse. Indeed,
passing from the consumption of the tradition to the production of verse is
for Fresca nearly as thoughtless, as automatic, as passing from the consumption of tea and chocolates to the production of bodily waste. And examples
of her automatism abound. The speaker notes of Fresca that "when restless
nights distract her brain from sleep / she may as well write poetry, as count
sheep" (62–63). As mechanical as counting, Fresca's poetic creation is practically somnambulistic. And yet hers is a style that cautious critics cannot afford
not to endorse.

Like the disaffected speaker of "A Game of Chess," Fresca figures a threat
inherent in the very act of literary-historical recollection that Eliot in his critical writings prescribes. For her behavior is dangerously close to the behavior of Eliot's mature poet: she reads fairly widely from the Western European
tradition, and out of these excursions into literary history she creates her art.
Though one could argue that Fresca is perhaps too reliant on the Decadents, or
that she responds too emotionally to the texts she encounters (at least to those
texts written by the bemusing Scandinavians and the thrilling Russians), not
one of these criticisms is by itself sufficient to distinguish her practice from
Eliot's own. When in "Tradition and the Individual Talent" Eliot describes the
poet's mind as "a receptacle for seizing and storing up numberless feelings,
phrases, images, which remain there until all the particles which can unite to
form a new compound are present together" (*SW* 31), his preferred analogy is
to the chemical reaction that occurs between oxygen and sulfur dioxide in the
presence of platinum. But he also describes the process of poetic creation as
one of "consumption" and "digestion" (31). And he returns to this metaphor
in other writings. So, Eliot writes, the strength of the metaphysical poets is to
be found in their ability to "devour any kind of experience" (127), to "digest . . .
all the experience of the human mind" (101). And this strength cannot be the

possession of the Metaphysicals alone, for "if we are to digest the heavy food of historical and scientific knowledge that we have eaten we must be prepared for much greater exertions. We need a digestion which can assimilate both Homer and Flaubert" (43). Again, "the language which is . . . important to us is the language which is struggling to digest and express new objects" (87). The poet is stomach as surely as he is mind. And so, in addition to looking into the heart, "one must look into the cerebral cortex, the nervous system, and the digestive tracts" (129).

Eliot was not alone among the modernists in connecting artistic production to digestion and defecation. Joyce, from the time of his early "Paris Notebooks" (1903), also ruminated on art and excrement—"Can excrement . . . be a work of art? If not, why not?"—and did so as a way of understanding the relationship between artistic production, on the one hand, and automatic processes (both organic and mechanical), on the other. Joyce may have answered for himself that excrement could not be a work of art; nonetheless, as he developed as an artist, the increasingly scatological content of his writings along with their increasingly ambitious attempts to ingest their environment suggested to some of his readers that his works enjoyed a very different relationship to the digestive tracts. So Lewis in his "Analysis of the Mind of James Joyce" would write of *Ulysses* that Joyce had "collected like a cistern in his youth the last stagnant pumpings of Victorian Anglo-Irish life. This he held steadfastly intact for fifteen years or more—then when he was ripe, as it were, he discharged it, in a dense mass, to his eternal glory" (*Time and Western Man* 90). The result, Lewis concluded, was "a monument like a record diarrhoea" (90).

Like Eliot's poet-catalyst, like Lewis's Joyce, and (somewhat later) like Warhol before his "oxidation" paintings, Fresca sacrifices herself and her art to an impersonal (because automatic) process. Thus, she goes on digesting and scribbling, beguiled by her "flattering friends" and championed by "cautious critics." As a result, she dramatizes the confusion of good and bad, high and low, man (or woman) of talent and popular charlatan endemic to modernism and its afterlives. And she dramatizes as well the threat of proliferation and degeneration that characterizes the modern wasteland. Finally, Fresca reminds us that to recall literary history is to risk bringing it back in a fallen form, to risk being implicated in her crimes (or at least to wonder if one is implicated—for the artist himself may not know).

Eliot responds to Fresca, he responds to the cultural confusion that Fresca figures, with satire, and he charges satire with two related tasks. First, and most obviously, Eliot turns to satire to insist on a difference between his own poetic practice and the automatic processes that Fresca embodies. The real content of this difference between Eliot's and Fresca's creative recollections of literary history may be effectively indiscernible, and so the real difference between Eliot and Fresca may be indiscernible; but the very fact of Eliot's satirical presentation of Fresca introduces between them a formal distinction. By mocking Fresca, Eliot locates his own practice in a position of greater authenticity, or at least greater knowledge, even if at this point these terms are relatively empty. Eliot is different because he mocks (and not the reverse). That Fresca and Fresca's gloomy verse can be satirized points to a weakness of her verse that neither Fresca, nor her friends, nor her too cautious critics—nor the reader of the drafts of *The Waste Land*, who never actually encounters Fresca's verse—can perceive.

Second, once satire is in place in the poem, it provides the content for the formal differentiation that it engenders. And this content is satire itself. In other words, when Eliot satirizes Fresca's poetics, he also introduces a distinction between two ways of managing literary history, a distinction that, as we have seen, all of his references to digestion and catalysis leave confused. On the one hand, there is Fresca's own somnambulistic synthesis, which recollects and reproduces the tradition automatically. On the other hand, there is satire, which is distinguished by its ability to distinguish. Satire divides its objects— those that deserve mockery from those that do not—and it divides itself from its objects (even as it serves as a vessel of its objects' representation). Above all, satire divides itself from what cannot divide itself, from what cannot decide and thus from what cannot stand back and laugh. Although she is thrilled to hysterical fits by the Russians, Fresca cannot join in Baudelaire's (and Eliot's) Satanic laughter, for she is not psychically distinct from the texts that she consumes and repeats. Rather, she simply ingests, digests, and expels. Eliot, however, *qua* satirist, is essentially separate from his objects, his texts, himself; he stands apart from what he condemns.

Here the problem that Eliot faces and the solution that satire provides—and so the importance of satire to the composition of *The Waste Land*—comes into view. In *The Waste Land*, Eliot struggles to effect a poetic anamnesis of literary history, to collect together in a sufficiently strict form not only the products of the Western tradition but also the processes that gave rise to them, the generative cycles that lead from work to work. Increasingly, though, and the closer Eliot gets to his own present, literary history comes to appear under the twin signs of proliferation and decay: great works return degraded, men of talent die off only to be replaced by popular charlatans, and the modern European prepares himself for the fate of the Melanesians. This is the wasteland that *The Waste Land* describes. But in describing the modern wasteland, *The Waste Land* risks tumbling into it, risks appearing as another instance of a world in which poetic recollection issues in ever more waste. In this situation, cautious critics and flattering friends are of no help. Satire, however, as principle or as method, serves to distinguish *The Waste Land* from the wasteland that it recalls as surely as it separates Eliot from his degraded double. At least for a moment, then, *The Waste Land* could have been a tremendous work of satire.

## IV. The Dissolution of Satire

Pound, however, was unamused. Reflecting on the composition of *The Waste Land* in 1928, Eliot noted that Pound "induced me to destroy what I thought an excellent set of couplets; for, said he, 'Pope has done this so well that you cannot do it better; and if you mean this as a burlesque, you had better suppress it, for you cannot parody Pope unless you can write better verse than Pope—and you can't'" (*WLF* 127). The seventy-two lines of heroic couplets with which Eliot intended to begin "The Fire Sermon" were another casualty of *The Waste Land*'s self-proclaimed "sage homme," another cut in Pound's "caesarean" delivery of the poem.[12] Eliot accepted Pound's cuts. And if in 1928 he could still describe the excised couplets as "excellent," by 1929 he appears to have wholly internalized Pound's criticisms, warning aspiring poets that "if you follow Dante without talent, you will at worst be pedestrian and flat; if you follow Shakespeare or Pope without talent, you will make an utter fool of yourself" (*SP* 217).

Since the drafts of "The Fire Sermon" have become available, a number of critics have weighed in on Pound's decision, typically voicing their agreement with Pound that Eliot's attempt to revive the satirical mode had failed (albeit in each case for slightly different reasons). Building on the argument of Kenner's "Urban Apocalypse," Philip Cohen notes that "a comparison of *The Rape of the Lock* to Eliot's parody shows how mistaken Eliot was in his conception of Pope. Eliot has none of Pope's occasional playfulness and very real fascination with Belinda" (19). Cohen goes on to remark that the disgust with female physicality Eliot exhibits in this section tells us more about Eliot himself than about Fresca. David Ward, on the other hand, resists the temptation to put Eliot on the couch and states in language as direct as Pound's own that "the parody is for the most part nerveless and slack" (100). More recently, Louis Martz has combined these positions: the lines that Pound "slashed," he writes, are both "offensive" and "weak" (141).

Now, it is true that Eliot's couplets do not equal Pope's in wit or precision, and that Eliot descends into cruelty where Pope remains playful. Even if Pope could endorse the misogyny that informs lines such as "the same eternal and consuming itch / can make a martyr or plain simple bitch," Pope would have found a better way to put it. So Eliot's contemporary critics are probably right. But even as these critics endorse Pound's decision, they obscure the most interesting aspect of Pound's response: the claim that Eliot's intent in his couplets was to "parody Pope" or to produce a "burlesque" of Pope's style. Is Pound suggesting that Eliot's aim in his Popeian satire is, in fact, to satirize Pope? Here Pound's own language is not entirely clear. The term "parody" can be used as a synonym for "satire," suggesting ridicule by imitation; thus, "to parody Pope" would be to satirize him. Alternatively, "parody" can simply describe the creation of a work in the characteristic style of another work, something akin to pastiche. Eliot, in a 1921 essay on John Dryden, seems to favor the first definition, writing of Dryden that his method in "Mac Flecknoe" (1682) is "very near to parody; he applies vocabulary, images, and ceremony which arouse epic associations of grandeur, to make an enemy helplessly ridiculous" (SW 114). The term "burlesque" refers to irreverent imitation—again, something akin to satire, though not necessarily intended to belittle. Perhaps Pound simply miswrote—should have written "pastiche" for "parody" and "burlesque," or have written "Fresca" for "Pope." Or perhaps Pound said exactly what he meant: that Eliot's aim was to make Pope the butt of the joke.

On the surface, this suggestion that Eliot aimed to satirize Pope seems absurd. In an informed treatment of Eliot's relationship to the Augustans, Patrick Deane has taken it up as a possibility, only to reject it: "[I]t is surely clear that the Fresca episode is not a literary satire but a pastiche, its aim not primarily to mock a style, but rather to use that style—however unusual and outdated—to mock something else" (86). Pope himself wrote in the style of the ancients to take the wind out of his contemporaries' sails; it was no doubt clear to his readers that in his own parodies his satirical targets were not Homer and Horace and Milton but rather those "scribblers" who would claim their legacy. When in The Rape of the Lock, for example, Pope describes the titular theft of hair in terms and tones borrowed from Homer's description of Paris's abduction of Helen of Troy, his aim is to mock the smallness of his contemporaries by opposing to their own trivial affairs Homer's gigantomachia. Similarly, when Eliot mocks Fresca in the style of Pope, who would imagine that Pope himself is Eliot's target rather than the popular charlatans and credulous critics who populate the modern wasteland?

And yet, I want to claim that if Eliot was, in 1922, so ready to take Pound's advice and consign Fresca to the wastepaper basket, it is likely because Eliot recognized in Pound's response a (perhaps unintended) implication: whatever Eliot imagined himself to be doing when he drafted the first, Popeian couplets of "The Fire Sermon," the effect of these lines was—it had to be—to satirize Pope himself. Again, I am not certain that this is what Pound was saying, though Pound's comment that "you cannot parody Pope unless you can write better verse than Pope" does suggest a relationship of superiority—and so, potentially, of ridicule—rather than one of simple mimicry. But this is not really the issue. For as I have suggested, what is of key importance to Eliot in his deployment of satire is not so much the mocking laughter that satire evokes as the division that satire effects. And Pope himself must be implicated in this division. He must because he is part of literary history, part of the literary-historical wasteland that Eliot, in *The Waste Land*, satirically recollects. Again, Eliot recollects the same literary-historical tradition as Fresca; he differs from her, however, insofar as he recollects this tradition critically—satirically—rather than automatically. He uses satire as a way of keeping himself at one remove from his historical objects. But if Eliot uses satire not only to manage the dangerous proximity of this or that "other"—Fresca, for example, or the speaker who transforms *The Tempest* into a "Rag"—but also, and more importantly, to recollect critically literary history itself, where in this process do we locate Pope's own satires (or Horace's, or Juvenal's, or Swift's, or Lewis's)?

This is a real problem. Pope is a part of the literary-historical wasteland that satire is supposed to recollect, and so are Pope's satires; if they were not, Eliot would be unable to draw on them for the first seventy-two lines of "The Fire Sermon." If Eliot's Popeian satire is to differentiate *The Waste Land* from the literary-historical wasteland, then, it must differentiate *The Waste Land* from Pope; moreover, Eliot's Popeian satire must differentiate *The Waste Land* from Popeian satire. And here Pound's apparent confusion over the target of Eliot's satire is understandable. In *The Waste Land*, "Pope" (the satirical style) must help to separate *The Waste Land* not just from Pope (the poet, who is subject to literary history's proliferations and degenerations) but from "Pope" (the satirical style) as well; each is implicated in the tradition to be satirized, and each is capable of returning in a degraded form. As Pound perhaps recognized, Pope (like "Pope") is necessarily intended in Eliot's "burlesque" because Pope (like "Pope") is very much a part of the literary-historical wasteland that *The Waste Land* describes. Eliot's satire must, therefore, satirically distinguish satire from itself.

If satire is to remain the model for a critical recollection of the tradition, it can only do so by at a certain point becoming the satire of satire. But if this is the case, the promise of satire to separate poets from dunces, to separate Eliot from Fresca, or to separate *The Waste Land* from the wasteland, becomes muddled. What becomes of satire, with its "gratifyingly idealized . . . coherence of self and other" (Bogel 46), when "self" and "other" are not just dangerously similar but necessarily the same thing? The closer Eliot comes to approximating the masterful satire of Pope, the more difficult it becomes to distinguish Eliot from Pope, or to distinguish Eliot's satire of satire from Pope's satire. In *The Waste Land*, then, satire (of satire) ends up inviting the dangerous proximity of literary history (including satire) that it was supposed to manage. The relatively stable system of differences promised by satire as a generic form dissolves into a vertigo of undecidable self-parody, a state of affairs akin to what Friedrich Schlegel, in a discussion of the related operations of irony, described as "eine permanente Parekbase" (a permanent parabasis; 18:85).

Satire is absent from the finished version of *The Waste Land* because in the early drafts of the poem, those drafts cut to ribbons by Pound, its work proves undecidable. In these drafts, we cannot establish, finally, whether what we read is satire, or satire of satire; consequently, there is no way to establish whether the poem has successfully distinguished itself from the literary-historical repetitions that it dramatizes, whether Eliot is satirizing Pope (as he must) or simply repeating him. This confusion is the fate of *The Waste Land* insofar as it seeks within literary history an immanent principle for the ordering of literary history—a project that seems increasingly akin to the Munchausen trick of lifting oneself by one's own hair. On the other hand, if literary history cannot be successfully recollected and managed by an immanent consciousness or generic technique, the only strategy left is to transcend it. It was, I suspect, an awareness of this fact that motivated Eliot's turn to the "mythical method," in essence a turn to a principle outside of or prior to the tradition in which every satirical gesture, no matter how self-critical, must remain.

## CHAPTER 3

# MYTH

**EARLY IN THE PREVIOUS CHAPTER** I noted in passing the exchange between T. S. Eliot and Eliot's friend Richard Aldington over the artistic merits of James Joyce's *Ulysses*. Aldington, recall, published in the April 1921 issue of *The English Review* "The Influence of Mr. James Joyce," a critical assessment of Joyce's novel in which he charged Joyce with setting the impressionable young on a path to "Dadaisme" and "imbecility" (333), even as he admitted that *Ulysses* was a "remarkable achievement" (331).[1] On 14 September 1920, seven months before the essay appeared in print, Aldington had contacted Eliot about the possibility of publishing a response:

> Suppose I publish my article in the E.R., will you answer it? The discussion would be interesting and, which is more important, would draw attention to Joyce. You could publish your reply simultaneously in the *Dial*. Let me know what you think. Meanwhile I'll keep my manuscript here and not send it to [Austin Harrison, the editor of *The English Review*] until I hear what you say. I feel rather pleased with my suggestion, no doubt selfishly, because it would be an honor if you answered me, but also, I hope, because it is a means of bringing "Ulysses" before the public and arousing curiosity. (qtd. in Kittredge 339–340)

Given that he attacks *Ulysses* for what he suggests will be its "deplorable" effect on young writers—"If I had a younger friend who wanted to write . . . I would conceal from him the works of Mr. Joyce" ("Influence" 341)—it is strange to see Aldington conspiring with Eliot to raise Joyce's profile. Nonetheless, this is

Aldington's proposal. Though his response to this proposal is lost, Eliot apparently agreed to pen a rejoinder. He was, however, characteristically slow getting started. In a letter to John Quinn from 9 May 1921, Eliot writes that "I have promised to reply to an article by Aldington deprecating [Joyce's] influence; but that was in the April *English Review*, and I have not yet begun" (*L* 1:558). And in a letter to Joyce himself from 21 May of the same year, after thanking Joyce for having sent to him the "Circe," "Eumaeus," and "Oxen of the Sun" episodes of *Ulysses*, Eliot claims (falsely) to have only just now heard about Aldington's essay and promises to write a letter to *The English Review* in response (1:562). No letter ever appeared. Eliot's response, "*Ulysses*, Order, and Myth," with its now famous description of Joyce's "mythical method," was eventually published in the November 1923 issue of *The Dial*, more than three years after Eliot was first contacted by Aldington.

History has been kinder to Eliot's response than to Aldington's provocation, which has become little more than a footnote to "*Ulysses*, Order, and Myth." And contemporary readers are surely more likely to accept Eliot's verdict—that *Ulysses* is "the most important expression which the present age has found" (*SP* 175)—than Aldington's—that *Ulysses* is, finally, "a libel on humanity" ("Influence" 338). Eliot's response is significant, though, not because it finds Eliot anticipating the critical consensus on *Ulysses*, nor because it presents a wholly original characterization of Joyce's method; that Joyce "[manipulates] a continuous parallel between contemporaneity and antiquity" (*SP* 177), for example, had already been observed by the French writer Valery Larbaud, with whose work Eliot was familiar, having translated it for the inaugural issue of *The Criterion*. Rather, Eliot's response to Aldington is significant because it affords Eliot the opportunity to restage (and so reassert) the break with a certain variety of modernism—Aldington's variety and, for a time, Eliot's as well—that he had already accomplished with *The Waste Land*. In this restaging, Aldington is an ideal foil, a kind of stand-in for Eliot's own past self. Like Eliot, Aldington had put in his time in the "school of Ezra"; indeed, along with his fellow poets Pound and H.D. (the latter Aldington's erstwhile spouse), he was a member of the original troika of *Imagistes*, named into existence by Pound in the British Museum's tearoom in the late spring or early summer of 1912.

The disagreements between Aldington and Eliot were not, of course, just theatrics. Despite the fact that they had much in common personally and artistically, Aldington made no attempt to hide from Eliot his problems with Eliot's poetry,[2] writing to Eliot in the summer of 1919 that, though he considers Eliot "the only modern prose writer of criticism in English . . . I feel compelled to add that I dislike your poetry very much; it is over intellectual and afraid of those essential emotions which make poetry" (*L* 1:382). And when he turns his attention to Joyce's novel, Aldington attacks it for qualities that, at least to an unsympathetic reader, would seem to describe Eliot's poetry as well:

> A style which is allusive, derived, full of quotations, is a bad style because it is pe-
> dantic and lifeless; and a style which is affected, strained for effect, incomprehen-
> sible, is a bad style because the only reason for using words is to make ourselves
> understood. Merely to astonish simple-minded people with profound-looking
> imbecilities is not literature; it is playing the fool in print. ("Influence" 340)

Aldington's remarks on *Ulysses* anticipate the response that at least some baf-fled critics would have to the appearance of *The Waste Land*. The American critic Gorham Munson, for example, describes the "esotericism" of Eliot's poem as an instance of "deliberate mystification" (157). For, Munson continues, given the emotions that Eliot was attempting to convey, "classical lucidity was entirely possible" (159). And in a review published in the *Manchester Guardian*, Charles Powell writes similarly that in *The Waste Land* "meaning, plan, and intention alike are massed behind a smoke-screen of anthropological and literary erudi-tion, and only the pundit, the pedant, or the clairvoyant will be in the least aware of them" (156).

In spite of Aldington's implicit or explicit criticisms of his work, Eliot saw clearly that he still shared with Aldington sufficient common ground to make dialogue, however mediated, practicable. The banner under which this dialogue would be carried out, both Eliot and Aldington called "classicism," a slippery term of singular importance to English-language modernism. So, Eliot: "I think that Mr. Aldington and I are more or less agreed as to what we want in principle, and agreed to call it classicism. . . . We are agreed as to what we want, but not as to how to get it, or as to what contemporary writing exhibits a tendency in that direction" (*SP* 176). What is classicism for Aldington and for Eliot? In the same letter in which he solicits Eliot's response to his criticisms of *Ulysses*, Aldington provides his own characterization of classicism: "[C]lassic style—sobriety, preci-sion, concision—is and must be the most beautiful thing in literature and devia-tions from it are retrogression" (qtd. in Kittredge 339). And he essentially repeats this characterization in the Joyce essay, lamenting the "tendency of modern literature—I mean the experimental, non-commercial kind—towards vulgarity and incoherence and away from distinction and sobriety" and recommending to young writers practice in "clarity, sobriety, and precision" (qtd. in Kittredge 341). We can hear in Aldington's account of classicism echoes of Pound's second principle of imagism (which, Pound notes, was agreed on by H.D., Aldington, and himself): "[U]se absolutely no word that does not contribute to the presentation" (*LE* 3). And we can hear as well echoes of T. E. Hulme's polemical (and now canonical) "Romanticism and Classicism" (1911): "[T]he great aim [of classicism] is accurate, precise and definite description" (78).

Clarity, sobriety, precision, concision, distinction—Eliot's own description of classicism is less precise, less definite than Hulme's or Aldington's. Indeed, it is almost aggressively unspecific. As Eliot writes:

> Classicism is not an alternative to "romanticism," as of political parties, Conservative and Liberal, Republican and Democrat, on a "turn-the-rascals-out" platform. It is a goal toward which all good literature strives, so far as it is good, according to the possibilities of its place and time. One can be "classical," in a sense, by turning away from nine-tenths of the material which lies at hand and selecting only mummified stuff from a museum—like some contemporary writers, about whom one could say some nasty things in this connection, if it were worthwhile (Mr. Aldington is not one of them). Or one can be classical in tendency by doing the best one can with the material at hand. (*SP* 177)

With these remarks, Eliot seems less interested in providing classicism with a positive definition than in purging the term of its familiar associations. He rejects the opposition of classicism to romanticism underscored by Hulme. He rejects as well the tendency to collapse aesthetic classicism into a broader social program (as in the *nationalisme intégral* of Charles Maurras, for example).[3] For, Eliot goes on, "the fact that the term ["classicism"] is applied to literature and to the whole complex of interests and modes of behavior and society of which literature is a part" only results in "confusion" (177). Finally, he rejects the commonplace equation of classicism with what Nietzsche called "antiquarian history," with the refusal of the contemporary world in favor of "mummified stuff from a museum." In sum, classicism can be neither a set of precepts—Aldington's "clarity, sobriety, and precision," for example—nor an inventory of conventions. If anything at all, it is an empty ideal—"a goal toward which all good literature strives"—or perhaps an honorific—"so far as it is good."

In Hulme's sense or in Aldington's, classicism describes the aims and techniques of that division of the London avant-garde with which Eliot was most closely associated during the 1910s. By effectively emptying the term of meaning,

Eliot thus separates himself both from his peers and from his recent past. Now, it is true that nowhere in "*Ulysses*, Order, and Myth" does Eliot state as his goal the lustration of classicism. Nonetheless, it is not terribly difficult to see why an assault on Aldington's version of classicism might be necessary to Eliot's poetic aims. I described in the last chapter the problems Eliot encountered when he attempted to provide his long poem with a principle of order. I imagine that the effect of Eliot's accepting Aldington's precepts, accepting Aldington's notion of classicism, would have been to make these problems insurmountable. The classicism that Aldington prescribes suits H.D., and it suits Pound (at least through *Cathay* and *Lustra*), and it certainly suits Aldington himself (though even he would move away from it with his 1924 "jazz poem," *A Fool i' the Forest*). For Eliot, however, classicism has reached its breaking point already in "Gerontion," if it ever really characterized his poetic project. At any rate, it is of no help in describing his ambitions in *The Waste Land*.

Though he may go on using the term, Eliot has to separate himself from what Aldington means by classicism. And so, to return to my earlier claim, it is in "*Ulysses*, Order, and Myth" that Eliot restages the break he first effected with *The Waste Land*. "Myth," which serves as the centerpiece of "*Ulysses*, Order, and Myth," names (after the fact) this break. Now, I want to pause here to emphasize the difference between what I am claiming and the more familiar version of the claim that Eliot's method in *The Waste Land* is the "mythical method" that he outlines in "*Ulysses*, Order, and Myth," which method involves "manipulating a continuous parallel between contemporaneity and antiquity" and so on. Again, what Eliot describes as Joyce's "mythical method" is taken more or less wholesale from Larbaud's characterization of the structural parallelism that Joyce maintains between the *Odyssey* and *Ulysses*, a characterization developed by Larbaud in close contact with Joyce himself (which is not, of course, to deny Larbaud's own critical acumen). When Eliot introduces into his discussion of Joyce the "mythical method," he provides Joyce's strategy in *Ulysses* with a name, a past—it originates, Eliot avers, with Yeats—and a future—it is "a method which others may pursue after [Joyce]" (*SP* 177). But having accepted the accounts of Joyce and Larbaud, he does not add to it much else. Consequently, if we attempt to transfer what Eliot has to say about the "mythical method" to *The Waste Land*, we do not get very far. Eliot, too, juxtaposes the new (centrally, though not exclusively, modern London) and the old (centrally, though not exclusively, the wasted landscapes described in the myth-critical investigations of Jessie Weston and Sir James Frazer).[4] This is true, but banally so. And it tells us very little about how the new and the old are manipulated in *The Waste Land*, how literary-historical chaos is therein transformed into poetic order. But if we cannot explain how this occurs, if we cannot explain how myth enables us to pass from chaos to order, then we cannot be certain that what we encounter in the poem *is* order, that we have not just honored the poem's esotericism or incoherence with a new name.

I think that it is more useful to begin by recognizing that, for Eliot, "myth" names, first of all, an interruption of the narrative of literary modernism—an interruption of "classical" modernism, in the sense that Aldington would have understood this term—and that this interruption effectively separates Eliot from his immediate past and from his London milieu. Doing so, we observe the recurrence of a strategy that appeared in the previous chapters of this book, a strategy in which Eliot attempts to manage the "futility and anarchy" of a history that is, at once, literary and personal, and to do so by dividing himself and his poetry from it. In *The Waste Land*, this strategy of division takes priority over the strategy of juxtaposition, but the former is not necessarily opposed to the latter. Indeed, when Eliot incorporates the archaic into the body of his long poem, he does so not to force the collapse of historical distance or to reveal that all moments in the literary tradition are (finally, fatefully) equivalent. Rather, his aim is to establish in *The Waste Land* a moment or a space outside of the historical world that *The Waste Land* describes, one from which this world might be ordered, controlled. This aim is not so different from the aim that motivated Eliot's earlier turn to satire: to effect, regarding literary history, a position of critical detachment. But in the final version of *The Waste Land*, it is radicalized, figured as a suspension of or an exit from literary history itself (one that is, nonetheless, murkily replayed in Eliot's own exit from classicism).

What I mean by all of this will, I hope, become clearer as the chapter progresses. Here, however, I should pause to note that my reading of Eliot's poetic project does stop with *The Waste Land* (before moving on to a discussion of Walter Benjamin's own response to the problem of historical representation); that is to say, I do not include in my treatment of Eliot's writings a reading of Eliot's second masterpiece, *Four Quartets* (1936–1942, 1943). The reason is that, while *Four Quartets* is no doubt a singular poetic achievement, and while it does address some of the same issues that have concerned me in my discussion of Eliot's writings thus far and will continue to concern me in this chapter—particularly the possibility of suspending literary-historical time and thus of exiting literary history[5]—*Four Quartets* does not seem to me (as *The Waste*

*Land* emphatically does) a crisis poem. The struggle with history that Eliot initiates already with "Prufrock" and that culminates in *The Waste Land* is absent from *Four Quartets*. I am not certain if this change of poetic outlook is a product of Eliot's religious awakening, or if it evidences a rapprochement with classicism (in Aldington's more traditional sense of the term). Whatever the cause, Eliot's real struggle with literary history reaches its limit in and ceases with *The Waste Land*. Let us then turn to *The Waste Land*, so as to pose the question of what, in the poem, literary history means.

## I. A Poem Including History

In its first publication in the October 1922 issue of *The Criterion*, the same issue that concludes with Eliot's translation into English of Larbaud's lecture on *Ulysses*, *The Waste Land* appears without dedication, epigraph, or explanatory notes. The reader thus progresses without disturbance from title, to section heading ("The Burial of the Dead"), to the poem's memorable first lines: "April is the cruelest month, breeding / Lilacs out of the dead land, mixing / Memory and desire, stirring / Dull roots with spring rain" (1–4). These lines establish the poem's frame as well as its literary-historical matter, and they do so by way of a double allusion. First, and most obviously, they recall the opening lines of Chaucer's *Canterbury Tales*: "Whan that Aprill, with his shoures soote / The droghte of March hath perced to the roote / And bathed every veyne in swich licour, / Of which vertu engendred is the flour" (1–4). By beginning with an allusion to Chaucer's April showers, Eliot, as Maud Ellmann has neatly noted, "invokes the origin of the tradition as well as the juvenescence of the year" (263); he underscores his poem's concern with both poetic and natural first things. As I pointed out in the previous chapter, Eliot did not initially intend to begin his poem with cruel April. He planned, rather, to begin with a loose narrative of a pub crawl in Boston. By replacing this scene of his own recent American past with a gesture to Chaucer's European Middle Ages, Eliot also replaces one history—personal, proximate—with another—impersonal, archaic—a choice he reaffirms at various moments during his and Pound's editing of *The Waste Land* by canceling an epigraph taken from Conrad, for example, and by rejecting a title drawn from Dickens, as well as by multiplying his references to earlier and often non-Western sources.

The second allusion contained in the poem's first lines seems to contradict these choices, however, moving the substantial center of these lines forward again in history—at least as far forward as the nineteenth century—and west again across the Atlantic. Here I am referring to Eliot's apparent allusion to Whitman's elegy for the then recently assassinated Lincoln, "When Lilacs Last in the Dooryard Bloom'd" (1865). The appearance of Whitman's poem in the first section of *The Waste Land*, signaled by Eliot's reference to "breeding / Lilacs out of the dead land," is underlined by its return in the "water-dripping song" from *The Waste Land*'s final section, "What the Thunder Said":

> If there were the sound of water only
> Not the cicada
> And dry grass singing
> But sound of water over a rock
> Where the hermit-thrush sings in the pine trees
> Drip drop drip drop drop drop drop
> But there is no water. (352–358)

Though the setting of these lines is distant from Whitman's dooryard—Eliot locates us in a mythical nonspace rather than in mournful 1860s America—they nonetheless recall Whitman's elegy: ". . . solitary the thrush, / The hermit withdrawn to himself, avoiding the settlements, / Sings by himself a song" (21–23).[6] And so, with the song of the hermit-thrush echoing back from "What the Thunder Said," the first lines of *The Waste Land* declare that Chaucer's flowers, before they became Eliot's, passed through Whitman's hands. It was there that they took on their specific form as lilacs as well as their funereal airs.

Two allusions, then, and from very different moments in the history of English literature. But if the allusion to Chaucer reflects Eliot's interest in beginnings, what does Eliot gain from the allusion to Whitman? How, in *The Waste Land*, are Chaucer and Whitman catalyzed? In a 1926 review essay "Whitman and Tennyson," after comparing the dispositions of the two nineteenth-century writers—"[T]here is," Eliot notes, "fundamentally, no difference between the Whitman frankness and the Tennyson delicacy"—Eliot pauses to oppose Whitman's weakness as a thinker to Whitman's strength as a poet: "[W]hen Whitman speaks of lilacs or of the mocking-bird, his theories and beliefs drop away like a needless pretext" ("Whitman and Tennyson" 426). This remark is as close as Eliot ever came to celebrating the bard of democracy in one of his essays, and it is worth noting here the care with which Eliot separates Whitman's poems (presumably "When Lilacs Last in the Dooryard Bloom'd" and "Out of the Cradle Endlessly Rocking") from the "theories and beliefs" with which they are entangled. A year later, in a letter responding in print to a reader skeptical of his comparison of Whitman to Tennyson, Eliot takes the opportunity to emphasize once more what he does and does not find of value in Whitman: "[H]e was," Eliot writes, "a great master of versification, though much less reliable than Tennyson. It is as a verse maker that [Whitman] deserves to be remembered; for his intellect was decidedly inferior to that of Tennyson. His political, social, religious and moral ideas are negligible" (*L* 3:529). Whitman might mean for Eliot a nation or the set of values associated with it—Eliot rejects the latter, at least, as the "clap-trap in Whitman's content" (Intro 362)—but also, and more importantly, Whitman means a particularly noteworthy moment in the development of English-language verse, a style of versification deserving of remembrance.

Now, remembrance is not the same thing as affirmation; and book-ending Eliot's 1926–1927 writings on Whitman are other short writings in which Eliot rejects the notion that Whitman had any real influence on his own or Pound's modernist verse experiments. Here is an example from 1928:

> I did not read Whitman until much later in life [that is, much later than 1908–1909, the period when Eliot was especially interested in Laforgue and Elizabethan drama], and had to conquer an aversion to his form, as well as to much of his matter, in order to do so. I am equally certain—it is indeed obvious—that Pound owes nothing to Whitman. This is an elementary observation; but when dealing with popular conceptions of *vers libre*, one must still be as simple and elementary as fifteen years ago. (Intro 362)

And here is an earlier example, from 1917 (the same year as Eliot's "Reflections on *Vers Libre*") and again addressing Whitman's alleged influence on Pound:

> There are influences, but deviously. It is rather a gradual development of experience into which literary experiences have entered. These have not brought the bondage of temporary enthusiasms, but have liberated the poet from his former restricted sphere. There is Catullus and Martial, Gautier, Laforgue and Tristan Corbière. Whitman is certainly not an influence; there is not a trace of him anywhere; Whitman and Mr. Pound are antipodean to each other. (*CC* 177)

Not a trace. And yet, and despite the pains that Eliot takes to separate Pound from Whitman, to break Pound's 1916 "Pact" ("I make a pact with you Walt Whitman— / I have detested you long enough"), and so to stop attempts to read transitively from Whitman to Pound to Eliot himself, Whitman is there in *The Waste Land*. There is still the matter of the lilacs. For better or worse, "Whitman" is the name for an event in the history of verse, an event that is, again, deserving of remembrance (while all those aspects of the Whitmanian ideology are just as well forgotten).

And of course Chaucer can be approached in much the same way, as an event in the history of English-language verse forms. In light of this approach, my claim is that the co-presence in the poem's first lines of Chaucer and Whitman establishes within the poem two moments on a literary-historical continuum. Between these two moments unfolds a certain narrative of literary history, or better, a certain narrative of the history of English-language verse forms as a synecdoche for literary history in general. This narrative stretches from the codification of iambic pentameter with Chaucer to this form's (indeed, to every fixed form's) collapse with Whitman. Chaucer and Whitman, alpha and omega: this is the same narrative as was set forth in 1910 by Charles W. Eliot—president of Harvard (1869–1909) and cousin of T. S.—in his three-volume *Complete English Poetry, Chaucer to Whitman* (40–42). T. S. Eliot almost certainly would have owned this edition, compiled as it was by his cousin and published during his own time as a student at Harvard (1909–1914). And he likely would have agreed with the entirely reasonable understanding of the history of English poetry that this edition presents. By beginning in *The Waste Land* with Chaucer and Whitman, Eliot thus figures the "complete" history of English poetry in a few dense lines. He does so, however, not by binding his poem to this or that moment in literary history—to Chaucer's European Middle Ages, or to Whitman's American nineteenth century, or even to his own London present—but by taking up poetically the movement of literary history itself, a history that is both dynamic (for in moving from Chaucer to Whitman we move from past to near present, from England to America, and perhaps from order to chaos) and apparently natural. I shall return to this latter point in a moment.

By moving from Chaucer to Whitman, Eliot presents *The Waste Land* from its very first lines as "a poem including history." The phrase originates with Pound, who used it in his 1934 essay "Date Line" to characterize the ambitions of epic (*LE* 86), repeating it in a slightly altered form ("a poem *containing* history") in a 1962 *Paris Review* interview with Donald Hall where he wondered about the possibility of such a thing: "[T]he past *epos* has succeeded when all or a great many of the answers were assumed, at least between author and audience, or a great mass of audience. The attempt in an experimental age is therefore rash" (Plimpton 75). Because Pound and Eliot were working on similar problems, attempting ostensibly similar things, and working together so closely during the 1910s and early 1920s, it is useful to compare the image of literary history presented in the first lines of *The Waste Land* to the image of literary history presented by Pound himself in the first lines of the *Cantos*, if only to see how Pound's phrase—"a poem including/containing history"—has its meaning transformed between Pound and Eliot.

Let us start with Pound. Canto I begins:

And then went down to the ship,
Set keel to breakers, forth on the godly sea, and
We set up mast and sail on that swart ship,
Bore sheep aboard her, and our bodies also
Heavy with weeping, and winds from sternward
Bore us onward with bellying canvas,
Circe's this craft, the trim-coifed goddess.
Then sat we amidships, wind jamming the tiller,
Thus with stretched sail, we went over sea till day's end.
Sun to his slumber, shadows o'er all the ocean,
Came we then to the bounds of deepest water,
To the Kimmerian lands, and peopled cities
Covered with close-webbed mist, unpierced ever
With glitter of sun-rays
Nor with stars stretched, nor looking back from heaven
Swartest night stretched over wretched men there.
The ocean flowing backward, came we then to the place
Aforesaid by Circe. (1–18)[7]

These lines, which translate from book 11 of Andreas Divus's 1538 Latin translation of Homer's *Odyssey*, are in no way a simple example of literary-historical borrowing. Although they begin in the midst of things ("And then went down to the ship . . ."), they also begin at the very beginning, with what Pound believed to be the oldest section of one of the original works of the Western tradition: it "shouts aloud that it is *older* than the rest" (*Letters* 274). Pound's lines describe Odysseus's descent into Hades, an instance of the Greek rite of *nekuia*, and so they both thematize and enact Pound's own communion with the dead. That these lines translate a translation of their source—and do not only translate it, but submit it to the conventions of Old English alliterative verse as well—could suggest that this communion, while perhaps necessary, is also necessarily impure, mediated both by thousands of years of history and by the limitations that this history places on the poet's tools (on his verse forms, on his language, and so on). Or it could suggest that the tradition is essentially continuous, that, thanks in part to the work of translators such as Divus and Pound, an unbroken line can be drawn from the *Odyssey* to *The Exeter Book* to Pound's own modernist present. For our purposes, either reading will do.

The literary-historical themes that Pound ruminates on in the *Cantos*—tradition, innovation, repetition, inheritance, and belatedness—appear as well in *The Waste Land*. Still, the ways in which the past is taken up in the two poems (or at least in their first lines) differ significantly. When Pound begins the *Cantos* with the conjunction "And . . . ," he indicates a direct, if complex, filiation between his poem and the *Odyssey*, a filiation borne out by the ability of readers to recognize Homer's epic in spite of the countless corruptions, translations, and reimaginings that it has undergone—corruptions, translations, and reimaginings that are in some sense present from the poem's origin, insofar as we are dealing with an initially oral form that survived for centuries through its repetitions. Pound's poem is simply the next moment in this ongoing series, a series that, from the first retellings of Odysseus's voyage to whatever additions Pound will make to his own definitively unfinished epic, remains open to literary history at both ends. This serial openness of Pound's poem—openness to a tradition already in progress as well as to a tradition to come—is key, and it is underscored throughout the *Cantos*, insofar as each canto does not so much end as fade out, pointing to the next member of the series. So, to return to canto I, the last lines read: "Venerandam, / In the Cretan's phrase, with the golden crown, Aphrodite, / Cypri munimenta sortita est, mirthful, orichalchi, with golden / Girdles and breast bands, thou with dark eyelids / Bearing the golden bough of Argicida. So that:". Had any writer before Pound thought to conclude a poem with a colon? In the aforementioned interview with Hall, looking back on the composition of *The Cantos*, Pound notes that the problem he faced in writing the poem "was to get a form—something elastic enough to take the necessary material. It had to be a form that wouldn't exclude something merely because it didn't fit" (51).

An openness to a changing tradition or to what does not "fit," an openness characteristic of Pound's poem, *The Waste Land* refuses—a fact, however, that the density of literary-historical allusion characteristic of *The Waste Land* belies. This claim needs to be sorted out. When I say that *The Waste Land* refuses the openness of Pound's *Cantos*, I do not mean that *The Waste Land* refuses literary history. It hardly needs saying that Eliot's poem, like Pound's, shores its share of fragments. And what Kenner said about the *Cantos*—that the latter is "a gestalt of what it can assimilate"—is also true of *The Waste Land*, as far as it goes. Nonetheless, and despite the fact that practically anything can be assimilated by *The Waste Land*, the form of Eliot's poem is, I want to claim, fixed in a way that Pound's is not. Unlike the *Cantos*, where there is a real sense that the poem itself is constantly changing (as the cantos accumulate), that the poem is in fact a moment in a grander transformative process, and that the poem (or rather, the continuing tradition of which the poem is part) will, through the creation of new works, continue to change, *The Waste Land* does not admit of progress or transformation. The literary history that *The Waste Land* assimilates is altered— this is absolutely true—but *The Waste Land* itself remains constant. Another way to say this: Pound's poem is coincident with literary history, moving and changing along with it, while Eliot's poem actually does contain literary history, maintaining it within itself as a single operation. To contain literary history, however, *The Waste Land* must present literary history as something essentially closed (though its borders may be hard to find) and as something concluded (though its contents may still move). Literary history is able to take this form in *The Waste Land* because *The Waste Land* derives its form not from literary history's own cumulative development, from the translations and commentaries and rewritings that interest Pound, for example, but from an order external to literary history, from the cyclical, natural processes of seasonal transformation and organic decay. These processes became more pronounced in the poem's definitive draft, displacing as a result the stratum of human history or folding the latter into themselves.

Let me return here to the first lines of *The Waste Land*, with their allusions to Chaucer and to Whitman, for these lines are paradigmatic of what I am describing: "April is the cruelest month, breeding / Lilacs out of the dead land, mixing / Memory and desire, stirring / Dull roots with spring rain." As I have suggested, these lines comprise a literary-historical development, one with a beginning (Chaucer) and an end (Whitman). Appropriately, then, they progress from April—a month of new life—to a wintry resolution. The next lines read: "Winter kept us warm, covering / Earth in forgetful snow, feeding / A little life with dried tubers" (5–7). A natural beginning leads on to a natural end. And yet the syntax of these lines works against their literal sequence and so against the above reading, twisting their literary-historical matter into a form befitting their seasonal vehicle. The enjambed participles that punctuate the first three lines ("breeding," "mixing," "stirring") indeed root us in the present, from which, presumably, everything will follow. The third line's reference to "memory and desire" divides this present, directing us simultaneously to the past and to the future. To remember we must locate ourselves before the moment of remembering; to desire we must project a satiation that would follow after the moment of desiring. We remain at this temporal crossroads momentarily; the next lines of the poem send us backward in time: "Winter kept us warm, covering." The familiar repetition of present participles binds these lines to those that preceded them, while the principal clause's shift in tense—winter *kept* us warm—signifies that we have moved into April's past. Before April, there was the winter; before the winter there was, presumably, an autumn, preceded by summer—"Summer surprised us, coming over the Starnbergersee / With a shower of rain . . ." (8–9)—preceded by an earlier April, and so on. We thus enter a cycle with no real beginning and no real end.

*The Waste Land* incorporates into its substance motion, then, but motion of a peculiar sort. How are we to understand it? It is cyclical, endless, characteristic of both literary history and natural history. In his lectures on Shakespeare given at the Surrey Institute in 1808, Samuel Taylor Coleridge described as the "one great principle . . . common to all the fine arts" the ability to unite "images, notions, or feelings conceived as in opposition to each other"; and he pointed specifically to the seeming contraries "infinite change and ineffable rest" (*Notes and Lectures upon Shakespeare* 43). William Wordsworth, his friend and romantic confederate, provided a poetic version of this vision in the Simplon Pass episode of book 6 of *The Prelude*: "The immeasurable height / Of woods decaying, never to be decayed, / The stationary blasts of waterfalls . . ." (624–626). These are, Wordsworth continues, the "types and symbols of Eternity, / Of first and last, and midst, and without end" (635). Somewhat closer to our own present, in "The Double Vision of Michael Robartes," Yeats imagined a "mind" that "moved yet seemed to stop / As 'twere a spinning-top" (43–44). Again, infinite change and ineffable rest: perhaps Eliot inherits this manner of thinking. Something similar seems to be at stake not only in the form of *The Waste Land* as a whole—for what is seasonal change but a kind of revolution in stasis?—but also in some of the poem's most memorable images: the perpetually decomposing Sybil of the poem's epigraph; the endless throng of doomed souls crossing London Bridge; the drowned sailor, Phlebas the Phoenician, forever rising and falling on an undersea current. Each achieves it effect by uniting in a single figure movement and rest, time and eternity.

And yet, between Wordsworth's "gloomy Pass" and *The Waste Land*, much has changed. We do not, in the latter, pass from mutability to eternity, from infinite change to ineffable rest; rather, mutability itself becomes eternal: to be is to decay. And this equivalence of being and decaying is the other side of the treatment of (literary) history in *The Waste Land*. Whitman is not only the repetition of Chaucer's verse revolution; he is, in some sense, the latter's falling to waste. The poem thus presents the coadunation of a closed, cyclical process—the repetition of seasons and the repetition of literary-historical moments—with a degenerative process, a process of both organic and cultural decay. These two operations, repetition and decay, intermingle, as in the image of the sprouting corpse from "The Burial of the Dead": "That corpse you planted last year in your garden, / Has it begun to sprout?" (71–72); or, in "A Game of Chess," in the poem's locating procreation (parenthetically) within a discussion of aging, sickness, and death:

> You ought to be ashamed, I said, to look so antique.
> (And her only thirty-one.)
> I can't help it, she said, pulling a long face,
> It's them pills I took, to bring it off, she said.
>
> (She's had five already, and nearly died of young George.)
> The chemist said it would be alright, but I've never been the same.
> You are a proper fool, I said.
> Well, if Albert won't leave you alone, there it is, I said,
> What you get married for if you don't want children? (156–164)

Birth and death are bound together. The same sentiment would be voiced, a few decades later, by Samuel Beckett's Pozzo: "They give birth astride of a grave, the light gleams an instant, then it's night once more" (103); and glossed by Beckett's Vladimir: "Astride of a grave and a difficult birth. Down in the hole, lingeringly, the grave digger puts on the forceps" (104).

So, repetition and decay. I described something similar in the last chapter, noting that already in the drafts of *The Waste Land* the poet's attempts to recollect literary history—to recollect it through rewritings, allusions, or simply through the necessarily tradition-bound act of artistic creation—are implicated in a process of cultural degeneration, one typified by the movement from Shakespeare's *Tempest* to "That Shakespeherian Rag," and thus from the high to the low. This movement is still present in the final version of *The Waste Land*; however, what was in the drafts still fundamentally a cultural (or at times more specifically literary-historical) process is, in the published version of the poem, naturalized. At the level of the poem's content, this naturalization of literary history appears in the commingling of the literary with the organic, in the images of sprouting corpses and sick fertility that proliferate in the poem; while at the level of form this naturalization of literary history is of a piece with what Franco Moretti has described as Eliot's gradual "emancipation of polyphony from anthropocentric motivation" (*Modern Epic* 196), a process of depersonalization in which the literary fragments that *The Waste Land* comprises are separated from whatever speaking subjects could be said to pronounce them. So, Moretti writes, from the drafts of the poem to the final version we move from "Unreal city, *I have sometimes seen and see,* / Under the brown fog of *your* winter dawn / A crowd flowed over London Bridge, so many . . ." to "Unreal city / Under the brown fog of winter dawn / A crowd flowed over London Bridge, so many . . ." (qtd. in Moretti, *Modern Epic* 186). From draft to final version, everything that would indicate that these lines are the property of a particular speaker is eliminated. The result is that the repetition-degeneration that Eliot describes—from winter to spring, from birth to death, or from Chaucer to Whitman—no longer appears as the contingent effect of the wrong sort of people writing the wrong sort of poetry; rather, it appears as the necessary extension of an impersonal because natural logic, one that provides the poem with its order and the contents of the poem with their significance.

## II. Narrative Ends in Myth

I need to interrupt the discussion of *The Waste Land* that I have been developing up to this point in order to make a small (but, I think, significant) shift of focus. Thus far I have attempted to describe how Eliot manipulates literary history so as to produce an image of the latter compatible with "a poem including history," a poem whose form decides in advance that, within it, every literary-historical event fits. I want to shift my focus, then, from the naturalized vision of literary history that Eliot develops to the implications of this vision for our conception of literary modernity, where the latter describes the sense of progress, or rupture, or novelty usually associated with the modernist project. Doing so will allow me both to address a prevalent reading of *The Waste Land*—one that tends to conflate the problems that Eliot faces in his composition of the poem with the solutions that he tries—and to come back to the question of the mythical method, so as to ask how the latter really helps us to make sense of *The Waste Land*'s complicated relationship to modernism.

At the beginning of this chapter, I noted that most of what Eliot has to say about the mythical method in "*Ulysses*, Order, and Myth"—that its practitioner "[manipulates] a continuous parallel between contemporaneity and antiquity" (*SP* 177), for example—had been adumbrated already by the French writer Valery Larbaud in Larbaud's own work on Joyce's novel, work that Eliot translated for *The Criterion* and cites approvingly in "*Ulysses*, Order, and Myth." Larbaud's aim in this work was to provide readers with a rough guide to the parallels between Homer's ancient world and Joyce's dear dirty Dublin. And in this sense, Larbaud's project has been carried on by expositors of Joyce's novel up to the present day. In "*Ulysses*, Order, and Myth," Eliot does not add much in the way of explicative detail to Larbaud's analysis. He does, however, suggest a possible explanation for Joyce's turn to the ancient world, and so for Joyce's mobilization of the mythical method. Joyce, Eliot avers, being "in advance of [his] time, felt a conscious or probably unconscious dissatisfaction with the form [of the novel]," recognized that "the novel, instead of being a form, was simply the expression of an age which had not sufficiently lost all form to feel the need of something stricter." As a result, Eliot continues, Joyce rejected the "narrative method" for the mythical method. The latter promises its practitioner "a way of controlling, of ordering, of giving a shape and a significance to the immense panorama of futility and anarchy which is contemporary history" (*SP* 176), a task at which the narrative method presumably fails.

The mythical method replaces, or ought to replace, the narrative method. In the passages I cited above, Eliot is describing the transition from one way of composing a work of literature or ordering the stuff of (literary) history to another. With its juxtaposition of old and new, Grail Quest and urban decay, *The Waste Land* effects this transition. But there is, I think, another way to take Eliot's claim that narrative ends in myth, one that comes into better focus when we detour, temporarily, from Eliot's remarks on the mythical method to the reception of Eliot's long poem. We can start with the poem's first reader. In a July 1922 letter to Felix E. Schelling, his former teacher at the University of Pennsylvania, Pound writes of *The Waste Land* that "[it] is I think the justification of the 'movement,' of our modern experiment, since 1900" (*Letters* 180). In some quarters at least, Pound's verdict has been hard to displace. Citing it in the final chapter of his definitive *Genealogy of Modernism: A Study of English Literary Doctrine 1908–1922*, Michael Levenson writes that he is "inclined to

concur" (168), and he goes on to treat *The Waste Land* as reconciling the con-
flicting demands of modernism as they had been articulated over the previous
decade and a half, as the culmination of the "modern experiment." With Pound
and Levenson, then, as justification or as culmination, *The Waste Land* serves
as a kind of capstone to the project of literary modernism, at least as it had been
carried out since 1900 or 1908. But if this is the case, if *The Waste Land* is the
goal toward which literary modernism was moving all along, then *The Waste
Land* must also be located at (or as) this project's conclusion.

Compare the enthusiastic characterizations of *The Waste Land* proffered by
Pound and Levenson to some of the more ambivalent statements on the poem
voiced by Eliot's American contemporaries William Carlos Williams and Hart
Crane. First, Williams, in his autobiography:

> These were the years [that is, the years leading up to 1922] just before the great
> catastrophe to our letters—the appearance of T. S. Eliot's *The Waste Land*. There
> was heat in us, a core and a drive that was gathering headway upon the theme
> of a rediscovery of a primary impetus, the elementary principle of all art, in the
> local conditions. Our work staggered to a halt for a moment under the blast of
> Eliot's genius which gave the poem back to the academics. We did not know
> how to answer him. (146)

Williams goes on: "[O]ut of the blue *The Dial* brought out *The Waste Land* and
all our hilarity ended. It wiped out our world as if an atom bomb had been
dropped upon it and our brave sallies into the unknown were turned to dust.
. . . We were stopped, for the moment, cold" (174). *There was heat in us . . . but
the poem stopped us cold.* And now Crane, in a letter to Gorham Munson composed soon after *The Waste Land* was published: "What do you think of Eliot's
*The Wasteland* [*sic*]? I was rather disappointed. It was good, of course, but so
damned dead" (105). What does Crane mean in calling the poem dead? Is it that
*The Waste Land* lacks optimism? vitality? futurity? Williams accepts the mag-
nitude of Eliot's achievement—it is like the blast of an atom bomb—but sees
the upshot of this achievement as the interruption of poetic progress. Crane,
on the other hand, affects disinterest, though his own struggle to answer Eliot
would be more troubled than Williams's, would end with (poetically, biographi-
cally) complicated results.[8] In each case, though—and for Pound and Levenson no less than for Williams and Crane—there is a sense that, with *The Waste
Land*, something that was moving forward is culminated, halted, stopped dead.
And so we confront an ending of a different sort: not the end of the narrative

method and its replacement by the mythical method, but the end of the very
literary-historical narrative in which the transition from narrative to myth is
supposed to occur.

Let me turn, finally, to two more responses to Eliot's poem, and to its relationship to historical narrative. Despite their being composed decades apart,
they say roughly the same thing, make roughly the same connection between
the form of Eliot's poem and its effect on literary history. The first appears in
Joseph Frank's seminal 1945 study, "Spatial Form in Modern Literature," not a
study of Eliot per se but of a certain tendency in literary modernism of which
Eliot's project in *The Waste Land* is exemplary. In spatial form, Frank writes, as
in myth,

> past and present are seen spatially, locked in a timeless unity which, while it
> may accentuate surface differences, eliminates any feeling of historical sequence
> by the very act of juxtaposition. The objective historical imagination, on which
> modern man has prided himself, and which he has cultivated so carefully since
> the Renaissance, is transformed in these [modernist] writers into the mythical
> imagination for which historical time does not exist—the imagination which
> sees the actions and events of a particular time merely as the bodying forth of
> eternal prototypes. These prototypes are created by transmuting the time-world
> of history into the timeless world of myth. (63)

The second passage appears in Moretti's more recent "From *The Waste Land* to
the Artificial Paradise":

> *The Waste Land*'s construction materials . . . reveal themselves in a double light:
> as "fragments" and "incomplete meanings" when judged with reference to liter-
> ary tradition; as "functions" and "adequate signifiers" when attention is shifted
> to the poem, or to myth. *The Waste Land*'s construction therefore involves the
> reader in two simultaneous evaluations: on one hand, it makes history seem an
> accumulation of debris, a centrifugal and unintelligible process; on the other,
> it presents mythic structure as a point of suspension and reorganization of this
> endless fugue. . . . This is a radical devaluation of history. . . . It is a question
> of overturning the very way in which Western civilization has conceived the
> historical process. History must no longer be seen as irreversible as regards the
> past, and mainly unpredictable as regards the future, but as a cyclical mecha-
> nism, which is, therefore, fundamentally static: it lacks a truly temporal dimen-
> sion. (*Signs* 222)

Both Frank and Moretti move easily from the intraliterary manipulation or devaluation of history to its extraliterary effects. Frank moves from what he describes early in his essay as a literary technique in which "syntactical sequence is given up for a structure depending on the perception of relationships between disconnected word-groups" (14) to this technique's implication in a "mythical imagination for which historical time does not exist." Moretti moves from the structuralist jargon of "functions" and "adequate signifiers" to the "overturning [of] the very way in which Western civilization has conceived the historical process" and, finally, to the association of *The Waste Land* with the "exhaustion of literature's raison d'être and its historical function within Western culture" (209). Under the heading of myth, then, or following Eliot more closely, under the heading of the mythical method, both critics move from the end of the narrative method, to the devaluation of historical sequence in favor of anachronistic parallelism, to the end of the literary-historical project that is supposed to inform all of these operations.

Perhaps there is a confusion of registers here, a confusion shared by all of the poets and critics I have mentioned, and a slippage from what *The Waste Land* describes to what *The Waste Land* effects. But if this is so, it is a confusion or a slippage that the poem invites. As I claimed above, the image of history exhibited by *The Waste Land* is of something closed, concluded. The poem freezes the history that it contains, or it permits this history only false movement. What is eliminated, then, by the transformation of history into myth—if that is what we want to call Eliot's imposition of a cyclical, ostensibly natural structure onto the literary-historical matter of *The Waste Land*—is, first of all, a certain narrative quality of history, a quality that allows history to be viewed "as irreversible as regards the past, and mainly unpredictable as regards the future." But this suppression of narrative within *The Waste Land* has proved hard to separate from the suppression of narrative without, from the effect of the poem on the narrative of literary modernism. The reason, I suspect, for this blurring of inside and outside is that *The Waste Land* does not itself admit the legitimacy of this distinction. The poem includes history. And from within the poem, from within the experience of *The Waste Land* and the conviction of its quality that this experience inspires, one cannot imagine a (historical) movement beyond *The Waste Land*. The poem insists, then, through the real or proleptic inclusion of all of (literary) history within itself, that there is nothing (historically, aesthetically) beyond it, nothing but more of the same.

On the other hand: "the essence of modernism resides in its refusal to re-gard a particular formal 'solution,' no matter how successful or inspired, as definitive. . . . This is tantamount to the realization that if the dialectic of mod-ernism were to come to a halt anywhere once and for all, it would thereby be-tray itself" (Fried 235–236). So writes the art historian and critic Michael Fried, describing in an early work the open-endedness of the modernist project, the impossibility of this project's culmination. *The Waste Land*, however, presents itself as a work of literary modernism whose response to the problem of liter-ary history (and, so, to the problem of literary modernism) is definitive (in the term's strict etymological sense: from the Latin *definire*—to bound, end, or terminate [*OED*]). And so it presents an image of history after which the mod-ernist project appears impossible. It is this image of history that is registered by *The Waste Land*'s readers—Pound, Williams, and Crane; Frank, Levenson, and Moretti—when they portray *The Waste Land* as the climactic or catastrophic end to the modernist project. Faced with the poem, they glimpse an ending and halt (albeit momentarily) before finding another path. Perhaps this means that Eliot betrays the modernist project; or rather, that through Eliot's long poem, the modernist project betrays itself, and does so by imagining that it could "come to a halt anywhere once and for all." At any rate, the result is that *The Waste Land* occupies vis-à-vis modernism the liminal status usually re-served for beginnings and endings.

I am more interested, finally, in Eliot's relationship to these issues than in the responses of Eliot's contemporaries or later critics. And for Eliot, what I have described as the mythical ending of narrative is something complicated, both a solution and a problem. Before he turned to myth, recall, Eliot turned to satire to solve the problems that he faced in his composition of *The Waste Land*. Satire promised to divide Eliot's own critical-creative act from the de-generate cultural productions that provided his long poem with its content. Satire failed in this task, though; and it failed because it was too much a part of—indeed, was finally indistinguishable from—the literary-historical waste that it was supposed to manage. Turning to myth, Eliot avoids this problem. Like the satirical method, the mythical method promises to control, to order, the anarchy of literary history. Myth, however, unlike satire, is not and can-not be a part of this history. This point needs to be understood correctly. It is no doubt true that the particular myths retold by Homer or Ovid or Edith Hamilton are continuous with the great story of European literature, part of the "mind of Europe" (to borrow Eliot's metaphor from "Tradition and the

Individual Talent"). Nonetheless, again, *qua* mythic, they cannot be a part of this history. For myth imposes a vision of history absolutely incompatible with narrative presentation; one that "lacks a truly temporal dimension"; one for which "historical time does not exist"; and so one that refuses the before and after on which accounts of literary tradition depend. Between the time of narrative—irreversible, unpredictable—and the "time" of myth—cyclical, closed—there can be no conciliation. From the vantage of narrative, myth can only be thought as narrative's (definitive) end; from the vantage of myth, narrative is not thought at all.

And this, for Eliot, is both a solution and a problem. In *The Waste Land*, Eliot operates on the narrative of literary modernism much as he operates on the moments of literary history that this narrative comprises. Just as he cuts lines from Webster or Baudelaire free from their textual or historical contexts, he cuts this narrative's joints, denies the progressive continuity of its moments. He thus divides *The Waste Land* from (literary) history (or at least from this history as it has been "cultivated so carefully since the Renaissance" and perfected in the nineteenth century). But in doing so he makes the existence of *The Waste Land* something effectively unfathomable. For how could something timeless, something that disallows the possibility of any becoming, come to be? If *The Waste Land* is not one more moment in the cyclical, degenerative process that *The Waste Land* describes—and if it is, then the mythical method merely repeats the failure of the satirical method—then it is not clear how *The Waste Land* can be a poem at all, can be something produced and something that might itself produce or transform a history. Eliot's very real conservative tendencies—and I mean here personally conservative, not artistically conservative—have, I believe, tended to obscure this problem, have encouraged readers of *The Waste Land* to assume that, insofar as the poem's soon-to-be-self-described Anglican, classicist, royalist author has made real novelty appear impossible, he has achieved his goal. Terry Eagleton writes of *The Waste Land* that "behind the back of this ruptured, radically decentered poem runs an alternative text, which is nothing less than the closed, coherent, authoritative discourse of the mythologies that frame it. The phenomenal text . . . is merely the meat with which the burglar distracts the guard-dog while he proceeds with his stealthy business" (150). In other words, Eliot's aim all along was to establish something like a modern myth: closed, coherent, authoritative. I am not so sure. Perhaps this is true of the man who suffered. But of the mind that creates? All we can do, though, to controvert Eagleton and all those other readers sure that Eliot was "in no way

. . . subject to the fascination of the 'appeal of the new'" (Moretti, *Signs* 223), to show, rather, that Eliot himself struggled with his own ostensibly successful replacement of time with space, history with myth, is to return to *The Waste Land*.

## III. Now and Forever

The problem that *The Waste Land* presents to its author is the problem of inscribing within the poem—a poem that apparently allows nothing to originate within it, nothing to exist outside of it—the act that should have brought the poem into existence. In other words, Eliot must establish within his long poem a moment of real creation, one uncompromised by the cyclical-degenerative operations to which every moment in the poem is submitted. Now, in the broader context of European modernism, this desire for an uncorrupted moment or pure poetic act is not so unusual. Karl Heinz Bohrer, who has probably done the most to theorize the exceptional moment—the instant, *Augenblick*— as one of literary modernism's controlling figures, writes that a fascination with "the moment that is no longer identical with history began in the early romantic period (Friedrich Schlegel, Friedrich Schleiermacher, Heinrich Von Kleist), found its previously undiscovered theorist in Friedrich Nietzsche, and was put through aesthetic and conceptual variations by modern authors like Marcel Proust, James Joyce, Robert Musil, and Walter Benjamin" (*Suddenness* vii–viii). The modernist moment takes different forms—Joyce's "epiphanies," Woolf's "moments of being," and the Surrealists' "shock," for example. But in each case, it exists in a problematic or antagonistic relationship to the degraded moments that surround it, to what Woolf called "moments of non-being," by virtue of its greater authenticity or its greater reality. Both Eliot and his long poem are absent from Bohrer's studies, most likely because Eliot, insisting that historical scholarship is at the origin of poetic creation, fits so uncomfortably into most conceptions of a modernist avant-garde (even one as expansive as Bohrer's). Here, though, we ought to distinguish Eliot's valorizing of the tradition in his critical writings from his turn to the archaic in *The Waste Land*. If the former is on the side of continuity, the latter is on the side of rupture. Indeed, it is through his turn to the ancient world, his incorporation into *The Waste Land* of not only the form but also the content of myth that Eliot develops a version of the exceptional moment *qua* sovereign poetic act.

In my discussion of the mythical method up to this point, I have focused on how this method enables Eliot to provide literary history with shape and significance, albeit by interrupting the narrative form that this history conventionally takes. In this formulation, the particular matter of literary history—the specific passages or literary allusions out of which Eliot constructs *The Waste Land*—is less consequential than this history's (spatial) form. Here I have remained fairly close to some of the most canonical conceptions of poetry's relationship to history, conceptions that I tried to outline in the introductory chapter of this book: poetry submits the stuff of history to categories of "probability and necessity" (Aristotle), to "unchanging forms" (Shelley). And it is these categories or forms, not the particular content of the poem, that make poetry something—Aristotle again—"more philosophical" or more universal than history. Insofar as, in *The Waste Land*, every bit of literary history fits, the specific fragments of literary history that Eliot shores should not matter too much to the shape of the poem as a whole. And yet Eliot does associate the mythical method not only with a certain form—the form of spatial juxtaposition rather than narrative progression—but also with a certain content. The latter, the content, he describes somewhat vaguely as the co-existence within the mythically structured work of the contemporary and the antique, which elements are manipulated by the artist in a "continuous parallel." The model, again, is Joyce, but as Eliot worked on *The Waste Land* in 1921–1922, he made his poem conform to these principles, expanding in it the role of the ancient world. At some point, Eliot replaced the original title of the poem, "He Do the Police in Different Voices," from Charles Dickens's *Our Mutual Friend* (1864–1865) with *The Waste Land*, apparently an allusion to Weston's retelling of the Grail legend; replaced the poem's original epigraph, "The horror! The horror!" from Joseph Conrad's *Heart of Darkness* (1899), with an untranslated Greek and Latin passage from the *Satyricon*; and increased the number of references to non-Western sources, sources whose distance from Eliot's own present is signaled both by their age and by the fact that, for the most part, they remain, like the epigraph, in their original languages: "Datta. Dayadhvam. Damyata. / Shantih Shantih Shantih" (432–433).

Why does the mythical method require a specific (antique) content, rather than merely requiring a specific (spatial) form, such that Conrad had to give way to Petronius, Dickens to Arthurian legend, and so on? At least some of Eliot's replacements were made at Pound's behest; and Pound, recommending the excision of the Conrad epigraph in a letter from 24 January 1922, makes his point simply: "I doubt if Conrad is weighty enough to stand the citation" (Eliot, *L* 1:625). By turning to ancient sources, non-Western sources, Eliot does lend his poem a certain weight, a claim to global significance that the poem would lack if its spiritual center were to remain modern London. But he also follows a path not so different from the one that many other modernist artists were following. Eliot composed *The Waste Land* during the same period, "the period 1918–1930," as Julian Stallabrass observes, "that saw primitivism established as an important theme in writing on art and anthropology" (95). Over the last few decades, but with a special energy since the Museum of Modern Art's controversial 1984 exhibition *"Primitivism" in 20th Century Art: Affinity of the Tribal and the Modern*, critics have studied the imbrication during the first half of the twentieth century of the demand to "make it new" and the demand to "make it old," make it primitive, where the latter connotes purity, authenticity. The appearance of the primitive in the literature and visual art of modernism is too large a topic to address here in any kind of detail, and I do not intend to try, though it is at least worth noting the coincidence of modernism with the birth of anthropology and anthropological tourism. Constricting our historical scope to the year of *The Waste Land*'s publication, for example, we see that Eliot's poem shared the spotlight in 1922 not only with *Ulysses* and *Jacob's Room*, but also with Bronisław Malinowski's *Argonauts of the Western Pacific* and Robert Flaherty's work of "salvage ethnography," the film *Nanook of the North*. Of course, when Eliot turns to Ovid or Augustine, his retreat into the past does not have the same ethnographic resonances as Picasso's use of Iberian masks in the *Demoiselles*, or of Eliot's own racial masquerade in his unpublished poems about "King Bolo and his Big Black Bassturd Kween."[9] Still, Eliot's turn to the ancient world in *The Waste Land* shares with other modernist forays into the real or imagined past the assumption that the nonmodern (or the non-Western as a stand-in for the nonmodern) promises the modern artist a position from which he might evaluate the world as it exists or project a different world. As to the questions of how and why the nonmodern is imbued with this promise, Eliot's answers vary from those of his contemporaries. The similarities and the differences are instructive.

In the conclusion to his *Postmodernism*, Fredric Jameson provides as good an explanation of the how's and why's of modernist primitivism as we are likely to find. While I must remain agnostic concerning the larger framework on which this explanation depends and on this larger framework's ability to make sense of Eliot's project in *The Waste Land*, I do believe that Jameson sheds light on certain temporal dynamics of modernist primitivism that are (also) at play in Eliot's poem. Modernism, Jameson explains, is the "cultural logic" of an unfinished process of modernization. A work like Arno Mayer's *The Persistence of the Old Regime* shows that during the period of literary modernism there remained parts of Europe still relatively untouched by capitalism, regions that still found peasants living under feudal (or something akin to feudal) conditions, subordinate to an aristocracy and surviving by working the land without the benefit of twentieth-century technology. Within the first-world imaginary, the political and economic "backwardness" of these locales was transformed into a temporal difference, one illuminated by Ernst Bloch's conception of the "synchronicity of the nonsynchronous" (*Gleichzeitigkeit des Ungleichzeitigen*): "not everyone is present in the same Now" (22). Similarly, the African Congo (seen from the vantage of the Dutch colonizer) and the Tahitian village (seen from the vantage of the French postimpressionist) appeared to exist at a different, earlier moment in history. Because these spaces presented a visible alternative to capitalist modernity—this is Jameson's claim—they became sites of utopian hope for modernist artists, who would use them to "dream [their] way back to an older time" (Bloch 22) and, from this older time, to project a different future. Thus the sometimes contradictory temporal dynamics of modernist primitivism. On the one hand, the primitive must be separated off from history. It cannot be a question for Gauguin of how Mataiea actually fits into the late nineteenth-century world system, for example, for to think about the primitive in these terms would interfere with its functioning as a blank space of utopian imagining. On the other hand, the primitive must be a part of history, for it must really exist as an earlier moment on the same historical continuum that could (but does not necessarily have to) lead up to the present.

We find in Eliot's turn to myth something akin to this odd relationship to the (distant) past. The form of spatial juxtaposition on which *The Waste Land* depends is an ideal vehicle for the Blochian "synchronicity of the nonsynchronous": rather than "handicrafts alongside the great cartels, peasant fields with the Krupp factories or the Ford plant in the distance" (Jameson, *Postmodernism* 307), Eliot gives us, for example, Tiresias in modern London:

> At the violet hour, when the eyes and back
> Turn upward from the desk, when the human engine waits
> Like a taxi throbbing waiting,
> I Tiresias, though blind, throbbing between two lives,
> Old man with wrinkled female breasts, can see
> At the violet hour, the evening hour that strives
> Homeward, and brings the sailor home from sea,

The typist home at tea-time, clears her breakfast, lights
Her stove, and lays out food in tins. (215–223)

And we find alongside Eliot's juxtaposition of the new and the old the notion
that the truly antique exists both inside and outside of history, a position that
Eliot famously attributes to Tiresias: "Tiresias, although a mere spectator and
not indeed a 'character,' is yet the most important personage in the poem, uniting all the rest" (*TAWL* 72n218). We should, of course, take this claim with a
grain of salt. Though Eliot presents Tiresias as a force of literary-historical uni-
fication, Tiresias is himself a literary-historical allusion, having passed through
the hands of Homer, Sophocles, Ovid, and Dryden before he was taken up by
Eliot himself. It is hard to see, then, how he could be expected to stand apart
from what he "sees." Nonetheless, the dual position of the antique with regard
to literary history is worthy of attention.

At this point, then, we can look more closely at the appearance of antiquity
in Eliot's poem, can turn to the most plainly mythical section of the poem, the
final section, "What the Thunder Said." The setting is the blighted landscape of
Arthurian legend. Here is roughly the first half of the second stanza:

Here is no water but only rock
Rock and no water and the sandy road
The road winding above among the mountains
Which are mountains of rock without water
If there were water we should stop and drink
Amongst the rock one cannot stop or think
Sweat is dry and feet are in the sand
If there were only water amongst the rock
Dead mountain mouth of carious teeth that cannot spit
Here one can neither stand nor lie nor sit
There is not even silence in the mountains
But dry sterile thunder without rain
There is not even solitude in the mountains
But red sullen faces sneer and snarl
From doors of mud-cracked houses (331–345)

These lines lack forward movement. They double back on themselves: ". . . only
rock / Rock . . ."; ". . . the sandy road / The road . . ."; ". . . among the mountains / Which are mountains. . . ." And their tone is distinctly sorrowful. They
describe the unhappy experience of "those hooded hordes swarming / Over

endless plains, stumbling in cracked earth" (368–369), which hordes recall the doomed souls flowing over London Bridge in "The Burial of the Dead": "A crowd flowed over London Bridge, so many, / I had not thought death had undone so many" (61–62).

In "The Poetry of Drouth," a discussion of *The Waste Land* that appeared in *The Dial* only a month after the publication in the same magazine of Eliot's poem, Edmund Wilson presents a reading of "What the Thunder Said," and of the poem as a whole, that is of interest not only for its attention to Eliot's mythical sources but also for its articulation of a thesis about *The Waste Land* that has remained virtually unquestioned in the critical literature. Recalling the spring rains of "The Burial of the Dead" from the bleak vantage of "What the Thunder Said," Wilson writes the following:

> There were rain and flowers growing then. Nothing ever grows during the action of the poem and no rain ever falls. The thunder of the final vision is "dry sterile thunder without rain." But as Gerontion in his dry rented house thinks wistfully of the young men who fought in the rain, as Prufrock longs to ride green waves and linger in the chambers of the sea, as Mr Apollinax is imagined drawing strength from the deep sea-caves of coral islands, so in this new poem Mr Eliot identifies water with all freedom and illumination of the soul. He drinks the rain that once fell on his youth as—to use an analogy in Mr Eliot's own manner—Dante drank at the river of Eunoë that the old joys he had known might be remembered. (146)

*Pace* Wilson, I am not sure that most readers would accept the claim that "no rain ever falls" in *The Waste Land*, though I suppose that it depends on how one reads the opening stanza's reference to "spring rain." Nor do I expect most readers to agree that, within the poem, Eliot "identifies water with all freedom and illumination of the soul." April—the month of the spring rains—is "the cruelest month"; we "fear death by water" and see its effects on the drowned Phlebas the Phoenician; and the Thames, when it appears, is incorporated into a vision of Hell, doomed souls "flowing" over it like water. Wilson, though, is hardly alone in finding in "What the Thunder Said" an association of the longing for rain with the longing for redemption. So, Michael North: "The rest of ['What the Thunder Said'] is littered with 'empty cisterns and exhausted wells,' dried-up sources of water that are clearly parallel to the 'empty chapel' bereft of its god. But just these exhausted sources give rise to 'voices singing out,' to lightning and finally to rain" (*Political Aesthetic* 104); and Lyndall Gordon: "Gerontion and, later, a pilgrim in

*The Waste Land*, are poised at the extremity of a dry season, waiting for rain, the traditional sign of spiritual fertility. 'We would see a sign!' Gerontion says in the words of Lancelot Andrewes, and his wish is answered by the thunder's message and promise of rain at the end of *The Waste Land*" (167–168).

Given what I have said about Eliot's modeling of literary-historical repetition and decay on the cycle of the seasons, it is, I hope, clear why it might be a problem to treat the rain as a figure for the redemption of the modern world. The horror of the modern wasteland is, after all, coded in the poem as a kind of perverse fecundity—corpses sprout, memories return monstrous. After a few hundred lines of seasonal rebirth-as-degeneration, and despite the melancholy tone of "What the Thunder Said," the cracked earth of sterile desert spaces ought to seem positively utopian. That it does not, however, and that instead we end up wishing for rain (and doing so in the excellent company of Wilson, North, Gordon, and so many other readers of Eliot's poem), means that something has changed between this section of the poem and the four that preceded it.

Let us pick up the stanza that I was quoting above. It continues:

If there were water
And no rock
If there were rock
And also water
And water
A spring
A pool among the rock
If there were the sound of water only
Not the cicada
And dry grass singing
But sound of water over a rock
Where the hermit thrush sings in the pine trees
Drip drop drip drop drop drop drop
But there is no water (346–359)

More of the same: the desire for water voiced in these lines persists, becomes more desperate. As Jewel Spears Brooker notes, "if water is not to be found, if the sound of water is not to be heard, then the sound of the hermit thrush will suffice" (177). The latter is not itself present, of course, and so even the apparent allusion to Whitman remains at the level of mere wishing. In a letter to Ford Madox Ford from 14 August 1923, Eliot writes that "There are I think about thirty *good* lines in *The Waste Land*, can you find them? The rest is ephemeral." Ford replied immediately, admitting that he could not find them and denouncing the "cruelty" of Eliot's question. In a letter from 4 October, Eliot explains himself: "[A]s for the lines I mention, you need not scratch your head over them. They are the 29 lines of the water dripping song in the last part" (*WLF* 129). These twenty-nine lines—the lines that run from "Here is no water but only rock" to "But there is no water"—stand apart from the rest of the poem. They ask to be read differently (and so they have been). But what does this mean? Where do they stand?

A hypothesis: the twenty-nine or thirty "*good* lines" to which Eliot directs Ford stand apart from literary history, apart from the tradition, apart from the mind of Europe. This claim should be understood in two senses. On the one hand, these lines stand apart from literary history because they locate us *before* literary history, at least as the latter appears in *The Waste Land*. And, indeed, the same can be said of much of "What the Thunder Said." There are still allusions to Dante, to Shakespeare, to Webster's "White Devil," and to Hesse's *Blick ins Chaos*. But interspersed with these more proximate bits of literary history are those moments when *The Waste Land* "silences its Western noise with Eastern Blessings" (Ellmann 273), leads us back to a time and a place that resist translation into the language of the present. "Da. Dayadhvam. Damyata. / Shantih shantih shantih": Eliot writes of these last lines of the poem, "Shantih. Repeated as here, a formal ending to an Upanishad. 'The Peace which passeth understanding' is a feeble translation of the content of this word" (*TAWL* 74n433).[10] We thus reach a language before our contemporary idiom, a language that frustrates poetic translation. And thus we reach a moment before the beginning of literary history, before the April rains with which the poem commences. On the other hand, though, these lines stand apart from literary history in the sense that they locate us *outside* of literary history, outside of the poem that includes this history. The space described in "What the Thunder Said" is a space untouched by the rains that coincide with the cyclical movements of the modern wasteland, an arid, timeless space in which nothing occurs.

Both chronologically prior and spatially outside: if the first vision of the desert space still holds open the possibility of a temporal, narrative development, of a movement, however hard to fathom, from aridity to rain, the second denies this movement and maintains instead a vision of pure, timeless sterility. These two visions are entirely incompatible, as different from one another as history and myth. Either we can pass from the desert to the wasteland (to *The Waste Land*) or we cannot. If we can, then the desert will always already have been part of literary-history's cycles (for these cycles have no beginning and no end); if we cannot, if there can be no contact between myth and history, then the possibility of *The Waste Land* cannot be safeguarded. Nonetheless, it is through the articulation of these two visions that Eliot attempts to inscribe within *The Waste Land* the poem's possibility. He succeeds in bringing them together, albeit only for a moment, in an image of real creation, perhaps the only one of its sort in the poem. The key lines read: "Only a cock stood on the roof-tree / Co co rico co co rico / In a flash of lightning. Then a damp gust / Bringing rain" (391–394). The drought is interrupted, the desert landscape transformed. Only after can the poem truly begin: "April is the cruelest month . . ."

Appropriately, the image itself is double: the onomatopoeic crowing of the cock, on the one hand, and the flash of lightning, on the other. The first, the crowing of the cock, has been read as an allusion to Peter's denial of Christ: "[T]he cock crows as it did when Peter wept tears of penitence" (Kenner, *Invisible Poet* 174); and it has been read as an allusion to the daylight disappearance in *Hamlet* of the murdered king's spirit, which spirit "faded on the crowing of the cock" (qtd. in Haughton 167); and it has been read as a figure for "the return to sexual potency" (Miller 125; Davidson 130). I would like to suggest another possibility, however. The cock, I submit, and despite the haziness of Eliot's allusion, is most likely the avian seer and protagonist of Chaucer's "Nun's Priest's Tale," Chauntecleer. In addition to being the sole rooster of any real literary merit, Chauntecleer belongs in the world of *The Waste Land*. He reminds us "[t]hat dremes been significaciouns / As wel of joye as of tribulaciouns / That folk enduren in this lif present. / Ther nedeth make of this noon argument, / The verray preeve sheweth it in dede" (159–163). His prophecies—like the prophecies of Tiresias, Madame Sosostris, and the Cumaean Sybil—figure a closed future, warn Chauntecleer himself to fear death by *vulpes*. Appearing in Eliot's poem, he foretells the April rains with which *The Waste Land* begins, and so foretells his own maker's "shoures soote." He thus returns us to the beginning, to the beginning of the history of English poetry, from Chaucer to Whitman as well as to the "beginning" of Eliot's poem. The ends meet: from "a damp gust / Bringing rain" to "April is the cruelest month" *The Waste Land* closes the circle.

The presence of Chauntecleer in the desert of "What the Thunder Said" means that even myth is already incorporated into literary history, folded into the latter's diurnal course as surely as is Chauntecleer himself. The flash of lightning, though, is an image of another sort. It appears as something without precedent, as something seemingly impossible within the sterile desert scene. There is, perhaps, some question as to whether it appears at all. Wilson, again, could hear only the "dry sterile thunder without rain" and could conclude that "no rain ever falls" in *The Waste Land*, that nothing ever happens. But there it is: "In a flash of lightning. Then a damp gust / Bringing rain." Is the lightning an image of real creation, then, insofar as it apparently originates from somewhere other than the desert space that it interrupts? It seems more correct to call it an image of division. It divides sterility from productiveness, the barrenness of the desert from the abundance of literary history. And so it divides the poem from itself, divides *The Waste Land* from the sovereign—because unhistorical, atemporal—act that brings this poem into existence. Less a figure within the poem than a jagged line dragged across the page—and so a relative of the pen marks with which Pound scored Eliot's drafts—the flash of lightning, however lucky, is finally only a catachresis for the impossible transition between two incommensurable spaces: the one temporal, historical, seasonal, literary; and the other timeless, mythic. The lightning marks their nonrelation.

And this is where the poem leaves us. History, in *The Waste Land*, remains the realm of (literary historical) production, however fallen its products, while myth remains something apart from history, the space where nothing—not history and certainly not literary history—happens. Eliot can try to affirm both history and myth in *The Waste Land*, but it is not at all clear that he can really bring them together—a fact marked, again, by the impossibility of representing in a single figure the act that would overcome their difference. Of course, the *legacy* of this fact—the fact of the lightning flash and of the insight into Eliot's struggle with history that the lightning flash provides—is something else entirely, is the story of this fact's reintegration by careful critics into one of the most familiar narratives of literary modernism: the narrative (happy or sad) of Eliot's traditionalism (a narrative for which *Four Quartets* offers a much more certain testimony). *The Waste Land*, however, refuses this narrative, and so remains within literary modernism a poem of crisis, a kind of death in the middle of life.

# PART 2

# KILLING TIME, WALTER BENJAMIN

## CHAPTER 4

# ORDER

**IN A LETTER** to his friend Gerhard (later, Gershom) Scholem dated 1 February 1918, Walter Benjamin describes a shift in his plans. Having intended to write his dissertation on Immanuel Kant's philosophy of history and, more particularly, on the status within that philosophy of the "infinite task" (*C* 103–104), Benjamin expresses to Scholem his frustration at having discovered that "it is virtually impossible to gain any access to the philosophy of history using Kant's *historical* writings as a point of departure" (116). He concludes his letter by pointing to the "Idea for a Universal History with a Cosmopolitan Aim" (1784) as evidence of Kant's failure, pausing for a jab at his former teacher at the University of Freiburg, the neo-Kantian Heinrich Rickert—Rickert's method, Benjamin notes, is "modern in the worst possible sense of the word"—and wishing Scholem "all the best from me and my wife." Two months later, another letter to Scholem makes it clear that Benjamin's earlier plans to write on Kant and history are very much a thing of the past. He outlines for his friend a new dissertation topic. He will focus on the early German romantic conception of art criticism, will seek to show that "only since romanticism has the following view become predominant: that a *work* of art in and of itself, and without reference to theory or morality, can be understood in contemplation alone" (119). At least initially, Benjamin reserves for Kant a place in this new project, for, he notes, "Kant's aesthetics constitute the underlying premise of romantic art criticism." Soon enough, though, Benjamin accepts that there may be no place for Kant in his dissertation; indeed, he accepts that the romantics' "historically and fundamentally important congruence [*Koinzidenz*] with Kant . . . may prove impossible to demonstrate in 'dissertationlike' format" (125). This would, apparently, be the case: Benjamin's dissertation, *The Concept of Art Criticism in German Romanticism* (*Der Begriff der Kunstkritik in der deutschen Romantik*), successfully defended at the University of Bern in June 1919, contains scant reference to Kant, focusing instead on the importance to *Frühromantik* of the subjective idealism of J. G. Fichte.[1] Kant, it would seem, has given way to the post-Kantians (to Fichte, Novalis, and the Schlegels, if not yet to Hegel or Marx).

Benjamin's decision to abandon Kant's philosophy of history as a dissertation topic has not enjoyed the same attention paid to other philosophical reversals, to Martin Heidegger's *Kehre*, for example, or to the long crisis that divided Ludwig Wittgenstein's career between the *Tractatus* and the *Philosophical Investigations*.[2] Perhaps the reason for this inattention is simply that Benjamin did not yet have in 1918 a stable position to disavow or a fully developed philosophical program to which his later writings could act as a counterpoint. Or perhaps the reason is that Benjamin's decision to move on from Kant now seems to us so natural, so necessary, and thus not so much a reversal as an advance. Benjamin's movement from Kant to post-Kantian idealism (and finally, in his later works, to Marx) is, after all and excepting a few detours, the movement of German—of modern—thought itself.[3] Benjamin's philosophical-political ontogeny would, therefore, effectively reproduce the phylogeny of one version of modern intellectual history, the history that begins in 1781 with the publication of the first *Critique*, passes through Hegel and Marx, and coincides finally (and in a confusion of levels) with Benjamin's own project.

It is this characterization of Benjamin's itinerary—*von Kant bis Hegel (bis Marx)*[4]—that I hope to call into question in what follows, and for two, related reasons. First, it does not seem to me that it quite fits the facts, at least not insofar as it purports to describe Benjamin's relationship to Kant and Kantianism at the end of the 1910s. Benjamin, for his part, shows no sign of having treated his decision to move on from Kant as a philosophical one and still less as anything like the result of a natural, irreversible development. In the same February 1918 letter in which he announces to Scholem his change of scholarly plans, and despite his frustration with Kant's philosophy of history, Benjamin stresses that his reason for turning away from Kant is not philosophical but professional, and that he is only putting Kant down in order to pick him up again:

> Mathematics and any further grappling with Kant and [the Marburg neo-Kantian Hermann] Cohen have to be put off. The development of my philo-

sophical ideas has reached a crucial stage. As difficult as this might be for me, I have to leave it at its current stage in order to be able to devote myself to it completely and with complete freedom after I have taken my examination. If obstacles to the completion of my doctorate should crop up, I shall take that to mean that I should work on my own ideas. (*C* 119)

Referring to the informal mathematical studies that he was undertaking alongside Scholem as well as to his and Scholem's joint reading of Cohen's early work, *Kants Theorie der Erfahrung* (1871, 2nd ed. 1886), a text singularly important to the neo-Kantian movement, Benjamin emphasizes to Scholem his reluctance to take leave of these matters and his intention to return to them—to return to "[his] own philosophical ideas"—after completing his dissertation. All of this is a matter of intellectual history. It has been addressed with considerable care in the work of Peter Fenves and, most recently, in Howard Eiland and Michael Jennings's detailed study of Benjamin's life and thought. I shall return to Benjamin's early engagement with Kantianism in a moment, but my aim is not, finally, to present an exhaustive account of this engagement. Rather, I am more interested in how Benjamin's mature thought maintains within itself a subterranean current of Kantianism (in the same sense that Louis Althusser could find in Marx a "subterranean current" of Epicurean or Lucretian materialism). This Kantianism, I want to claim, decides the terms even of Benjamin's late critique of historicism.

And this leads me to my second objection to readings of Benjamin's philosophical itinerary that impose on it the development of modern German intellectual history. In his late critique of historicism, in what he calls (in a self-conscious echo of Kant's characterization of his own project) his "Copernican revolution in historical perception" (*AP* K1,2), Benjamin famously denies the legitimacy of just this sort of developmental narrative, denies that progress is a valid historical category. He writes in *The Arcades Project* (*Das Passagen-Werk*), for example, of his intent "to demonstrate a historical materialism which has annihilated within itself the idea of progress" (N2,2), and he locates his theses "On the Concept of History" ("Über den Begriff der Geschichte") under the sign of the criticism of the concept of progress. But this rejection of historical progress marks as well Benjamin's earliest writings. He introduces one of his first published texts, "The Life of Students" ("Das Leben der Studenten"; 1914), with the observation that "there is a view of history that puts its faith in the infinite extent of time and thus concerns itself only with the speed, or lack of it, with which people and epochs advance along the path of progress," only to conclude that this view of history reveals "a certain absence of coherence and rigor in the demands it makes on the present" (*SW* 1:37). And this refusal of the concept of progress colors not only Benjamin's reading of the philosophical tradition but also his reading of particular figures within the tradition. When he indicates to Scholem his disappointment with Kant's historical writings, Benjamin is most likely disappointed with Kant's own faith in progress, a faith evidenced by remarks such as the following, from the eighth thesis of Kant's "Idea for a Universal History": "One can regard the history of the human species in the large as the completion of a hidden plan of nature to bring about an inwardly and, to this end, also an externally perfect state constitution, as the only condition in which it can fully develop all its predispositions in humanity" (8:27). And from very early on, Benjamin reserves some of his harshest criticisms for Hegel, whose own teleological vision of history exacerbates the defects of Kant's: "[T]he Hegel I have read . . . has so far totally repelled me. If we were to get into his work for just a short time, I think that we would soon arrive at the spiritual physiognomy that peers out of it: that of an intellectual brute, a mystic of brute force, the worst sort there is: but a mystic, nonetheless" (*C* 112–113). *A mystic of brute force* . . . Here Benjamin expands on his initial assessment of Hegel's thought, communicated to Scholem at the beginning of 1918: "Hegel seems to be awful!" (108).

My point here is just that it seems somewhat perverse to impose on Benjamin's career the very notion of historical progress that Benjamin spent so much of his career resisting. I shall describe in depth Benjamin's critique of progress in this book's fifth and sixth chapters, focusing on Benjamin's interest in anecdote (Chapter 5) and allegory (Chapter 6) as alternative modes of "doing history." In these chapters, certain affinities between Benjamin's project and Eliot's should become clearer, and particularly the fact that for Benjamin, as for Eliot, the question of historical representation turns out to invite a specifically literary response. Here, though, I want to set up these later arguments by addressing in more detail Benjamin's early struggle with Kantianism. Most particularly, I want to address Benjamin's attempt to replace Kant's transcendental philosophy—Kant's ostensibly complete description of the conditions of human cognition—with a "doctrine of orders" (*Lehre von den Ordnungen*), a system of interlinked but nonidentical structures of knowledge-experience. This project ought to be read not only as a revision of Kantianism (though it is certainly that) but also as a deepening of Kantianism. It finds Benjamin taking seriously Kant's claim that human experience is constitutively finite and expanding this notion of constitutive finitude to include the Kantian transcendental itself, leaving the latter open to transformation through its encounters with a material, historical outside.

Benjamin first alludes to his desire to revise Kantianism in "On Perception" ("Über die Wahrnehmung"), an unpublished philosophical fragment composed in 1917; and he treats this project more thoroughly in "On the Program of the Coming Philosophy" ("Über das Programm der kommenden Philosophie"). This latter essay was likewise unpublished during his lifetime, though Benjamin gave a version of it to Scholem as a (slightly belated) birthday gift in December 1917 (adding an additional section to the essay at some point in March 1918) (Scholem, *Walter Benjamin* 62). Because these early writings establish the program for—or the "prolegomena" to—Benjamin's later critique of historical reason, it is necessary to read them carefully.

## I. The Kantian Vespiary

At the very beginning of "On the Program of the Coming Philosophy," Benjamin writes the following:

> The central task of the coming philosophy will be to take the deepest intimations it draws from our times and our expectation of a great future, and turn them into knowledge [*Erkenntnis*] by relating them to the Kantian system. The historical continuity that is ensured by following the Kantian system is also the only such continuity of decisive and systematic consequence [*entscheidender systematischer Tragweite*]. (*SW* 1:100)

Here, Benjamin effectively repeats a remark that he makes to Scholem in a letter from October 1917: "[I]t is my firm belief that, in keeping with the spirit of philosophy . . . , there will never be any question of the Kantian system's being shaken and toppled. Rather, the question is much more one of the system's being set in granite and universally developed" (*C* 97).[5] The philosophy of the future will be Kantian or it will not be. And yet, even as he underscores the singular importance of cleaving to Kantianism, Benjamin refuses to argue for a bare repetition of Kant's own claims. He continues his letter to Scholem by noting that, though the philosophical core of Kant's system must indeed be protected, a "great number" of "Kantian minutiae . . . may have to fade away" (97). Similarly, he writes in "On the Program of the Coming Philosophy" that "it is of the greatest importance for the philosophy of the future to recognize and sort out which elements of the Kantian philosophy should be adopted and cultivated, which should be reworked, and which should be rejected" (*SW* 1:101–102).

Benjamin argues, then, that any engagement with Kantianism will also need to be a decision on Kantianism, a decision on what in Kantianism is living and what is dead. And what, after all, could be a better way to follow Kant—the philosopher who (as Heine wrote) introduced to the world of ideas the guillotine, who located philosophy itself under the sign of *critique* (of *Kritik*, from κρίνειν, to cut or divide, or to decide)—than to cut into his system, to engage this system critically? A similarly decisive affirmation of fidelity to Kant appears in a lecture course delivered by Martin Heidegger in 1927–1928: "We are for Kant against Kantianism" (*Phenomenological Interpretation of Kant's "Critique of Pure Reason"* 120). We are, therefore, for a certain spirit of Kant against all of those self-proclaimed "Kantians" who have betrayed their master (perhaps by merely following him). As a result—and this is Heidegger again, now reflecting on the challenges presented by the Kantian text in his 1929 *Kant and the Problem of Metaphysics*—"every interpretation must necessarily use violence," for only through a certain interpretive violence can we hope to get at the "decisive content" (*entscheidenden Gehalt*) of Kant's writings (141). But who are these Kantians from whom Kant must be divided? Why is a decision on the Kantian legacy such an urgent task, a task shared by Benjamin, by Heidegger, and indeed by so many other thinkers during the early years of the twentieth century?

At this point, some historical background is probably necessary. Like Heidegger (who was only three years his senior), Benjamin carried out his most sustained engagement with Kant's transcendental philosophy during a moment of crisis in German intellectual life that was also (and a fortiori) a moment of crisis in the reception of Kant's thought. On the one hand, neo-Kantianism, having risen to prominence following the slow disintegration of speculative idealism and the definitive discrediting of romantic alternatives to mainstream experimental science, was now itself in decline, on its way to being supplanted by phenomenology, *Lebensphilosophie*, and an assortment of other linguistically and empirically minded programs.[6] On the other hand, even at this late moment in its history, neo-Kantianism continued to enjoy within the German university system a considerable influence. Its relative resiliency, like its rapid ascent, was at least in part an effect of its modesty. Rather than reproduce the metaphysical flights of fancy characteristic of the writings of Hegel or Schelling, the neo-Kantians began by accepting as given the claims of the em-

pirical sciences—the so-called fact of science (*das Faktum der Wissenschaft*)—
and, for the most part, sought only to articulate and clarify the logic behind
these claims. As a result, as Frederick Beiser has recently noted, they treated
"the fundamental task of philosophy as, in a word, epistemology," where the latter names a "second-order reflection on the basic concepts, methods, and presuppositions of the empirical sciences" (*After Hegel* 37). Ernst Cassirer marks
this neo-Kantian rallying point in a short essay dedicated to his teacher Hermann Cohen, the founder of the Marburg School of neo-Kantianism and the
figure whose writings on Kant had the most immediate and profound effect on
Benjamin's thought: Cohen, Cassirer writes, moved beyond Kant himself in his
realization that "the transcendental question should be directed at mathematical natural science first" ("Hermann Cohen" 97).

At least initially, it was the desire to bring transcendental philosophy in
line with mathematical natural science that motivated the revisions to Kant's
doctrine undertaken by the neo-Kantians. The most important of these revisions—for Benjamin's purposes and so for our own—was carried out by the
members of the Marburg School, that is, by Cohen and his epigones. It involved
nothing less than the revision of Kant's faculty psychology, his partitioning of
cognition into the faculties of (sensible) intuition and (logical) understanding.
The Marburg neo-Kantians rejected the separation of the intuition—the receptive faculty of space and time—from the understanding—the active faculty of
conceptual articulation—and instead derived "the *a priori* formal structures in
which the object of knowledge becomes possible . . . from the logical faculty
of the understanding and from this faculty alone" (Friedman, *Parting of the
Ways* 28). They carried out this revision of Kantianism owing in part to their
suspicion that, by reserving a separate place for sensibility among the cognitive faculties, Kant had betrayed a residual psychologism, a conflation of the
universal laws of thought with the relative laws of human psychology.[7] This
conflation of the logical with the psychological could only impede access to the
purely logical knowledge that philosophy ought to pursue. And so the Marburg
School neo-Kantians developed instead a strictly "logical idealism," a version
of transcendental philosophy purged of all psychologistic residue, purged of
all reference to human sensibility. As a result of this lustration of sensibility,
the notions of the passivity of the human subject and the necessary givenness
of the object of experience were eliminated as well (Köhnke 181). Cohen, for
example, in the same text in which he announces that "Kant discovered a new
concept of experience" (3), explains that by "experience" he means only the

result of a priori acts of logical construction, acts exemplified by the construction of mathematical idealities according to objective principles and so not the result of the passive reception of sensations.

Like Heidegger, Benjamin was a student (albeit a poor one) of the neo-Kantian Heinrich Rickert.[8] His correspondences during the 1910s are littered with references to now mostly forgotten luminaries of the neo-Kantian movement. And as I noted above in passing, he undertook alongside Scholem in the summer of 1918 a close reading of Cohen's *Kants Theorie der Erfahrung*.[9] With regard to neo-Kantianism's philosophical program, however, Benjamin was decidedly ambivalent. He endorsed neo-Kantianism's "abolition of the strict distinction between the forms of intuition and the categories [of the understanding]" (*SW* 1:95), for this distinction, he notes, is only a "metaphysical rudiment" in Kant's work, one in need of correction. He endorsed as well the neo-Kantians' antipsychologistic interpretation of transcendental philosophy; in fact, he wondered if neo-Kantian antipsychologism had gone far enough—if it had not, perhaps, continued to model the cognizing consciousness on the empirical consciousness (1:103). Benjamin rejected, however, what he construed as neo-Kantianism's scientism and, in his later writings (and with a special vehemence), its progressivism (Eiland and Jennings 102).[10] Indeed, his direct pronouncements on neo-Kantianism are rarely positive. Concerning Cohen, for example, a remark in a letter to Scholem from January 1921, a few years after Cohen's death and during a period when Benjamin was at work on the "Critique of Violence" ("Zur Kritik der Gewalt"), is typical: "I had to deal with [Cohen's] *Ethik des reinen Willens* to be able to write ['Critique of Violence']," Benjamin notes. "But what I read there really depressed me. Cohen's sense of the truth was clearly so strong that he was required to make the most unbelievable leaps in order to turn his back on it" (*C* 173). Perhaps it was reading Cohen alongside Scholem that prompted Benjamin to turn against the neo-Kantian approach to philosophy, for we read among Scholem's notes the following: "One can only critique good works[;] that is the reason why no one has yet written the absolutely negative critique of Cohen's *Kants Theorie der Erfahrung*. This book proves only one thing absolutely[:] that it is impossible to understand Kant today" ("On Kant" 444).

Despite his reservations about the orthodox neo-Kantian reading of transcendental philosophy, Benjamin seems never in his early writings to have considered articulating his philosophical program in other than Kantian terms. Peter E. Gordon has the following to say about the character of German phi-

losophy around the time of the First World War, and he presents an apt characterization of the situation in which Benjamin found himself during this period:

> [A]lthough the neo-Kantian schools still dominated the German universities,
> many students were now inclined to see their idealist training as mere prepa-
> ration. It was a common sentiment that one must return to the source-texts
> themselves, not bothering with previous academic interpretation. Rather than
> reject the older canon, they aimed to force it to speak in a new way. (*Rosenzweig
> and Heidegger* 31)

Gordon is thinking here of the work of Heidegger and of Franz Rosenzweig, but
his observation suits Benjamin's early writings as well. Though Benjamin does
not share with Heidegger the obsession with framing his philosophical project as the recovery of a buried tradition, Benjamin does return to his (Kantian)
source-text—"looking on each letter as a *tradendum* to be transmitted" (*C* 98)—
rather than settle for the academic interpretations provided by the neo-Kantians,
and he does so with the aim of forcing this text to speak in a new way.

Keeping this return to Kant in mind, let us look again at "On the Program
of the Coming Philosophy." Here is a relevant passage (and note Benjamin's
readiness to engage with transcendental philosophy on neo-Kantianism's own
essentially epistemological terrain even as he challenges neo-Kantianism's core
assumptions):

> The problem faced by Kantian epistemology, as by every great epistemology, has
> two sides, and Kant managed to give a valid explanation for only one of them.
> First of all there was the question of the certainty of knowledge [*Erkenntnis*] that
> is lasting, and, second, there was the question of the dignity of an experience
> [*Erfahrung*] that is ephemeral. For universal philosophical interest is continually
> directed toward both the timeless validity of knowledge and the certainty of a
> temporal experience that is regarded as the immediate, if not the only, object of
> that knowledge. (*SW* 1:100–101)

The terms into which Benjamin divides Kantian (and indeed every great) epistemology—"knowledge" and "experience"—are some of the most contested
in the history of philosophy, the source of conflicts between and within ra-
tionalisms and empiricisms throughout the modern era. And "experience" in
particular is one of the master terms in Benjamin's own writings, crucial to
his 1930s discussions of capitalist modernity, in which discussions he opposes
*Erfahrung* (experience reflected on, incorporated into oneself) to a fragmen-

tary, impoverished *Erlebnis* (punctual, lived experience). In the above passage, though, Benjamin is most likely responding to and rejecting Cohen's use of the term "experience" in *Kants Theorie der Erfahrung*. If Cohen's conception of experience effectively folds experience into logic, giving experience over to mathematical natural science and so over to the certainty of (one version of) timeless knowledge, it also instances the one-sidedness with which Benjamin charges Kantian epistemology more generally. It neglects, in Benjamin's terms, the *dignity* of experience.

In the passage cited above, however, Benjamin faults not only Cohen and the neo-Kantians but also Kant himself for having failed to recognize the rights of "temporal" or "ephemeral" experience, for having failed to recognize what every great epistemology must recognize: the two-sidedness of cognition, the real coexistence within cognition of both knowledge and experience. Now, on the surface this criticism seems to be unfounded. One need go no further than Kant's oft-cited remark in the "Transcendental Logic" that "thoughts without content are empty, intuitions without concepts are blind" to find within critical philosophy a defense of the ephemeral (*CPR* A51/B75). Lacking ephemeral intuitions, our timeless concepts would remain hollow shells. Nonetheless, Benjamin insists that the Kantian notion of experience is limited in just this sense. And thus he contrasts with Kant's "brilliant exploration of the certainty and justification of knowledge" Kant's failure to provide the epistemological foundation for a "new and higher kind of experience" (*SW* 1:102). So, where has Kant gone wrong?

Benjamin's point here—and this is really the motive force of Benjamin's challenge both to Kant and to neo-Kantianism—is that within the Kantian framework the form that ephemeral experience can take is decided in advance. As a result, the dignity of ephemeral experience is missed. Kant, Benjamin explains, and "especially in the *Prolegomena* [*to any Future Metaphysics*]," suffered from a limited and limiting notion of experience insofar as he derived "the principles of experience from the sciences—in particular, mathematical physics"; and yet, "as an experience or a view of the world, it was of the lowest order" (1:101). Setting off from the assumption that the only valid experience is the experience described by the natural sciences (and specifically, by Newtonian mechanics), Kant—who, alas, "shared the horizon of his times"—allowed this particular experience to determine the form of the transcendental structures themselves, allowed it to determine the character of categorical knowledge in transcendental philosophy. The upshot: only experience amenable to the quantifying demands of natural science would be recognized as valid in the Kantian system. The neo-Kantian revision of Kant's epistemology only exacerbated this problem: attempting to bring Kantianism in line with more recent developments in the sciences, transforming transcendental philosophy itself into a second-order reflection on the fact of science, the neo-Kantians produced, finally, "an extreme extension of the mechanical aspect of the relatively empty Enlightenment concept of experience" (1:105).

Benjamin rejects the one-sided epistemology characteristic of (neo-)Kantian scientism, and he rejects as well the enervation of experience to which it gives rise. He does not, however, oppose to this scientism an equally one-sided irrationalism, a metaphysics of the will or of life. Peter Fenves describes lucidly this double refusal:

> [Benjamin] borrows, as it were, the pathos of contemporaneous *Erlebnis*-discourse [as it appears in the vitalist philosophies of thinkers from Nietzsche and Bergson to Wilhelm Dilthey and Martin Buber], which summarily repudiates the "mechanical-mathematical" experience of the physical sciences; but he does not then expend this pathos in evocations of the higher life that awaits whomever [*sic*] has enough courage to break out of the narrow confines of Kantian critique in particular and Western rationalism in general. "On the Program of the Coming Philosophy" evinces none of the intoxicated talk of an eruptive "breakthrough" that Thomas Mann memorably recounts in the wartime discussions among students of theology at the University of Munich who had read their Feuerbach and their Nietzsche. (*Messianic Reduction* 156)

While scientism neglects experience in favor of (a certain version of) timeless knowledge—one derived surreptitiously from mechanical-mathematical experience—irrationalism dissolves all knowledge into disarticulated experience. Neither the scientism of the neo-Kantians, then, nor the irrationalism or mysticism that had begun to appear an attractive alternative to so many of Benjamin's contemporaries can secure a really two-sided epistemology, and thus neither can serve as a foundation for the philosophy of the future.

Between this epistemological Scylla and Charybdis, Benjamin charts his course, one summed up in a remark with which he concludes that portion of the "Program" finished and presented to Scholem in December 1917: "[E]xperience is the uniform and continuous multiplicity of knowledge" (*SW* 1:108). The real force of this assertion, how it describes a deepening rather than a simple overturning of the Kantian program, will be my concern in the next section.

For now, though, I want to call attention to how Benjamin here seeks to reverse the relative priority usually afforded to knowledge and experience and to do so without simply reducing one to the other. On the one hand, knowledge will remain distinct from experience as the source of the latter's principles. On the other hand, knowledge will no longer simply describe that timeless, certain, and singular structure under which a variety of experiences are grouped and judged. Rather, knowledge must be made multiple, so that it coincides with the essential multiplicity of experience; and it must be made passive, so that it is opened up to transformative encounters with domains of experience that lie outside of it. In the next section, I shall discuss in more detail each of these projected revisions of Kantianism—what we might refer to as Benjamin's democratization and finitization of Kantianism.

## II. The Doctrine of Orders

In "On the Program of the Coming Philosophy," Benjamin proposes to transform the Kantian notion of experience by reforming the Kantian table of categories, the a priori structures of knowledge that provide experience with its formal conditions. He describes this project in the following terms:

> Just as the Marburg school has already begun with the sublation of the distinction between transcendental logic and aesthetics (even though it is possible that an analogue of this distinction must return on a higher level), so must the table of categories be completely revised, as is now generally demanded. In this very process, then, the transformation of the concept of knowledge will begin to manifest itself in the acquisition of a new concept of experience, since the Aristotelian categories are both arbitrarily posed and have been exploited in a very one-sided way by Kant in light of mechanical experience. (*SW* 1:106)

In order for Kantian epistemology to admit of a "new concept of experience," Kant's table of categories must be "completely revised." This revision Benjamin presents both as continuous with the neo-Kantian recasting of Kant's faculty psychology—that is, with the neo-Kantian "sublation of the distinction" between the understanding and the intuition—and as the necessary response to a general (and unattributed) "demand." This demand, if we take it as registering a frustration with Kant's failure to motivate his blanket adoption of Aristotle's logical categories, reaches back at least to Hegel, who writes in the *Science of Logic* that "[Kantian philosophy] *borrows* the categories, as so-called root notions, for the *transcendental* logic, from the subjective logic in which they were adopted empirically. Since it admits the latter fact, it is hard to see why transcendental logic resolves to borrow from such a science instead of directly resorting to experience" (*SL* 613). And it reaches forward to (for example) P. F. Strawson, who, in the analytical reconstruction of Kant that he lays out in *The Bounds of Sense*, expresses "serious doubts" about the "primitive" logical forms that Kant's table of categories is supposed to supply (78).[11] Benjamin shares with both philosophers the notion that what Kant presents as a structure of certain or timeless knowledge is in fact open to revision. But he differs from both philosophers as to the form that this revision should take.

Benjamin elaborates on the character of his projected revision of Kant only a few lines later:

> First and foremost, one must consider whether the table of categories has to remain in its present isolation and lack of mediation, or whether it could not take a place among other members in a doctrine of orders [*Lehre von den Ordnungen*] or itself be built up to such a doctrine, founded upon or connected to primal concepts [*Urbegriffe*]. Such a doctrine of orders would also comprise that which Kant discusses in the transcendental aesthetic, and, furthermore, all the basic concepts [*Grundbegriffe*] not only of mechanics but also of geometry, linguistics, psychology, the descriptive natural sciences, and many others, to the extent that these concepts had a direct relation to the categories or the other highest ordering concepts of philosophy [*höchsten philosophischen Ordnungsbegriffe*]. (*SW* 1:106–107)

Kant's table of categories can be maintained, then, but only insofar as it is relativized, freed from its "present isolation" and located among other "basic concepts" in a "doctrine of orders." Scholem notes that "the terms *Ordnung* [order] or *geistige Ordnung* [intellectual order] were among [Benjamin's] most frequently used in [the late 1910s]. In the presentation of [Benjamin's] own thought, they usually took the place of 'category'" (*Walter Benjamin* 69). Scholem's explanation is helpful insofar as it marks a relationship between "category" and "order" in Benjamin's thinking, but it also risks obscuring Benjamin's more radical claim that the doctrine of orders he describes is intended to subsume the table of categories, which latter will "take a place among other members in [the] doctrine of orders." And here one should keep in mind the broader meaning of "*Ordnung*," which suggests not just an arrangement but an arrangement according to rank (as in the Latin *ordo*), as well as a sense of exponentiation, such that we could say that the doctrine of orders is of a higher power than the table of categories, or that the former relates to the latter as an exponent relates to its base.

In the "doctrine of orders," the "basic concepts" that compose Kant's table of categories (which are, again, nothing other than the basic concepts of the mathematical natural sciences) should coexist alongside the basic concepts of "geometry, linguistics, psychology. . . ." And Benjamin later adds to this list the basic concepts of "art, jurisprudence, and history" (*SW* 1:107), and then of "theology" and "metaphysics" (1:108). For from each of these "sciences" can be drawn a set of ordering concepts, which should in turn make possible a particular sphere of experience. Howard Caygill has elucidated the relationship between the Kantian table of categories and Benjamin's doctrine of orders with his own concept of "double infinity": "the transcendental infinity of possible marks on a given surface (or perceptions within a given framework of possible experience) and the speculative infinity of possible bounded but infinite surfaces or frameworks of experience" (4). Each individual order constitutes a "transcendental infinity" insofar as an infinite number of experiences are possible within that order *qua* transcendental structure. Kant's own table of categories provides one such "infinity" insofar as it preconditions an infinite number of possible experiences (albeit experiences formally determined by mathematical science); history is another "infinity," psychology still another, and so on. The second, "speculative" infinity describes the potentially unlimited number of possible sites of inscription, the extension of the list that Benjamin begins to sketch: geometry, art, jurisprudence, metaphysics, theology . . .

Benjamin aims, then, to make knowledge multiple by deriving from preconstituted domains of experience basic concepts and using these concepts to construct a system of interlinked but nonidentical orders. Once we have this project in mind, we can better understand some of Benjamin's more cryptic statements about the task of philosophy, for example, Benjamin's now well-known response to Scholem's question of whether the philosophy of the future should include as well the "mantic disciplines in [its] conception of experience": "a philosophy that does not include the possibility of soothsaying from coffee grounds and cannot explicate it cannot be a true philosophy" (qtd. in Scholem, *Walter Benjamin* 73). The domain of experience present in "soothsaying" and the other mantic disciplines possesses, presumably, basic concepts, concepts that might coexist with the Kantian table of categories in a doctrine of orders. A philosophy that bars this domain of experience remains, then, still one-sided, unable to realize fully the multiplicity of—and thus the dignity of—experience.

More importantly, Benjamin's project of positioning Kant's table of categories within a doctrine of orders helps us to understand the central (but fluc-
tuating) place that language occupies in Benjamin's writings during the 1910s.
After imagining in the "Program" a future philosophy that would account for
"all the basic concepts not only of mechanics but also of geometry, linguistics,
psychology, the descriptive natural sciences, and many others," Benjamin notes
that "outstanding examples here are the principles of grammar" (*SW* 1:107). He
develops this point as follows:

> Just as Kantian theory itself, in order to find its principles, needed to be con-
> fronted with a science with reference to which it could define them, modern
> philosophy will need this as well. The great transformation and correction
> which must be performed upon the concept of experience, oriented so one-
> sidedly along mathematical-mechanical lines, can be attained only by relating
> knowledge to language, as was attempted by Hamann during Kant's lifetime.
> (1:107–108)

Gesturing to the pietistic philosopher J. G. Hamann's linguistic "metacritique"
of Kantianism, Benjamin argues that "a concept of knowledge gained from
reflection on the linguistic nature of knowledge will create a corresponding
concept of experience which will also encompass realms that Kant failed truly
to systematize" (1:108).[12] He thus presents language as constituting a system of
knowledge, an order, akin to Kant's own transcendental system yet possessing a
greater scope, a greater ability to account for the sorts of experiences foreclosed
by Kantianism. And so Benjamin apparently looks back to his 1916 essay "On
Language as Such and on the Language of Man" ("Über die Sprache überhaupt
und über die Sprache des Menschen"), wherein he develops a notion of "language as such," "pure language" (*reine Sprache*), to describe something like a
transcendental field without—*pace* Kant—a subject or an object, a field of pure
"communicability" (*Mitteilbarkeit*) (*SW* 1:72).

There are certainly continuities between Benjamin's interests in "On Language as Such," on the one hand, and "On the Program of the Coming Philosophy," on the other, not least of which is his persistent concern with "the
fact that all philosophical knowledge has its unique expression in language"
(*SW* 1:108). In a recent study of Benjamin's work and thought, and pointing to
passages like the one I just cited, Uwe Steiner writes that "the 'Program' directly
continues ideas developed in 'On Language as Such and on the Language of
Man,' a treatise completed barely a year earlier" (40). Moreover, a number of the

most astute readers of Benjamin's project have insisted on the centrality even to Benjamin's last writings of the early reflections on language. Giorgio Agamben, for example, in his aptly titled "Language and History: Linguistic and Historical Categories in Benjamin's Thought," traces an unbroken line of philosophical argument concerning the status of a "redeemed humanity" from "On Language as Such" all the way forward to Benjamin's 1940 theses "On the Concept of History" (*Potentialities* 43).

Though it is no doubt true that "the early theory of language is of exceptional significance in Benjamin's oeuvre" (Steiner 41), I want to claim, nonetheless, that the notion of language that Benjamin sets forth in "On Language as Such" risks concealing something central to the particular role that language plays in the "Program." The earlier essay is organized by the opposition that Benjamin establishes between an Adamic language that communicates only the fact of communicability and a postlapsarian human language, one instrumentalized and divided among different linguistic communities. In the "Program," however, language is crucial to the doctrine of orders not so much because, in its perfected state, it opens onto an experience of the absolute—which still seems to be Benjamin's hope in the earlier essay—but because language is itself a figure for the multiplicity of orders. For just as a variety of languages can coexist, so too can a variety of orders. This fact comes through most clearly in an unpublished fragment on "Language and Logic" ("Sprache und Logik"; 1921), in which Benjamin revises some of his earlier remarks on language. Against his prior assertion that translation is necessary as a consequence of humanity's fall "from the paradisiacal state that knew only one language" (*SW* 1:71), Benjamin writes that "the multiplicity of languages is not the product of decadence any more than is the multiplicity of peoples, and indeed is so far removed from any such decay that we might be justified in asserting that this multiplicity expresses their essential character" (1:273). Languages, like orders, gain nothing from their being represented as symptoms of some Babelic muddle or as fragments of a lost whole; rather, multiplicity is their essential character. And for this reason, Benjamin can treat language as one order among others—can include linguistics alongside history, psychology, and so on—*and* can present language as a model for the doctrine of orders itself. Language allows for—or perhaps essentially entails—a multiplicity, an infinity, of different languages; and in each of these languages, an infinite number of things can be said.[13]

As I suggested above, the revision of Kantianism that Benjamin undertakes in "On the Program of the Coming Philosophy" has as its upshot not only the democratization of transcendental philosophy—that is, the multiplication within a philosophical "doctrine" of distinct but equally valid transcendental orders—but also the introduction into transcendental philosophy of a particular notion of passivity. Indeed, it is through the latter that Benjamin underwrites the former, secures for his doctrine of orders its condition of possibility. Now, when I say that Benjamin *introduces* into transcendental philosophy a notion of passivity, I do so to stress that Benjamin does not simply return to Kant's own position concerning the constitutive passivity of experience. Before the revisions of transcendental philosophy carried out by the neo-Kantians, which had the effect of eliminating from transcendental philosophy the distinction between intuition and understanding (and hence between affection and construction, passivity and spontaneity), Kant had made all cognition originate in the finite subject's passive reception of sensations. Heidegger had a related notion of passive receptivity in mind when he wrote that, with Kant, "we come to know the genuine meaning of the finitude of the subject for the first time" (*Kant and the Problem of Metaphysics* 277). Benjamin, however, is no more interested than the neo-Kantians in the receptive faculty of finite, human subjects. Moreover, Benjamin rejects as inadequate to modern philosophy—indeed, rejects as an "epistemological mythology"—the "notion, sublimated though it may be, of an individual living ego which receives sensations by means of its senses and forms its ideas of the basis of them" (*SW* 1:103).

Benjamin develops an alternative notion of passivity, indications of which we can glimpse in two, seemingly unrelated remarks. I already cited each of them above in support of slightly different claims. The first remark follows (parenthetically and as a kind of *correctio*) Benjamin's endorsement of the neo-Kantian "sublation of the distinction between transcendental logic and aesthetics": "[I]t is possible," he writes, "that an analogue of this distinction must return on a higher level." (*SW* 1:106) The second remark immediately precedes Benjamin's insistence that modern philosophy must put itself in dialogue with the fact of language: "Just as Kantian theory itself, in order to find its principles, needed to be confronted with a science with reference to which it could define them, modern philosophy will need this as well" (1:107). While the first remark suggests that an equivalent of the distinction between the intuition and the understanding—the origin of passivity in Kant's philosophy and one of the main targets of the neo-Kantians' corrections—must reappear within modern philosophy (albeit at a "higher level," one distinct from that of the cognizing consciousness), the second remark provides the first with its content. Every philosophy must develop out of a confrontation with a domain of experience—a preconstituted "science"—external to it; every philosophy must, therefore, remain passively receptive vis-à-vis its own outside. The "higher level" at which passivity returns is, then, the level of the system of modern philosophy itself. The latter is made subject to "confrontations," to constitutive encounters. These encounters are essential both to the varied orders that Benjamin describes and to the "doctrine" that comprises them. They are essential to the former: just as Kant's table of categories was conditioned by the preconstituted science of Newtonian mechanics, orders based on history, linguistics, psychology and so on will be conditioned by their respective sciences and will see their basic concepts derived from these sciences. And they are essential to the latter insofar as, again, Benjamin makes clear that modern philosophy as a whole, the coming philosophy for which he provides the blueprint, is or ought to be conditioned by a confrontation with language.

By introducing into transcendental philosophy this radical notion of passivity—in other words, by making transcendental philosophy into something that is itself finite rather than treating it as an unchanging system that describes how unalterable structures of knowledge make particular finite experiences possible—Benjamin anticipates a number of later continental philosophical attempts to think together transcendental form and historical genesis, a problematic that binds together (for example) Michel Foucault's "archaeological" reflections on the historical a priori, Jacques Derrida's early interrogations of the necessarily material inscription of mathematical idealities, and more recently, Alain Badiou's work on the relationship between "Being" and "Event." It is beyond the scope of this chapter and this book to discuss these diverse projects in any kind of detail. In each case, however, what is at stake is the mutability (rather than the simple dissolution) of a structure that seems, at first glance, singular, certain, and timeless.

### III. A Historical A Priori

Benjamin never really completed the philosophical project that he outlines in "On the Program of the Coming Philosophy," at least not in the terms that he establishes therein. And I suspect that, even early on, Benjamin must have recognized how difficult the completion of the task that he set before himself would have to be. Again: "[J]ust as Kantian theory itself, in order to find its principles, needed to be confronted with a science with reference to which it could define them, modern philosophy will need this as well." To revise Kantian theory, to recast the Kantian system as a doctrine of orders, would entail something akin to rewriting the *Critique of Pure Reason*, and not just once but over and over again, confronting the passively receptive skeleton of transcendental philosophy with linguistics, with theology, with history, and so on, all in an attempt to derive a multiplicity of orders, a multiplicity of articulations of knowledge-experience. Whatever his considerable talents, Benjamin was, fundamentally, a critic, closer in temperament to Friedrich Schlegel, really, than to Hegel or Kant—which is just to say that Benjamin probably lacked the disposition for the sort of sustained philosophical labor that the project he outlines in the "Program" would have required. And so his program remained just that: a program, and not the coming philosophy itself.

For all its promise, the doctrine of orders appears only briefly in Benjamin's early writings. It fades away quickly; and in his late writings references to it seem to be entirely absent. If we can say anything about these late writings in general, it is that they demonstrate a movement away from philosophical abstraction and toward lived experience, a movement encapsulated by Benjamin's assertion that "the eternal is, in any case, far more the ruffle on a dress than some idea" (*AP* B3,7). Or, as Adorno would have it: "[Benjamin's] philosophy indefatigably breaks its teeth on the core" (*Prisms* 225), on the irreducible "that-ness" of the object-world. At any rate, from the mid-1920s through the 1930s, Benjamin changes his focus; his work begins to address subjects that appear at first glance less epistemological or metaphysical than historical, sociological, or even psychological. Still more surprising, the empirical subject, excised from his early writings, returns with a vengeance, as his more abstract reflections on knowledge and experience give way to discussions of prostitutes, flâneurs, gamblers, and melancholics: a litany of human types. This shift is, at least in part, politically motivated. In a letter from 1924, Benjamin describes to Scholem his plans to "generate a 'politics' from within myself" (*C* 258). In another letter to Scholem, written two years later, he notes his readiness to "leave the purely theoretical sphere" and perhaps join the Communist Party (300). We find Benjamin on the cusp of his Marxist phase.

I shall turn to Benjamin's writings from the 1920s and 1930s in the next chapters. Before doing so, however, and by way of conclusion, I want to return to what I said in my introductory remarks: despite the relative dearth of explicit references to Kant in Benjamin's writings after the 1910s,[14] Benjamin's early struggles with Kantian philosophy continued to influence (albeit as an underground current) his later historical and political writings. And so the familiar claim that Benjamin's work "can be divided into two phases: an early period of metaphysical-theological interests, and a later period with a Marxist orientation" (Steiner 7) has to be rethought. As evidence of continuity between these two phases of Benjamin's work, as a place where the division between Benjamin's early fascination with Kantianism and his later turn to politics, technology, urban space, and so on becomes blurry, Benjamin's work from the period during and immediately following his completion of his dissertation on *Frühromantik* is noteworthy. It is not so much that the work of this period allows us to say that Benjamin remained interested in Kant two or three or four years after he was supposed to have put Kant down (for this would be a small thing, after all); rather, this work suggests, through its blending of themes from different moments in Benjamin's career, the possibility that these themes can coexist, that Benjamin's Kantianism and his political-historical concerns need not exclude one another.

I shall limit myself to two, small pieces of evidence in support of this claim, reserving its more detailed treatment for the sequel. The first appears in Scholem's 1975 memoir *Walter Benjamin: The Story of a Friendship*. In it Scholem recalls a conversation with Benjamin dating from the spring of 1919, when Benjamin was close to completing his dissertation on *Frühromantik*. Having recently been introduced by Hugo Ball to the Marxist theorist Ernst Bloch (whose first book, *The Spirit of Utopia*, had appeared in print only months earlier), Benjamin told Scholem that "Bloch had him [Benjamin] in mind as the specialist on the 'theory of categories' for a projected general survey of philosophy" (97). Bloch's project seems never to have materialized. Scholem's recollection is still noteworthy, however, and for several reasons. First, it provides some evidence of how Benjamin was perceived—or at least how he wanted Scholem to believe that he was perceived—by his interlocutors, including those interlocutors who possessed the philosophical acumen of Bloch: Benjamin was taken to be an expert in Kant's table of categories, in the Kantian doctrine of the a priori structures of human cognition. Second, Scholem's recollection has the tantalizing effect of suggesting that Benjamin, more than a year after he had expressed to Scholem his regret at having to set Kant down and devote himself to his dissertation, had returned—or was planning to return—to Kant; and suggesting as well that this return to Kant centered on—or would have centered on—an engagement with Kant's table of categories, essentially the same project that Benjamin outlines in the "Program."

Finally, Scholem's anecdote suggests that the minutiae of the Kantian system remained still central to Benjamin at one of the key moments of his politicization. Benjamin's relationship with Bloch was transformative, for even though he found in *The Spirit of Utopia* "enormous deficiencies," he also describes it in a letter to Scholem as "nevertheless, the only book on which, as a truly contemporaneous and contemporary utterance, I can take my own measure" (*C* 148). And he describes as well how "in conversation [Bloch] so often challenged my rejection of *every* contemporary political trend that he ultimately forced me to immerse myself in these matters, something I hope was worthwhile" (148). Benjamin intended to write a lengthy review of Bloch's book; it would be wonderful to have this piece of writing, since Bloch's articulation of the theological and the messianic so clearly anticipates the themes of Benjamin's own work, but it seems to have been lost (154, 156). For our purposes, though, what matters most is the suggestiveness of Scholem's claim that Benjamin's discussions of political matters with Bloch intermingled with Benjamin's plan to return to his earlier work on Kant's table of categories.

The second small piece of evidence I want to marshal in support of my claim for the continuity of Benjamin's interests from the 1910s into the 1920s concerns his fascination with the work of the utopian science fiction author and theorist of glass architecture, Paul Scheerbart. Benjamin first encountered Scheerbart's work of science fiction, *Lesabéndio*, in 1917, when he received it from Scholem as a wedding gift. He subsequently wrote a review, "Paul Scheerbart: *Lesabéndio*" (1918), which he left unpublished, in which he celebrates Scheerbart's eschewal of psychological interiority in favor of "the outermost surface of things" (*die äußerste Oberfläche der Dinge*; *GS* 618). He planned another discussion of Scheerbart, which was to have been included in a comprehensive work on politics, "The True Politician" ("Der wahre Politiker"), a product of the time he spent with Bloch, but this text seems to have been lost. Its only trace, with the exception of a few scattered fragments, is the 1921 essay "Critique of Violence." His enthusiasm for Scheerbart's work persisted, however. Benjamin completed "Experience and Poverty" ("Erfahrung und Armut"), which he published in *Die Welt im Wort* in December 1933; in it he compares Scheerbart positively to Jules Verne, writing that "unlike Verne, who always has ordinary French or English gentlemen of leisure travelling around the cosmos in the most amazing vehicles, Scheerbart is interested in inquiring how our telescopes, our airplanes, our rockets can transform human beings as they have been up to now into completely new, lovable, and interesting creatures" (*SW* 2:733). In 1939, Benjamin completed a brief study "On Scheerbart," written in French and again unpublished at the time of his death. In it, he says of *Lesabéndio* that here we discover the "image . . . of a humanity which had developed the full range of its technology and put it to humane use" (*SW* 4:386). Both of these texts from the 1930s reflect Benjamin's then pronounced interests in utopian social engineering and the transformative power of technology. Finally, Benjamin turned again to Scheerbart in his unfinished magnum opus, *The Arcades Project*. Here, Scheerbart appears in his guise as the utopian theorist of glass architecture (a topic that fascinated Benjamin and one on which Scheerbart had completed a short treatise in 1913) and as the "twin brother of Fourier" (*SW* 4:387).

I provide this sketch of Benjamin's continuing interest in Scheerbart (and *Lesabéndio* in particular) because Scheerbart's writings (and again, *Lesabéndio* in particular) provide a kind of allegorical rendering of the coexistence of Benjamin's earlier and later interests. *Lesabéndio* tells the story of the planet Pallas and the bizarre creatures that populate it, including the novel's eponymous hero, Lesabéndio, who undertakes the utopian project of constructing a tower forty-four miles high. His aim in doing so is to pass through a cloud that hides from Pallas the astral system that the planet occupies. This project results in Lesabéndio's demise, as he ascends beyond Pallas and is absorbed into the astral system that he has finally reached. Scheerbart does not present Lesabéndio's end as something tragic, however; rather, he writes that "[Lesabéndio] had the sense that he was gradually turning into a star" (221), and concludes the novel with a description of Lesabéndio's communing with the sun; the latter states that anything is possible "as long as we fear neither pain nor death!" (222). So we find in *Lesabéndio* an image of technological innovation resulting in the transformation of the individual, but also in the transformation of the species, for the tower Lesabéndio constructs is so large as to alter Pallas's center of gravity, which alters as a result the composition of the Pallasians' bodies (218). Benjamin returned repeatedly to this topic—that is, the transformation of the species through the transformation of technology—during the 1930s, in the canonical essay "The Work of Art in the Age of Its Technological Reproducibility" ("Das Kunstwerk im Zeitalter seiner technischen Reproduzierbarkeit"), published in differing French and German versions between 1935 and 1939, as well as in "On Some Motifs in Baudelaire" ("Über einige Motive bei Baudelaire"; 1940). In the latter, Benjamin describes the power of new technologies—both instrumental (traffic lights, for example) and artistic (cinema)—to "subject the human sensorium to a complex kind of training" (*SW* 4:328). And in the former, he locates modern media technologies at the very center of "the theory of perception that the Greeks called aesthetics" (3:120), pointing to these technologies' role in re-functioning the human sensory apparatus.

I suspect that most readers interested in Benjamin's use of Scheerbart have tended to read backwards from Benjamin's interests in the 1930s to his first encounter with Scheerbart in 1917. In doing so, however, they leave unanswered the question of why Benjamin was so immediately taken with *Lesabéndio* when the ideas he would draw from it would not become an explicit theme in his writings for another decade. It seems, then, like a good idea to bracket reference (temporarily) to Benjamin's later statements on technology and architecture—except as these appear as emergent themes in his writings from the 1910s—and to ask instead how Scheerbart's novel might have harmonized with Benjamin's earliest philosophical concerns. Given his interest in the 1910s in alternative structures of experience, it seems entirely possible that Benjamin would have found in Scheerbart's detailed description of creatures "new, lovable, and interesting," and utterly unlike ourselves, an imaginative concretization of some of the theories that he was in 1917 still approaching as abstract, epistemological problems.[15] Scheerbart's novel provides us with a glimpse of how Benjamin's earlier work on Kantian themes—his attempt to imagine alternative structures of knowledge that enable alternative structures of experience—might be translated from a more or less idealist (though Benjamin's earliest writings are only problematically idealist) to a more or less materialist register, how they might enter into dialogue with his growing interests in historical, political, and technological matters. From the vantage of Benjamin's revised Kantianism, Scheerbart's Pallasians present an alternative configuration of terrestrial sensory experience (as we witness in Lesabéndio's telescoping eyes) and an image of this experience as fundamentally mutable, open to wholesale transformation as a result of the whims of the individual or the pressures of the environment. But these themes are immediately interlaced with questions of technology, architecture, and collective existence more generally. This same interlacing controls Benjamin's later writings. It is just a matter, then, of seeing urban modernity as a kind of new Pallas.

## CHAPTER 5

# ANECDOTE

Human sensuousness is therefore embodied time.
——Karl Marx, *The Difference between the Democritean
and Epicurean Philosophy of Nature*

To write history means giving dates their physiognomy.
——Walter Benjamin, *The Arcades Project*

**WALTER BENJAMIN'S** most memorable remarks on the critical potential of
the anecdote appear in Convolute S of *The Arcades Project*, a section of Benjamin's unfinished masterwork ostensibly dedicated to "Painting, Jugendstil,
Novelty":

> The constructions of history are comparable to military orders that discipline
> the true life and confine it to barracks. On the other hand: the street insurgence
> of the anecdote. The anecdote brings things near to us spatially, lets them enter
> our life. It represents the strict antithesis to the sort of history which demands
> "empathy," which makes everything abstract. (*AP* S1a,3)

Commentators have typically interrupted the passage here. What have we
learned? The anecdote, an essentially "insurgent" form, serves "true life" by refusing the strictures of official history. It affirms the rights of the particular and
the transient against their incorporation into any *grand récit*. It resists abstraction, resists as well "empathy." The latter, Benjamin writes elsewhere, has as its
"origin . . . that indolence of the heart, that *acedia*, which despairs of appropri-
ating the genuine historical image as it briefly flashes by" (*SW* 4:391).

The critical studies of the anecdote that have appeared in the last few decades
have more or less endorsed Benjamin's description of the anecdote as a fundamentally antiauthoritarian form. Noting the etymology of "anecdote" (from the
Greek term ἀνέκδοτα, meaning "not given out," "not published"), Peter Fenves
writes that "the *an* of *anecdote* serves as an expression of determinate negation,

not as an indication of a zone of indetermination. What the *an* of *anecdote* negates is authority. Under no condition can *auctoritas* express itself anecdotally" (*Arresting Language* 153). And in what is probably the single best study of the historical fortunes of the anecdote, Lionel Gossman writes the following:

> From its earliest usage in the modern European languages . . . the term "anecdote" has been closely related to history, and even to a kind of counter-history. Procopius's *Anekdota* cover exactly the same years as his *History of the Wars*: 527–553 CE. But in the unpublished work, the secretary and companion of Belisarius, Justinian's famous general, exposes the censored, seamy underside, the *chronique scandaleuse*, of the reign he himself had presented in noble colors in his official history. (152)

A challenge to "official history," the anecdote is, from its origins, a minor form in the most emphatic sense.

The passage from Benjamin's *Arcades Project* that I cited above continues, however, with a remarkable illustration. After indicating the ability of anecdotes to "bring things near to us spatially," Benjamin presses on:

> The same technique of nearness may be practiced, calendrically, with respect to epochs. Let us imagine that a man dies on the very day he turns fifty, which is the day on which his son is born, to whom the same thing happens, and so on. If one were to have the chain commence at the time of the birth of Christ, the result would be that, in the time since we began our chronological reckoning, not forty men have lived. Thus the image of a historical course of time is totally transformed as soon as one brings to bear on it a standard adequate and comprehensible to human life. (*AP* S1a,3)

As a way of illustrating the counterhistorical potential of the anecdote, Benjamin opposes to our conventional conception of chronology what is "calendrically" most near: the finite course of forty human lives. As strange as this passage may seem, it is not without precedents. In his 1874 meditation *On the Advantage and Disadvantage of History for Life*, Friedrich Nietzsche asks, "[O]f what account, after all, are a couple of millennia (or expressed differently: the period of thirty-four consecutive lives of men calculated at sixty years each)?" (44). A year later, in one of his first published articles, "Über das Studium der Geschichte der Wissenschaften vom Menschen, der Gesellschaft und dem Staat," Wilhelm Dilthey uses a similar metric to determine that only fourteen generations separate him from the late Scholastics, and eighty-four from Thales (*Gesammelte*

*Schriften* 5:36–37). He explains the importance of measuring time by generations a decade later, and in terms that anticipate Benjamin's own: "[O]nly the historian who . . . builds history from these life-units . . . and who links together individual lives through the concept of generations, only he will be able to apprehend the reality of a historical whole in contrast to the lifeless abstractions which are usually drawn from the archives" (*Introduction to the Human Sciences* 85).

The question that I mean to address in this chapter concerns the affinity between these essentially human measurements of time and the critical potential of the anecdote, especially as it informs "the Copernican revolution in historical perception" (*Die kopernikanische Wendung in der geschichtlichen Anschauung*) that Benjamin attempts to carry out in his late writings (*AP* K1,2). With this goal in mind, I shall first want to revisit Benjamin's aborted plan to write his dissertation on Immanuel Kant's philosophy of history, for it seems to me that a version of this early project resurfaces in Benjamin's late critique of historicism—in his "critique of historical reason" (to borrow a phrase from one of Benjamin's near contemporaries).[1] Here, it will be necessary to distinguish the philosophy of history that Benjamin develops in dialogue with Kant's theoretical system, on the one hand, from Kant's own philosophy of history (which Benjamin evidently found abhorrent), on the other. Second, drawing on Benjamin's scattered remarks on the anecdote as well as on the dispute between Benjamin and Adorno over the question of mediation in "The Paris of the Second Empire in Baudelaire" ("Das Paris des Second Empire bei Baudelaire"), I want to ask how the anecdote came to appear to Benjamin to provide a critical model of historical representation, "critical" in the sense that it eludes the failings of both the classical rationalist and the empiricist approaches to our experience of the past. And third, I want to argue that this critical, anecdotal model of historical representation is explicated and concretized in Benjamin's late "physiognomies," that is, in his examinations of the gambler, the flâneur, the melancholic, and other modern historical types.

As I have already indicated, addressing these issues will mean prizing open Benjamin's *Arcades Project*, so let us now turn to this text.[2]

## I. The Critique of Historical Reason

Benjamin worked intermittently on *The Arcades Project*—"the theater of all my struggles and all my ideas" (*C* 285)—between 1927 (when he first began to collect the notes that the project would eventually comprise) and 1940, the year of his death by suicide in Portbou.[3] The result of his efforts: a work (though the term is perhaps infelicitous) of more than a thousand pages, one of the monuments of European modernism. Benjamin's method was, from the very beginning, self-consciously materialist. In a letter from March 1929, Benjamin describes to Scholem his intent "to attain the most extreme concreteness for an era"—the nineteenth century—and to do so through an examination of such objects and events as, for example, "children's games, a building, or a real-life situation" (348). He never wavers in this dedication to the concrete. Around 1934–1935, however, Benjamin also begins to characterize *The Arcades Project* somewhat differently, shifting his focus from the object of historical experience—the detritus of nineteenth-century culture—to the subject of that experience. The aim of his project, he explains, is nothing less than a "Copernican revolution in historical perception."

Benjamin describes this revolution in the following terms:

> Formerly it was thought that a fixed point had been found in "what has been"; and one saw the present engaged in tentatively concentrating the forces of knowledge on this ground. Now this relation is to be overturned, and what has been is to become the dialectical reversal—the flash of awakened consciousness. Politics attains primacy over history. The facts become something that just now first happened to us, first struck us; to establish them is the affair of memory. (*AP* K1,2)

This remark is shot through with the idiosyncratically surrealist-Marxist language of Benjamin's later career. The moment of revolutionary awareness is presented as an "awakening" from the dreamworld of capitalist modernity; history is subordinated to politics. Before addressing this language, though, I want to look more closely at Benjamin's use of the phrase "Copernican revolution."

Throughout *The Arcades Project*, Benjamin never misses an opportunity to bring together the celestial and the mundane, as in his use of J. J. Grandville's depiction of the rings of Saturn in *Un autre monde* (1844): "a cast-iron balcony on which the inhabitants of Saturn take the evening air" (*AP* 8); or in the account of his project that he provides to his friend Werner Kraft: "[A]s for me, I am busy pointing my telescope through the bloody mist at a mirage of the nineteenth century that I am trying to reproduce based on the characteristics that it will manifest in a future state of the world, liberated from magic. Naturally, I must first build this telescope" (*C* 516).

It seems likely, though, that the phrase "Copernican revolution" is, in *The Arcades Project*, doing (at least) double duty, and that, in referring to his critique of historical perception as aiming at a Copernican revolution, Benjamin has in mind not only Copernicus's own overturning of geocentrism but also Kant's well-known use of the same language to characterize the revolution effected by the *Critique of Pure Reason* (1781). Describing the need to make the intuition of objects conform to our cognition rather than the reverse, Kant notes that this solution to the problems of metaphysics "would be just like the first thoughts of Copernicus, who, when he did not make good progress in the explanation of the celestial motions if he assumed that the entire celestial host revolves around the observer, tried to see if he might not have greater success if he made the observer revolve and left the stars at rest" (*CPR* Bxvi).

The Kantian pedigree of Benjamin's use of the phrase "Copernican revolution" helps us to make sense of the passage I quoted above, where references to "the flash of awakened consciousness" and to the "facts" as an "affair of memory" turn the question of historical perception from what lies outside of us— empirical facts, the real stuff of history—to what lies within us—our cognition or our recollection of these facts. The "fixed point" of historical perception is thereby radically transformed (a topic that I shall address in greater detail in a moment). More polemically, and still following Kant, Benjamin's claim that we need a Copernican revolution implies that our understanding or experience of history has been, up to this point, precritical, which is tantamount to saying that we have not as yet really had history at all, at least not in any meaningful sense. In his preface to the *Metaphysical Foundations of the Doctrine of Right* (1797) and looking back to the publication of the *Critique of Pure Reason*, Kant makes this point about the state of philosophy before and after his own critical intervention: "It sounds arrogant, conceited, and belittling of those who have not yet renounced their old system to assert that before the coming of the critical philosophy there was as yet no philosophy at all. . . . Yet since, considered objectively, there can be only one human reason, there cannot be many philosophies." And so, Kant concludes, "anyone who announces a system of philosophy as his own work says in effect that before this philosophy there was none at all" (6:206–207). All philosophy before 1781 is precritical, which is to say, prephilosophical. Sticking to Kant's own classification of precritical positions, we might oppose Benjamin's truly critical approach to historical perception to the rationalist historicism of G. W. F. Hegel, on the one hand, and to the empiricist historicism of Leopold von Ranke and the so-called "critical school of history," on the other. Each would appear precritical—and thus prehistorical—from this side of Benjamin's Copernican revolution.

As I observed at the beginning of the previous chapter, Benjamin had initially planned to write his dissertation at the University of Bern on the topic of Kant's philosophy of history, only to realize that "it is virtually impossible to gain any access to the philosophy of history using Kant's *historical* writings as a point of departure" (C 116). Overt references to Kant's writings all but disappear from Benjamin's work after 1918; overt references to Kant's *historical* writings are entirely absent. By describing his critique of historical perception as a "Copernican revolution," however, Benjamin seems to return to his early project, or at least to that moment in his early scholarly development when he could, in one breath, affirm the superiority of Kantianism to every other philosophical program and assert that "the ultimate metaphysical dignity of a philosophical view . . . will always manifest itself most clearly in its confrontation with history" (98).

There are other indications that what appears in *The Arcades Project* to be a gesture to Kant is not just the result of a slip of Benjamin's pen. In a 1940 letter to Theodor Adorno's wife Gretel, composed mere months before his death, Benjamin writes of his very last reflections on history, the theses "On the Concept of History" ("Über den Begriff der Geschichte"), that "the war and the constellation that it brought with it have led me to set down certain thoughts which I can say that I have kept safe with me, indeed kept safe from myself, for some twenty years" (GB 6; qtd. in Eiland and Jennings 435; trans. modified). Why Benjamin has needed to conceal these particular thoughts (even from himself) when he could speak so openly about other matters is not entirely clear. By referring to them in a letter intended to introduce "On the Concept of History," however, which famously begins with the tale of the chess-playing automaton and the dwarf, who, concealed within it, pulls its strings, Benjamin cannot help but suggest that these thoughts—though perhaps "small and ugly" and thus needing to be "kept out of sight"—have been controlling his work for a long time. How long? Benjamin says some twenty years. But perhaps they have been at work a little longer. For if Benjamin returns in the theses to the concept of history, then he returns to his work of 1917–1918, to the moment of his early confrontation with Kant's philosophy of history.

To the moment of this confrontation if not exactly to the matter: I do not mean to suggest that Benjamin has, in his late writings, finally come around to accepting the theory of historical progress that Kant outlines in *The Idea for a Universal History, Toward Perpetual Peace*, and other related works. In both *The Arcades Project* and the theses "On the Concept of History" Benjamin attacks with a special vehemence the Kantian notion of "universal history" and of this history as an "infinite task." Though the theses have been read—rightly, I think—as a mediated response to Marx's *Eighteenth Brumaire*, they are no less a rejoinder to Kant's occasional writings on history. A leitmotif of Kant's *Idea for a Universal History*, for example, is the difficulty—but also the necessity—of reconciling ourselves to our own suffering, as well as to the suffering of our ancestors, so as to affirm the rational development of the species, a development to be completed at some future time. Compare this to Benjamin's remark in the twelfth thesis that the working class is "nourished by the image of enslaved ancestors rather than by the ideal of liberated grandchildren" (*SW* 4:394). To affirm the latter at the cost of the former—as Kant does—would be to "cut the sinews" of the revolution.

It is, therefore, even in the late 1930s, still "virtually impossible" for Benjamin "to gain any access to the philosophy of history using Kant's *historical* writings as a point of departure." The claim that I want to make, though, is a bit different. To anticipate the argument that I will present in what follows: when Benjamin returns to the concept of history, when he reveals (to his readers and to himself) the thoughts on history that he has kept concealed for some twenty years, he returns not to Kant's philosophy of history but to the philosophy of history and to (a certain version of) Kant, a version of Kant prepared by Benjamin's recasting of the table of categories as a "doctrine of orders" in "On the Program of the Coming Philosophy."

To understand better how Benjamin brings together Kantianism and the philosophy of history while still keeping at arm's length Kant's own philosophy of history, a short digression will first be necessary. We need to determine what a philosophy of history might look like insofar as it takes its cue not from Kant's hopeful predictions concerning the progress of the human species—again, the probable source of Benjamin's recoil from Kant's historical writings—but instead from Kant's Copernican revolution.[4] Fortunately, Kant himself provides us with a hint of what a properly critical model of historical perception might look like in one of his very late writings, the second of the three essays that make up *The Conflict of the Faculties* (1798), "An Old Question Raised Again: Is the Human Race Constantly Progressing?," or "The Conflict of the Philosophy Faculty with the Faculty of Law." It is not clear that Benjamin was familiar with this essay, which includes Kant's most sustained and sympathetic reflections on the French Revolution. When Benjamin refers in his correspondences to his early work on Kant's historical writings, he names only *The Idea for a Universal*

*History* and *Toward Perpetual Peace* (*C* 105, 116). Both of these essays appear in the eighth volume of the Akademie edition of Kant's writings, which includes as well *The End of All Things* and the Herder reviews but not *The Conflict of the Faculties* (which appears in the seventh volume). Benjamin did receive from his father-in-law a complete edition of Kant's writings at some point in 1919 (151), but by then he had (for the moment) put Kant down and begun to work on his dissertation on *Frühromantik*. Regardless, I am not interested in arguing that "An Old Question" influenced Benjamin's work on history, only in suggesting that the essay provides a model for what a critical philosophy of history might look like and thus sheds some light on what Benjamin may have been attempting in the 1930s.

In "An Old Question," Kant sets himself the task of locating "some experience in the human race which, as an event, points to the disposition and the capacity of the human race to be the cause of its own advance to the better, and (since this should be the act of a being endowed with freedom) to be the author of this advance" (7:84).[5] That is, Kant is looking for a phenomenal manifestation of mankind's moral—and so, noumenal—substrate, insofar as the latter, Kant argues, must be at the origin of real progress. And he turns to recent events in France. Or rather, he almost turns to them:

> The revolution of a gifted people which we have seen unfolding in our day may succeed or miscarry; it may be filled with misery and atrocities to the point that a right thinking human being, were he boldly to hope to execute it successfully the second time, would never resolve to make the experiment at such cost—this revolution, I say, nonetheless finds in the hearts of all spectators (who are not engaged in this game themselves) a wishful participation that borders closely on enthusiasm [*eine Teilnehmung dem Wunsche nach, die nahe an Enthusiasm grenzt*] the very expression of which is fraught with danger; this sympathy, therefore, can have no other cause than a moral predisposition in the human race. (7:85)

If Kant begins here with the "revolution of a gifted people," he does so only to withdraw from it, arguing that the violence of its means and the ultimate question of its success are irrelevant, that we must look instead to its spectators. When he turns to these spectators, however, his withdrawal recommences. These spectators, who are not themselves engaged, exhibit a participation that is only wishful and a sympathy that is not quite enthusiasm. Their detached complicity, their disinterested fidelity to the revolution's promise, is the legible sign of man's "moral predisposition," what Kant names the "sign of history" (*Geschichtszeichen*; 7:84).

Beginning with a concrete historical event, then, Kant idealizes it. He replaces the material with the mental, the engaged combatant with the sympathetic spectator. Out of this idealization, he generates a narrative of human progress. Nonetheless, and despite the fact that Kant's essay displays all of those historical themes that Benjamin finds most pernicious—empathy, abstraction, progress—"An Old Question" still goes some way toward revealing what a "Copernican revolution" in the domain of historical perception might look like. Here, Kant's delineation of the sign of history is of key importance. The sign of history, Kant explains, is not just a future-oriented intimation of progress, but "*signum rememorativum, demonstrativum, prognostikon*" (7:84), the sign of a recalling, a demonstrating, and a foretelling. Only as the successful articulation of past, present, and future can it assure us that "the human race has always been in progress toward the better and will continue to be so henceforth" (7:89). And this articulation of moments is also what is at stake in Kant's description of the sign as "a fragment of human history [*ein Stück von der Menschengeschichte*] that is drawn not from past but from future time" (7:79). The sign manifests in the present a future perspective on what will have been mankind's past. To remember the sign of history is, therefore, to remember a history that has been re-membered, that has seen its past, present, and future moments drawn together in a coherent, continuous narrative of human progress.

The sign of history is a sign of the orderliness of history, a sign of the synthetic unity of past, present, and future. The form that this historical synthesis takes cleaves to a very familiar Kantian logic. It bears striking similarities, for instance, to the functions of the imagination as Kant describes them in his precritical *Lectures on Metaphysics*. As Kant notes,

> A present appearance has representations of the past and of the time to come. But in my representations there is a series of the following representations, where the representations of the past relate to the present just as the representations of the present relate to the future. Just as I can go from the present into the past, I can also go from the present into the future. Just as the present state follows on the past, so the future follows on the present. This happens according to the laws of the reproductive imagination. (28:236)

The present image of an object includes with it a recollection of the object's immediate past as well as an anticipation of the object's immediate future. For this reason, the image of an object is never of a pure, present experience; it is, rather, always the product of a temporal synthesis. Kant thus divides the reproductive imagination into its functions as *Abbildung*, *Nachbildung*, and *Vorbildung*, that is, of the "illustration" of the present, the "imitation" of the past, and the "anticipation" of the future (28:235). Representational consciousness is the product of this threefold temporal synthesis, a point that Kant repeats and extends in the *Critique of Pure Reason*'s "Transcendental Deduction". In the latter text, another threefold temporal synthesis is enlisted to secure a priori not only the unity of the object of experience but also the transcendental unity of apperception, "the supreme principle in the whole of human cognition" and the foundation of the transcendental logic (B135).

And here we can return to the question of what it might mean to carry out a Copernican revolution in historical perception. If Kant's Copernican revolution names in the domain of metaphysics a shift from the object of experience to the transcendental conditions of this object's synthetic unity—and thus from what is known to the conditions of its being known—Kant's sign of history names in the domain of historical perception a comparable reorientation: a turning from the events of history to the source of their unity in the experience of the spectator-subject. At stake in each case is a change of perspective, a change of perception's "fixed point." It is clear, I think, to what degree Kant's introduction of the sign of history in "An Old Question" anticipates all those post-Kantian attempts to imbricate episodes in the history of the world with episodes in the history of the mind, projects epitomized by Hegel's historical idealism. And it anticipates as well the notion of the Copernican revolution in historical perception that Benjamin invokes in *The Arcades Project*, at least insofar as he attempts to redirect our attention from the facts of history to the role that these facts play for an "awakened consciousness."

Or rather, Kant's notion of the sign of history anticipates Benjamin's project up to a point. On the one hand, Benjamin follows Kant by shifting historical perception from the object of this perception to the subject. That is to say, like Kant, and whatever his commitment to developing a materialist philosophy of history, Benjamin still approaches history first of all as an epistemological problem. Tellingly, the title of the "methodological" portion of *The Arcades Project*, "On the Theory of Knowledge, Theory of Progress" (*Erkenntnistheoretisches, Theorie des Fortschritts*], couples epistemology (*Erkenntnistheorie*) and historiography. Moreover, Benjamin's theses do not concern history as such but the concept of history, the way that we represent history to ourselves as something unified, progressive, and so on. It is important to keep this epistemological dimension of Benjamin's historical project in mind, even if it suggests as well that this project maintains a certain proximity to (historical) idealism, for it serves as a bulwark against those readings of Benjamin's late writings that would attempt to translate them into empiricist or realist terms. Indeed, it seems particularly important to stress this point today, when so many strains of cultural criticism (historicisms old and new, materialisms old and new, thing theory, object-oriented ontology), in their symptomatic striving to develop interesting claims about familiar objects, have taken as their point of departure an ignorance or avoidance of epistemology.[6] Lenin famously remarked that "intelligent idealism is nearer to intelligent materialism than is stupid materialism."[7] Benjamin would likely have agreed.

On the other hand, though he may follow Kant in recommending a reorientation of historical perception, and though, in trying to effect this reorientation, he may pass through something akin to Kant's own version of historical idealism (at least as Kant articulates the latter in "An Old Question"), Benjamin cannot rest with idealism or with the claims about history that idealism brokers. Benjamin intends in *The Arcades Project* a materialist philosophy of history—an *intelligent* materialist philosophy of history, but a materialist philosophy of history nonetheless. At this point, then, I want to shift course and ask how Benjamin aligns his philosophy of history—and, more precisely, his anecdotal philosophy of history—with materialism without collapsing into a naïve (precritical, prehistorical) empiricism.

## II. Anecdote: Immediacy and Mediation

When Benjamin invokes anecdote as an alternative to the abstractions of official history, he takes care to locate anecdote under the sign of nearness. Anecdote, he writes, "brings things near to us spatially"; and it brings things near to us temporally, "calendrically," as well. In fact, anecdote brings things so near to us that the distance between these things and us effectively collapses. Thus, with anecdote, things "enter our life." Would it be accurate, then, to say that a defining characteristic of anecdote is immediacy, such that, if anecdote resists abstraction, it resists as well (conceptual, theoretical) mediation in favor of an immediate contact with its object? I introduce into the discussion of anecdote this question of immediacy not only to provide Benjamin's still vague notion of nearness with some philosophical heft—for the question of

(im)mediacy, of mediation (*Vermittlung*), is, after all, one of the fundamental questions of nineteenth-century German philosophy, and of the tradition
of dialectical thinking in particular—but also, and more importantly, because
the question of immediacy is absolutely central to the most famous response
to Benjamin's late project: Theodor Adorno's excoriation of Benjamin's long
1938 essay "The Paris of the Second Empire in Baudelaire." Now, in addition to
providing us with an example, in situ, of Benjamin's late method, "The Paris of
the Second Empire" is one of the truly great analyses of modernity, a model for
the "social history of art," for example, as it has been practiced by T. J. Clark
and others. Moreover, it seems to me that, when he responds to Benjamin's essay, Adorno gets just about everything dead wrong. Nonetheless, his response,
with its uncharitable charge of uncritical immediacy, presents us with a kind
of *via negativa*, one that we can follow on our way to a positive conception of
(Benjamin's conception of) anecdote.

In "The Paris of the Second Empire," Benjamin offers up one version of
what it might mean to bring things near. In this case, the things in question are
those that index the political and economic culture of mid-nineteenth-century
Paris, the things out of which Baudelaire has built his impossibly modern lyric
poetry. In a letter to Max Horkheimer—who, from 1926, was the director of the
Institut für Sozialforschung in Frankfurt am Main, and so, along with Adorno,
had the power to accept, or not, "The Paris of the Second Empire" for publication in the institute's *Zeitschrift für Sozialforschung*—Benjamin describes his
essay as both a "sociocritical interpretation of the poet" and an attempt to "set
down the decisive philosophical elements of *The Arcades Project* in what I hope
will be definitive form" (*C* 573–574). Despite the more fragmentary character
of *The Arcades Project*, what Benjamin says therein of his method is similarly
true of his method in his "miniature of the *Arcades*" (556), "The Paris of the
Second Empire": "Method of this project: literary montage. I needn't say anything. Merely show [*Nur zu zeigen*]. I shall purloin no valuables, appropriate
no ingenious formulations. But the rags, the refuse—these I will not inventory
but allow, in the only way possible, to come into their own: by making use of
them" (*AP* N1a,8).

Responding in a letter of 10 November 1938 to his receipt of Benjamin's
Baudelaire essay, Adorno begins by waxing poetic, writing that "I took very
seriously the idea of considering the Baudelaire piece as a model for the
*Arcades*, and approached the Satanic spot not unlike Faust as he drew near
the phantasmagoria of the Brocken, expecting to find many a riddle solved"

(*SW* 4:99). He admits, however, "a certain disappointment" at having realized that, in the essay, "motifs are assembled but not worked through" (4:99). From here, Adorno intensifies his criticisms, always coming back to the problem of mediation: "Let me express myself in the simplest and most Hegelian manner possible: If I am not much mistaken, this dialectic lacks one thing: mediation. There is a persistent tendency to relate the pragmatic content of Baudelaire's work directly to adjacent features of the social history of his time, especially economic ones" (4:101). And again: "[The essay] fails to do justice to Marxism because it omits the mediation by the total societal process and because, almost superstitiously, it attributes to materialist enumeration powers of illumination which are reserved solely to theoretical interpretation and never to pragmatic pointing [*pragmatischen Hinweis*]" (4:102). Adorno takes issue with Benjamin's apparent readiness to treat Baudelaire's poetry—he singles out Benjamin's reading of "L'âme du vin"—as though it offered an unmediated reflection of its socio-economic milieu. More generally, though, Adorno takes issue with Benjamin's method of "literary montage," his attempt to let his objects "come into their own" absent any plain conceptual framing. This method, Adorno notes, insofar as it "omits the mediation by the total societal process" issues finally in "a wide-eyed presentation of mere facts" (*die staunende Darstellung der bloßen Faktizität*). "Now as regards the fate of the work," Adorno concludes, "publication in the next issue of the *Zeitschrift* will not be possible" (4:103).

There is a lot going on in Adorno's criticism of Benjamin's essay, and not all of it is easily explained by the two figures' intellectual differences. Here is what Howard Eiland and Michael Jennings have to say about Adorno and Benjamin's personal relationship:

> Not long before [their exchange over "The Paris of the Second Empire"], Adorno had been Benjamin's disciple, composing a series of essays, plus a book on Kierkegaard, that were deeply indebted to Benjamin's work; delivering his in-augural lecture at Frankfurt ["The Actuality of Philosophy," presented on 7 May 1931] as an homage; and teaching his first seminar on the *Trauerspiel* book. Now, aware that Benjamin was wholly dependent on the institute for his livelihood, he felt that he could dictate not just the choice of subject matter but the intellectual tenor of Benjamin's work. (624)

And then there is the matter of Benjamin's friendship during the 1930s with the Marxist avant-gardist Bertolt Brecht, who was Benjamin's neighbor in Skovbo-strand, Denmark, during the period of Benjamin's most intense labor on the

Baudelaire essay. The possibility that Brecht's *plumpes Denken*, his "crude thinking" (not to mention his putative vulgar materialism), might influence Benjamin's work seems to have troubled Adorno greatly. Adorno had already indicated to Benjamin in a letter of 18 March 1936 his discovery of "sublimated remnants of certain Brechtian motifs" in Benjamin's "Work of Art" essay. These motifs Adorno describes as "disquieting" (Adorno et al., *Aesthetics and Politics* 121).

If we limit ourselves, though, to the content of Adorno's letter of 10 November 1938, there is still plenty to keep us occupied. Adorno's complaint that Benjamin's "dialectic lacks . . . mediation" is the complaint of a Hegelian— Adorno makes this allegiance explicit, indicating to Benjamin that he is putting his criticism in "the simplest and most Hegelian manner possible"—to one who has forgotten what is, literally, the first lesson of dialectical thinking: one must have (conceptual, theoretical) mediation; one cannot merely point.[8] What does this mean? In the very first moment of the *Phenomenology of Spirit*, the dialectic of "sense-certainty" (*sinnliche Gewißheit*), Hegel describes the impossibility of grounding knowledge of the world on the immediacy of empirical experience. The subject of sense-certainty, he explains, tries to do just that. It tries to grasp its object as a particular "this," a particular "here and now," for it assumes that this most direct contact with the object secures for it the most certain kind of knowledge. This unmediated relationship to the object is, however, impossible. The subject, the cognizing consciousness, must have recourse to conceptualization, to language, to all of those mediating forces that impose themselves between mind and world, in order to know the object at all. In fact, the harder the subject tries to establish an unmediated contact with its object, the more insistently mediation asserts itself. The proof: From the very moment that they are uttered, "this," "now," and "here"— seemingly the most immediately concrete designations—reveal themselves to be the most abstract. Everything is a "this," every moment a "now," and every place a "here." The subject's attempt to ground certain knowledge on sensory experience miscarries. Before the collapse of its attempt to know the world immediately, however—that is, before it passes to the next stage of consciousness—the subject, desperate, simply points at its object: "We must let ourselves *point* to it, for the truth of this immediate relation is the truth of *this* I which limits itself to a *now* or to a *here*" (*Zeigen* müssen wir es uns lassen, denn die Wahrheit dieser unmittelbaren Beziehung ist die Wahrheit *dieses* Ich, der sich auf ein *Itzt* oder ein *Hier* einschränkt; *PS* 63). Pointing is the last ditch effort of the subject to lay claim to the immediacy of a sensual experience (This! Now! Here!) that conceptual mediation—and, for Adorno, the mediation of the whole social process—has already made impossible. By pointing, the subject says nothing at all. One cannot merely point.

When he characterizes Benjamin's method in "The Paris of the Second Empire" as a "wide-eyed presentation of mere facts" or as "pragmatic pointing," Adorno almost certainly has in mind the Hegelian dialectic of sense-certainty. Benjamin, it would seem, has fallen behind this dialectic by cleaving to the methodological dictum that he articulates in *The Arcades Project*: "I needn't say anything. Merely show" (*Nur zu zeigen*); or—and this amounts to the same thing—I needn't say anything. Merely point. Adorno (after Hegel) offers to Benjamin a choice, then, a choice between *Denken* and *Zeigen*, between dialectical thinking and mere pointing. If Benjamin makes the correct choice, and if he revises "The Paris of the Second Empire" accordingly, perhaps his essay could eventually find its way into the *Zeitschrift für Sozialforschung*. As it stands, Adorno writes, "the work does not represent you as this work in particular must represent you. But as I am firmly and staunchly convinced that you are capable of producing an extremely powerful and penetrating manuscript on Baudelaire, I would ask you most earnestly not to press for publication of the present version but to write that other one" (*SW* 4:103).

Benjamin responds to Adorno's criticisms of his method in a long letter mailed from Paris on 9 December 1938. This letter includes gestures of appeasement (for, again, Adorno enjoyed all of the power at this point in their relationship), but it also includes some attempts on Benjamin's part to preserve his method in the face of Adorno's charges. These attempts are not, I think, very satisfying. For the most part, Benjamin wavers between two lines of defense. First, he claims that the problems Adorno is having with "The Paris of the Second Empire" will evaporate when the essay is read in the context of the larger project on Baudelaire. And second, he suggests that what Adorno calls the "wide-eyed presentation of mere facts" is part of a "philological" method essential to the project's "construction" (*Konstruktion*; 4:107). There have been efforts to locate in Benjamin's response a genuine alternative to Adorno's position. Giorgio Agamben, for example, reads in Benjamin's reference to "philology" the attempt to outline a nonmetaphysical alternative to dialectical mediation. While dialectical mediation, he explains, depends on a notion of causality "consistent with Western metaphysics," one that "[presupposes] the sundering of reality into two different ontological levels" (*Infancy and History* 119), what

Benjamin calls "philology" overcomes this division so as to exhibit the "direct and fundamental unity of subject matter and truth content" (123). Benjamin's position, Agamben goes on, is the only one that is really compatible with materialism (though Adorno, blinkered by Hegelianism, cannot see it). In any event, Adorno does not seem to have been impressed by Benjamin's response, and in "A Portrait of Walter Benjamin," an essay published in the collection *Prisms* a decade after Benjamin's death, he essentially repeats his earlier criticisms of Benjamin's method: "[H]is micrological and fragmentary method . . . never entirely integrated the idea of universal mediation, which in Hegel as in Marx produces the totality" (236); "his philosophy of fragmentation remained itself fragmentary, the victim, perhaps, of a method, the feasibility of which in the medium of thought must remain an open question" (238).

*Also sprach Adorno.* Let us return, then, to our still open question: Does the "micrological and fragmentary method"—what I want to call the anecdotal method—that Benjamin advocates in *The Arcades Project* and (perhaps) practices in "The Paris of the Second Empire" necessarily imply a "wide-eyed presentation of mere facts"? Does Benjamin hope to bring things near simply by pointing at them? Once again, what is at issue is the apparent lack of mediation in Benjamin's method in general and in his notion of anecdotal history in particular. Before deciding that Adorno's criticism hits its target, however, we should at least acknowledge that anecdote is still a certain sort of representation—or in Benjamin's terms, a certain sort of *Konstruktion*—of the thing or event that it describes; it is not and does not pretend to be a direct presentation of the thing or the event itself. And this is true not only of Benjamin's particular notion of anecdote, but also of anecdote more generally. In his essay on "The History of the Anecdote" (note the double genitive, such that anecdote is here the object of a history that may itself be anecdotal), Joel Fineman does an excellent job of underscoring the copresence in anecdote of nearness and distance, of (material) immediacy and (formal) mediation. "The anecdote," he writes, "is the literary form or genre that uniquely refers to the real" (57). And this means that, while the anecdote "produces the effect of the real, the occurrence of contingency, by establishing an event as an event within and yet without the framing context of historical succesivity" (61), the anecdote nonetheless "has something literary about it, for there are of course other and non-literary ways to make reference to the real—through direct description, ostention, definition, etc.—that are not anecdotal" (56). As a literary genre, anecdote necessarily participates in a formal, aesthetic construction of its object, albeit with the goal of producing the effect of the object in all of its material immediacy.

Benjamin, too, presents anecdote not only as a disruption of familiar forms of historical construction—though from the moment of Procopius's inaugural *Anekdota*, anecdote is certainly that—but also as a form of historical construction in its own right. This latter point comes through most clearly when Benjamin opposes anecdote to another, non-anecdotal reference to the real: the newspaper. In an earlier version of the fragment on the anecdote that I quoted at the beginning of this chapter, Benjamin elaborates on his opposition of anecdote to "the sort of history which demands 'empathy,' which makes everything abstract," by noting that empathy "is what newspaper reading terminates in" (*AP* I°,2). Although the newspaper only appears in the early sketch of Benjamin's remarks on the anecdote, it resurfaces in Benjamin's canonical essay of 1936 on the impoverishment of experience, "The Storyteller: Reflections on the Work of Nikolai Leskov" ("Der Erzähler: Betrachtungen zum Werk Nikolai Lesskows"): "Every glance at a newspaper," Benjamin writes, "shows that [experience] has reached a new low" (*SW* 3:143); for the newspaper reduces communication to "information" (3:147). It codifies "a viewpoint according to which the course of the world is an endless series of facts congealed in the form of things" (*AP* 14).

Anecdote is not another name for the information that appears in the pages of the newspaper. Nor does anecdote join in Ranke's project of writing history "as it actually happened" (*wie es eigentlich gewesen ist*; Ranke 57). For each remains at the level of mere facts and can hope to achieve no more than these facts' "wide-eyed presentation." If anecdote is a showing—"I needn't say anything. Merely show"—then it is a showing of a very peculiar sort. What does it mean, then, to represent history anecdotally?

The question is better posed, I think, in the following terms: What sort of historical perception, what sort of experience or cognition of historical events, invites anecdotal presentation? Benjamin provides us with the beginning of an answer to this question when, in the context of his remark on anecdote, he notes that "the image of a historical course of time is totally transformed as soon as one brings to bear on it a standard [or a "measure," *Maßstab*] adequate and comprehensible to human life" (*AP* S1a,3). Anecdote is a means of presenting an image (or a perception) of a history that has been submitted to a human measure. Or—and this is really the same thing—anecdote is a literary or subliterary genre through which the results of Benjamin's Copernican revolution in historical perception can be communicated; for the latter involves, finally, the submission of historical perception—and of temporal, spatial experience more generally—to a human measure.

### III. From the Doctrine of Orders to the Physiognomic Cycle

In a letter to Adorno dated 23 February 1939 and concerning projected revisions to the middle section of "The Paris of the Second Empire," Benjamin writes of his intention to "bring the chapter on the flâneur closer to the form that it took in the physiognomic cycle [*physiognomischen Zyklus*], where it was surrounded by studies of the collector, the counterfeiter, and the gambler" (*SW* 4:209). The exact phrase "physiognomic cycle" appears nowhere else in Benjamin's writings. Benjamin, however, is most likely referring here to a conception of *The Arcades Project* dating from the period 1927–1930. A canceled sketch of the project from this same period reads: "Armature of physiognomic studies: the *flâneur*, the collector, the counterfeiter, the gambler" (*AP* Q,10). Fairly early on in his work, Benjamin seems to have imagined that *The Arcades Project* would eventually coalesce as a series of portraits of urban types—again, centrally the flâneur, the collector, the counterfeiter, and the gambler—whose respective physiognomies would together form a grander physiognomy of capitalist modernity. In the extant version of *The Arcades Project*, only traces of this conception of the text survive. We have a short chapter on the collector (Convolute H) and a long one on the flâneur (Convolute M); we have scattered references to counterfeiters and gamblers (as well as to ragpickers, prostitutes, and other modern figures); and we have innumerable (albeit often somewhat loose) uses of the term "physiognomy." So, Edgar Allan Poe, in his "Philosophy of Furniture" as well as in his detective fiction, is described as "the first physiognomist of the domestic interior" (*AP* 9, 20); Hugo and Baudelaire provide a "physiognomy of the city" (*SW* 4:35); and the historian is bidden to discover the "physiognomy of romanticism" by studying an unnamed lithograph housed in the Cabinet des Estampes of the Bibliothèque Nationale (*AP* d3a,4).

Why "physiognomy"? Benjamin defines the term in "Demonic Berlin," a 1930 radio address on the work of E. T. A. Hoffmann:

> Like many other great writers, [Hoffmann] found the extraordinary not somehow floating freely in mid-air, but in quite specific people, things, houses, objects, and streets. As you may have heard, people who judge other people by their face, their walk, or their hands, or judge their character, their profession, or even

their fate by the shape of their head, are known as physiognomists. In this sense, Hoffmann was not so much a seer as someone who looked at people and things. And that is quite a good definition of the term "physiognomy." (*SW* 2:324)

Looking at people and looking at things, the physiognomist finds in them something extraordinary. He finds the extraordinary in the ordinary, then; but, above all, he finds it in the particular—in this person or that thing—rather than in a heaven of abstract ideas. By revealing the extraordinary in and as the particular, the physiognomist participates in what Benjamin calls "the true philological attitude," the attitude for which, famously, "the eternal . . . is far more the ruffle on a dress than some idea" (*AP* N3,2). And he participates as well, again, in what Adorno maligns as "the wide-eyed presentation of mere facts." Hegel would have agreed with Adorno's verdict. The former treats physiognomy (together with psychology and phrenology) as an example of a "science" that falls short in its striving for real knowledge: "The science of physiognomy," Hegel writes, "which is concerned with the person's presumed actuality [*vermeinte Wirklichkeit*] and seeks to raise the unconscious judging of natural physiognomy to the level of knowledge, is . . . something that has neither a foundation nor an end in sight" (*PS* 286). Fundamentally—this is Hegel's complaint—the physiognomist fails to adequately conceptualize mediation (in this case, the mediation of outer and inner life). We are on familiar ground, and I shall return to this point in a moment.

When he considers producing out of his archive of notes a physiognomic cycle focused on the figures who inhabit "The Paris of the Second Empire," Benjamin is most likely inspired not by his readings of Hoffmann but by his readings of Balzac, Poe, and Baudelaire. Each dedicates pieces of writing to the legibility or illegibility of modern urban life: Baudelaire, in "The Painter of Modern Life," documents for his readers the movements of the flâneur; Poe presents a nightmarish tale of the criminally unreadable "Man of the Crowd"; and Balzac offers up a series of vignettes on social life that launches in turn the nineteenth century genre of the "physiologics." The latter are pocket-sized paperbacks dedicated to recording the "types" (artists, bankers, merchants, nobility, prostitutes, and so on) that one is likely to encounter in the modern city. Dana Brand, describing these "early genres of urban legibility" (24), reads in them a "dream of social control . . . through the reduction of human diversity to a system of signs structured like a language" (25). Similarly, Benjamin notes that the physiologies might have reassured those readers who were troubled by the disorder of urban life: "Simmel's apt remark concerning the uneasiness aroused in the urbanite by other people, people whom, in the overwhelming majority of cases, he sees without hearing, would indicate that, at least in their beginnings, the physiognomies <correction: physiologies> were motivated by, among other things, the wish to dispel this uneasiness and render it harmless" (*AP* M16a,2). The slip in this passage—"physiognomies," later corrected to "physiologies"—is significant. It marks the proximity of these categories in Benjamin's work. But it also belies what is Benjamin's very different goal: not, through a practice of making-legible, to dispel the particular or render it harmless but to find in the particular *qua* particular a standard adequate to it.

This claim needs to be unpacked. The following passage, which appears in *The Arcades Project* in the collection of notes dedicated to the flâneur, sets us on the right course:

> It would be profitable to discover certain definite features leading toward the physiognomy of the city dweller. Example: the sidewalk, which is reserved for the pedestrian, runs along the roadway. Thus, the city dweller in the course of his most ordinary affairs, if he is on foot, has constantly before his eyes the image of the competitor who overtakes him in a vehicle. (*AP* M14,6)

Benjamin imagines the experience of the pedestrian who, moving along a city sidewalk, is passed by a "competitor" in a vehicle (in a carriage, for now, though other vehicles will show up soon enough). Presumably, the encounter is disconcerting. The reason: one way of experiencing the world—one characterized by a certain rhythm of life, a certain articulation of time and space—has found itself set against another. What seemed natural now seems relative. In having his sense of time and space transformed, the foot-traveler overtaken by the carriage is kin to the flâneur, who challenges himself with a different rhythm of life: "In 1839," Benjamin notes, "it was considered elegant to take a tortoise out walking. This gives us an idea of the tempo of *flânerie* in the arcades" (M3,8). Less comically, the flâneur is a forebear of the generation that Benjamin describes in nearly identical passages in "Experience and Poverty" and "The Storyteller": "[A] generation that had gone to school in horse-drawn streetcars now stood under the open sky in a landscape where nothing remained unchanged but the clouds and, beneath those clouds, in a force field of destructive torrents and explosions, the tiny, fragile human body" (*SW* 2:732; 3.144). Each figure—the shocked pedestrian with his eyes on the carriage, the flâneur who matches the pace of his tortoise, and the soldier stranded in no-man's-land—confronts the conditional nature of a form of experience that he had previously taken for granted.

Benjamin is hardly the first to find in the concrete image of bodies in motion a way to grasp the abstract notion of time (or even the first to do so by
invoking the deliberate pace of a tortoise).[9] Struggling with Zeno's paradoxes,
Aristotle in his *Physics* observed that, if we hope to understand time, we must
first determine "what exactly it has to do with movement" (219a3); and he settled finally on a definition of time as "the number of motion in respect of 'before' and 'after'" (219b1–2). Approaching the same issue from the other direction
in an early version of his transcendental system, Kant could afford the Newtonian laws of motion an a priori status, since motion is essentially the articulation of time and space.[10] Benjamin, however, is after something a bit different.
He is not—or not only—using the movement of carriages, and tortoises, and
pedestrians to represent something, namely, time, that is, properly speaking,
unrepresentable. Rather, he is making the stronger and more unusual claim that
time and space, categories of experience that we usually take to be invariable,
are in fact open to mutation or wholesale transformation as a result of their embeddedness in particular forms of life. The movements of the flâneur and others
instance this embeddedness, but they do not exhaust it.

Benjamin develops this point in a passage included in Convolute D of *The
Arcades Project* ("Boredom, Eternal Return"). He begins by urging his readers
(or reminding himself): "Rather than pass the time, one must invite it in"; and
he goes on to provide a short list of examples: "To pass the time (to kill time,
expel it): the gambler. Time spills from his every pore.—To store time as a battery stores energy: The *flâneur*. Finally, the third type: he who waits. He takes
in time and renders it up in an altered form—that of expectation" (*AP* D3,4).
An earlier version of the same passage differs only slightly: "Rather than pass
the time, one must invite it in. To pass the time (to kill time, expel it): to be
drained. Type: gambler, time spills from his every pore.—To store time like a
battery: the type, *flâneur*. Finally, the synthetic type (takes in the energy 'time'
and passes it on in altered form): he who waits" (O,78). Each of the figures
Benjamin mentions—the flâneur, the gambler, and the synthetic type—models
time's plasticity, its susceptibility to transformation, through a particular form
of life. In his scattered accounts of these figures, Benjamin elaborates on the
forms that this transformation takes. The gambler's game, for example, "passes
the time more quickly as chance comes to light more absolutely in it, as the
number of combinations encountered in the course of play (of *coups*) is smaller
and their sequence shorter" (O12a,2); the peregrinations of the flâneur result in
an "intoxication," an "anamnestic intoxication," in which "dead facts" overlap

with current perceptions (M1,5) and "far off times and places interpenetrate the landscape and the present moment" (M2,4). In his hashish experiments of the 1930s, Benjamin produces comparable effects on his own person: "Now the hashish eater's demands on time and space come into force. As is known, these are absolutely regal. Versailles, for one who has taken hashish, is not too large, or eternity too long" (*SW* 3:674). Time and space are compressed, stretched, broken, and recombined. But these transformations are only possible insofar as time and space have been "invited in" to life.

Here we can begin to appreciate the chasm that separates Benjamin's turn to physiognomy from what Hegel or Adorno would impugn as a wide-eyed presentation of mere facts. In his physiognomic studies, Benjamin does not assume an unmediated relationship between the outer and the inner, the real and the ideal, or the particular and the general. For, unlike Adorno and the tradition for which Adorno speaks, Benjamin does not assume that existence is divided into these discrete registers (such that they would then need to be mediated). Rather, Benjamin assumes the immanent identity of a form of experience—most basically, a certain organization of time and space—and a form of life—most basically, a collection of embodied movements or practices.[11] This identity—exhibited by the flâneur on his walks, the gambler at the gaming table, and the hashish eater in the Galerie des Glaces—is the culmination (if not, as I will suggest in the next chapter, the conclusion) of Benjamin's intelligent materialism, his struggle "to attain the most extreme concreteness for an era."

But it is also—perhaps more covertly but no less fundamentally—the culmination of Benjamin's intelligent idealism. By the latter, I mean the project of revising Kant's transcendental philosophy that Benjamin undertook in dialogue with Scholem and apparently left incomplete at the end of the 1910s. Benjamin, recall, set himself the task of saving Kant from neo-Kantian scientism by democratizing Kant's table of categories, by locating the table of categories in a "doctrine of orders" (*Lehre von den Ordnungen*) alongside orders derived from linguistics, aesthetics, theology, and so on. To read Benjamin's physiognomy of urban types as an extension of this project of revising Kantianism (as we must, if we do not want to leave Benjamin susceptible to Adornian charges of naïve realism) is to conceive of the flâneur and his fellow urban types as, at the same time time, concrete historical figures and loci of transcendental organization—as living orders (*Ordnungen*), in the technical sense that Benjamin gives this term.[12] Because these orders are multiple as well as particular, the problem of communication presents itself. Thus, anecdote: the latter promises a means of communicating the particularity of the irreducibly particular, communicating historical perception insofar as it has been submitted to a standard adequate and comprehensible to human life.

This standard, of course, is itself complicated. As yet I have avoided doing much to connect Benjamin's interest in physiognomy and the ability of physiognomy to make the problem of experience concrete to his complicated relationship to Marxism. The reason is in part that I intend to address his relationship to historical materialism in the next chapter, and to enter into this discussion now would make the present chapter unwieldy. And the reason is in part that his philosophical allegiances predate his political allegiances, and the former do more to explain the shape of the latter than the reverse. There is, however, a point of contact between his physiognomic analyses and his Marxism that is too essential to the argument that I am trying to develop to pass over without comment. Just as Benjamin presents his doctrine of orders as a challenge to a version of epistemology wholly determined by the worldview of the empirical sciences, he develops his physiognomy of types as a challenge to a regnant model of lived experience. In the latter instance, the model is that of life under industrial capitalism. Here, however, the analogy between Benjamin's doctrine of orders and his physiognomy of types can no longer offer us much guidance. For if he can find in the discourses of linguistics or theology the germ of an alternative epistemological order, capitalism does not so readily admit of an outside. As a result, the alternative forms of life and experience modeled by the different types are bound to appear both tenuous and contradictory.

On the one hand, in "Central Park" ("*Zentralpark*"; 1938–1939), a collection of notes toward a study of Baudelaire, Benjamin describes "games of chance, flânerie, collecting" as "activities pitted against spleen" (*SW* 4:171). In "spleen," a notion Benjamin wrests from Baudelaire to make his own, "time is reified: the minutes cover a man like snowflakes" (4:335). As Benjamin characterizes it—and as Benjamin's description of time as "reified" makes explicit—"spleen" describes a form of temporal experience very close to the one examined by the Hungarian Marxist Georg Lukács in his "Reification and the Consciousness of the Proletariat" (a work Benjamin singled out for praise[13]). Briefly: Lukács's claim is that, under industrial standardization, "[t]ime sheds its qualitative, variable, flowing nature; it freezes into an exactly delimited, quantifiable continuum filled with quantifiable "things" . . . : in short, it becomes space" (90). The movements of the human body are themselves reduced to the ticks of the stopwatch; every unnecessary action is eliminated. To pit oneself against "spleen," then, is to challenge the form of temporal experience under nineteenth-century industrial capitalism, the form of experience exemplified by the monotony of factory labor.

On the other hand, both the flâneur and the gambler are unstable figures, eventually to be absorbed by the forms of life that they both resist and prefigure. Of the flâneur, Benjamin writes:

> [He] becomes attuned to the commodity; he emulates it entirely. In the absence of any market demand for him—that is, of any price attached to his services—he makes himself at home in purchasability. In venality of this kind, the *flâneur* outdoes the whore; one might say that he takes the abstract concept of "For Sale"-ness on a stroll through the streets. He fulfills this concept only in his last incarnation: I mean, in the figure of the sandwich man. (*SW* 4:208)

Likewise, the gambler:

> Even the worker's gesture produced by the automated work process appears in gambling, for there can be no game without the quick movement of the hand by which the stake is put down or a card is picked up. The jolt in the movement of a machine is like the so-called *coup* in a game of chance. The hand movement of the worker at the machine has no connection with the preceding gesture for the very reason that it repeats that gesture exactly. (4:330)

So, the flâneur becomes the sandwich man; the gambler becomes the factory worker. Each passes over into the form of life—the spleen—against which his activities had been pitted.

Susan Buck-Morss has addressed these transformations and the insight that they provide into the nature of modern subjectivity in a very useful essay, "The Flaneur, the Sandwichman and the Whore: The Politics of Loitering." Her claim—and as we have seen, it is a claim well supported by statements that appear in Benjamin's writings—is that, although the existence of the flâneur was precarious even in the Parisian milieu that Benjamin examines, the flâneur does not so much disappear in the last days of the nineteenth century as "[explode] into a myriad of forms, the phenomenological characteristics of which, no matter how new they may appear, continue to bear his traces, as *Urform*" (104). That is to say, "if the *flâneur* has disappeared [from contemporary urban life] as a specific figure, it is because the perceptive attitude which he embodied saturates modern existence" (104). Flipping channels, on vacation, or online, we modern subjects are all offspring of the flâneur. Consequently, by studying his distracted wanderings, we come to recognize not only a historically specific form of life, but also the originary version of "our own consumerist mode of being-in-the-world" (105).

The flâneur as (an) originary form of consumerist subjectivity: Buck-Morss's reading is right, as far as it goes; but it is is one-sided. She risks obscuring those aspects of *flânerie* (of gambling, of collecting . . . ) that are "pitted against spleen" and so that are pitted against the very forms of modern subjectivity to which they nonetheless give rise. The origin is not—not at all—reducible to what it originates. In his doomed *Habilitationsschrift* on *The Origin of German Tragic Drama* (*Der Ursprung des deutschen Trauerspiels*; 1928), Benjamin develops a concept of origin that sheds light on this issue:

> Origin [*Ursprung*], although an entirely historical category, has, nevertheless, nothing to do with genesis [*Entstehung*]. The term origin is not intended to describe the process by which the existent came into being, but rather to describe that which emerges from the process of becoming and disappearance. Origin is a vortex [*Strudel*] in the stream of becoming, and in its current it swallows the material involved in the process of genesis. That which is original is never revealed in the naked and manifest existence of the factual; its rhythm is apparent only to a dual insight. (*OG* 45)

In these dense lines, Benjamin is careful to distinguish *Ursprung*, which he provides with a rather atypical meaning, from *Entstehung*, traditionally understood. The "rhythm" of *Ursprung* is only manifest to a "dual insight" insofar as *Ursprung* is itself never selfsame. Indeed, to be originary is to be split into extremes; and so a "science of the origin" would need to examine "the remotest extremes and the apparent excesses of the process of development" (*OG* 47).[14] The types Benjamin describes are indeed *Urforms* of contemporary capitalism, but what this means is that each type is a *Vexierbild*, a double image that contains both extremes of its development—flâneur and sandwich man, gambler and factory worker—where the former is irreducible to the latter.[15] To neglect this doubleness is to neglect either the ideological-critical dimension or the utopian dimension of Benjamin's project.

## IV. Conclusion

By providing time and space with "a standard adequate and comprehensible to human life," by "inviting [time and space] in[to]" human life, Benjamin displays his fidelity to Kant's revolution. But he gives this revolution another turn.

Time and space are indeed "in" subjects, but these subjects cannot be reduced, as they still are reduced for Kant, to philosophical abstractions. Flâneurs and gamblers—like the forty men who illustrate Benjamin's remarks on anecdote— live, reproduce, and die. But life is not, for Benjamin, a neutral container. The time that it appropriates, it transforms. Like the lives of the gambler and the flâneur, then, the lives of Benjamin's forty men work on time; they construct it according to a different measure, and so they demonstrate that "life is a muscle strong enough to contract the whole of historical time" (*AP* N13a,1). If the result is a Copernican revolution in historical perception, the reason is not only that Benjamin is profoundly interested in questions of historical representation but also that all perception is, in truth, historical, bound up with a particular form of life. And this is what anecdote ought to transmit: a particular form of experience that cannot be separated from a particular form of life.

## CHAPTER 6

# ALLEGORY

[T]he situations did not change very frequently, but when
they did, they did so in a flash, like the appearance of the
print when a page is turned.

—Walter Benjamin, *The Origin of German Tragic Drama*

**WHAT DOES IT MEAN** that in his most radical presentation of the discontinuity of history, the ninth thesis "On the Concept of History" ("Über den Begriff der Geschichte"), Walter Benjamin turns to allegory? The lines in question, however familiar, merit quoting at length:

> There is a picture by Klee called *Angelus Novus*. It shows an angel about to move away from something he stares at. His eyes are wide, his mouth is open, his wings are spread. This is how the angel of history must look. His face is turned toward the past. Where a chain of events appears before *us, he* sees one single catastrophe [*Wo eine Kette von Begebenheiten vor* uns *erscheint, da sieht* er *eine einzige Katastrophe*], which keeps piling wreckage upon wreckage and hurls it at his feet. The angel would like to stay, awaken the dead, and make whole what has been smashed. But a storm is blowing from paradise and has got caught in his wings; it is so strong that the angel can no longer close them. This storm drives him irresistibly into the future, to which his back is turned, while the pile of debris before him grows toward the sky. What we call progress is *this* storm. (*SW* 4:392)

For Benjamin, who writes of his method, "I needn't *say* anything. Merely show" (*AP* N1A,8), the ninth thesis is surprisingly clear, concluding as it does with the key to its meaning: the new angel, ekphrastically transposed from Paul Klee's 1920 painting, sees what we cannot; he sees that progress is a lie that hides the single catastrophe of history. The angel himself is figured, fittingly, as a go-between—the word "angel" comes from the Greek ἄγγελος, a messenger—and as such, he is ideally suited to the work of allegory, to conveying one thing by saying or showing another. And yet the relative ease with which the angel communicates his message obscures an impossibility at the heart of the ninth thesis: though we may be told what the angel knows, we cannot see what the angel sees.

Nonetheless, what the angel sees and why this seeing invites an allegorical presentation will be my focus in what follows. A metaphysical either/or presents the greatest obstacle to this undertaking. In accord with the tradition, nearly all of Benjamin's readers have understood allegory as a fundamentally temporal form.[1] Two possible readings thus present themselves: on the one hand, a finitist reading in which allegory insists on the implacable decay of all life against the organic holism of the symbol; on the other, an infinitist reading in which allegory becomes the privileged figure for history's dialectical unfolding. Though each position finds ample textual support in Benjamin's diverse oeuvre and each has resulted in a number of powerful interpretations, neither has addressed what seems to me the most radical feature of Benjaminian allegory: its challenge to time as the latter manifests itself by ordering human history. As I shall suggest, the *Angelus Novus* is the privileged figure for this challenge, for his vision undoes the temporal forms through which human experience is given. Looking back to the discussion in the previous chapter of Benjamin's physiognomies, then, we might say that the angel is the final figure in the physiognomic cycle, and so the figure through which Benjamin completes his recasting of the Kantian theory of experience.

In his failed *Habilitationsschrift* on the German *Trauerspiel*, Benjamin develops the concept of allegory that will ultimately support his critique of historical reason. It is to this work, and to the allegorical mortification of time that it describes, that we now turn.

## I. The Temporal and the Timeless

The notion that allegory is essentially temporal, while not originating with Goethe, nonetheless finds in Goethe its most esteemed advocate. When Goethe distinguishes allegory from symbol and positions the former as the latter's denigrated antipode, he bases his distinction on the determining role of time. Benjamin begins his own discussion of baroque allegory by citing the following lines from Goethe:

> There is a great difference between a poet's seeking the particular from the general and his seeing the general in the particular. The former gives rise to alle-

gory, where the particular serves only as an instance or example of the general; the latter, however, is the true nature of poetry: the expression of the particular without any thought of, or reference to, the general. (qtd. in *OG* 161)

In Goethe's formulation, allegory corresponds to an image of the world that is flawed insofar as it is fractured, an image in which part and whole remain distinct. The allegorist seeks to reunite that which the (true) poet, with his recourse to symbol, sees holistically. His labor is, therefore, from the perspective of the poet, a false labor: he strives to bind general to particular mechanically,[2] failing to apprehend the "absolute identity of form and content on which the symbol insists" (*OG* 160). But to be condemned to wandering among allegorical fragments is, above all, to be condemned to time, as Goethe makes clear when he opposes the instantaneous vision of a symbolical "seeing" to the necessarily temporal process of allegorical "seeking."

The nearness of Goethe's formulation to wider trends in German romanticism and idealism is striking. As Terry Pinkard points out in his wide-reaching survey *German Philosophy 1760 to 1860*, at the turn of the nineteenth century "what is at stake in philosophy itself is not ultimately a matter of argument but a matter of vision—of viewing, seeing, *Anschauung*—an intuition of how we stand to ourselves and to the world in general."[3] Goethe's elevation of symbolical "seeing" over allegorical "seeking" is an example of the elevation of an immediate, intuitive vision of the whole over progressive, constructive argument. "It is," Pinkard continues, "the poet and the painter as the better artificers of such 'vision' who best grasp the absolute identity of mind and nature, not the natural scientist, bound as he is to discursive forms" (191). The natural scientist is bound to the "discursive" in the technical sense of being bound to the conceptual, as well as in the colloquial sense of being bound to the gradual movement of argument. To produce the artistic symbol is, on the other hand, to present the whole immediately through and in the particular. By arresting our endless seeking and replacing it with a single vision, by freeing us from time, the symbol manifests in the realm of art something akin to an "intellectual intuition" (*intellektuelle Anschauung*),[4] in which, as Hegel could write at the moment of his own greatest proximity to romanticism, "all opposition is suspended, all distinction between the universe as constructed by and for the intelligence, and the universe as an organization intuited as objective and appearing independent, is nullified" (*DFS* 111).

If the goal of Benjamin's *Trauerspiel* study is, at least in part, the recovery of allegory, to what extent are we justified in inscribing this recovery within the metaphysical problematic outlined above? To what extent, then, does Benjamin accept—if only to invert—the eighteenth- and nineteenth-century opposition of allegory to symbol, of temporal to timeless? "The measure of time for the experience of the symbol," Benjamin observes, "is the mystical instant [*das mystische Nu*] in which the symbol assumes the meaning into its hidden and, if one might say so, wooded interior" (*OG* 165). The time proper to the symbol, the *Nu*, corresponds to the moment of vision outlined above, a time opposed to the endless seeking of allegory. It is, then, no surprise that, as Benjamin acknowledges, the "decisive category of time . . . permits the incisive formal definition of the relationship between symbol and allegory" (166). From our current perspective, in which the romantic symbol's refusal of time in favor of an atemporal holism recalls the romantic ideology, the essential temporality of allegory appears much more appealing. By denying time, the symbol denies history; by insisting on organic holism, the symbol masks the imperfections of the real. Allegory, on the other hand, ought to undo the false totality that the symbol sustains by demonstrating the inevitability of the temporal, of an interminable seeking amid fragments—an appropriately modern response to a fundamentally romantic mystification.

Benjamin's readers have, therefore, been quick to emphasize the centrality of time to allegory. For Marxist critics like Fredric Jameson and Doris Sommer, the "battle cry is time, but the stakes are the dialectic" (Sommer 67). Benjaminian allegory, taken as a discontinuous temporal form, is identified as the privileged figure for an unresolved historical process, a dialectic in which the final reconciliatory moment has been indefinitely suspended, but a dialectic nonetheless. When he chooses to privilege allegory over symbol, then, Benjamin chooses history, though what the latter means outside of the nineteenth-century historicist framework that Benjamin explicitly rejects is left unremarked.[5] More satisfying but ultimately not so different have been those readings that treat Benjaminian allegory as insisting on the irreducibility of finitude over and against the positive infinity evoked by the symbol. In his seminar on Hegel's *Phenomenology of Spirit* from 1930–1931, Benjamin's contemporary Martin Heidegger expresses the consequences of such a reading: "For Hegel, being (infinity) is also the essence of time. For us, time is the original essence of being. These are not theses which can be simply played against each other antithetically" (*Hegel's "Phenomenology of Spirit"* 146).[6] Within the Hegelian dialectic, time describes the unfolding of thought and being in their infinite identity. For Heidegger, on the other hand, being is characterized by a temporal finitude that absolute idealism cannot overcome. This temporal finitude, the finitude of death, does not allow itself to be reimagined as a labor of the negative. Benjamin's association of allegory with death against the vitality of the organic symbol seems to follow from a similar insight: "This is the core of the allegorical way of seeing, of the Baroque, secular account of history as the Passion of the world, a world that is meaningful only in the stations of decay. The greater the significance, the greater the subjection to death, because death digs most deeply the jagged line of demarcation between physical being and significance" (*OG* 166). Allegory depicts a passing-away of the organic that the symbol must deny.

And yet, does this privileging of the historical over the eternal, or the temporal over the timeless, amount to an exit from romantic or idealist metaphysics? And even if it does, is it Benjamin's exit? In post-Kantian idealism, and above all in Hegel's mature philosophy, the distinction between "seeking" and "seeing," between human history and the completion of this history in absolute knowing, has never been secure. Indeed, we already find in Goethe's interpretation of allegory the germ of a reconciliation between the temporality of allegory and the timelessness of the symbol. The allegorist may find himself seeking amid particulars, but, Goethe notes, "whoever grasps the particular in all its vitality also grasps the general, without being aware of it, or only becoming aware of it at a late stage" (qtd. in *OG* 161). The time of allegory is the time between the act of grasping the particular and the awareness of having grasped the general; it is, therefore, the time between allegory and symbol, or between allegory and its own overcoming. In this sense, Benjamin can characterize Goethe's concept of the temporality of allegory as essentially "speculative" (*OG* 160).[7]

This equation of allegory with a historical dialectic, or with temporal finitude, against the punctuality or eternity of the symbol is not, however, so secure in Benjamin's writings. Certainly, critics who wish to insist on this equation can point to Benjamin's affirmative citations of the romantic authors Friedrich Creuzer and especially Joseph von Görres. The lines in question read: "We can be perfectly satisfied with the explanation that takes [the symbol] as a sign for ideas, which is self-contained, concentrated, and which steadfastly remains itself, while recognizing [allegory] as a successively progressing, dramatically mobile, dynamic representation of ideas which has acquired the very fluidity of time" (Görres, qtd. in *OG* 165). Görres's definition, although abjuring the disparagement of allegory that we find in Goethe, remains quite close to the latter's understanding of the relationship between symbol and allegory: "[T]hey stand in relation to one another as does the silent great and mighty natural world of mountains and plants to the living progression of human history" (qtd. in *OG* 165). Allegory still presents us with a kind of historical seeking, but this seeking now complements rather than distorts the timelessness of the symbol. Benjamin notes that this definition "puts many things right" (qtd. in *OG* 165), but while he essentially repeats the definition of the symbol that Görres provides—"the transfigured face of nature is fleetingly revealed in the light of redemption"—he considerably alters the definition of allegory: "In allegory," he writes, "the observer is confronted with the *facies hippocratica* of history as a petrified, primordial landscape. Everything about history that, from the very beginning, has been untimely, sorrowful, unsuccessful, is expressed in a face—or rather in a death's head" (*OG* 166). Although he passes from Görres's discussion of allegory as a temporal form to a figure of death, Benjamin first freezes what Görres had made fluid: the "living progression of human history" is petrified before it gives way to a grinning skull.

By petrifying history, Benjamin breaks decisively with the position of Goethe, Görres, and their critical heirs. But is it not true that to deny the temporality of baroque allegory is to deny this figure's historical-critical potential? Must allegory be treated as another means of obscuring our authentically temporal fate, such that the images of death that pervade baroque allegory are only photo negatives of eternity? Everything hinges on the question of what notion of time—if any—is appropriate to a petrified history. In shifting his focus from baroque allegory to the survival of the allegorical form in the nineteenth century, Benjamin outlines the effect on human temporality of the "allegorical intention," a uniquely destructive mode of viewing the world.

## II. Killing Time

Under the eyes of the great nineteenth-century historians, interchangeable events roll down the historical conveyor belt at regular intervals; Benjamin responds in *The Arcades Project* with a critique of historical reason. He frames this critique in "Convolute N" of the project, the title of which, "On the Theory of Knowledge, Theory of Progress" (*Erkenntnistheoretisches, Theorie des Fortschritts*), already insists on a coupling of epistemology (*Erkenntnistheorie*) and historiography. This section, the first to be translated into English, provides a methodological introduction to the work as a whole, or rather, it provides a negative introduction to the methodology that Benjamin will reject. The work aims to "demonstrate a historical materialism that has annihilated within itself the idea of progress. Just here, historical materialism has every reason to distinguish itself sharply from bourgeois habits of thought" (*AP* N2,2). What exactly Benjamin means by "historical materialism" will become clearer in a moment. First, however, it is necessary to specify that when Benjamin targets notions of historical progress, he does not oppose to them a Spenglerian pessimism. "Overcoming the concept of 'progress,'" he remarks, "and overcoming the concept of 'period of decline' are two sides of one and the same thing" (N2,5). This "same thing" is the overcoming of history *qua* "continuous" and "homogeneous" (N7a,2), a notion that grounds the previous century's attempts to secure a science of history, dialectical or other.

Benjamin thus contests what he terms the "epic" mode of writing history, a mode that he associates no less with Leopold von Ranke's insistence on depicting history "as it actually happened" (*wie es eigentlich gewesen ist*) than with Hegel's historical idealism (*SW* 3:262–263). Although he does not have much to say about the particular traits of epic as a narrative form, Benjamin most likely takes his notion of epic from Georg Lukács, who, in his pre-Marxist *Theory of the Novel*, valorizes epic as the form of artistic creation characteristic of the early Greek state:

> Happy are those ages when the starry sky is the map of all possible paths—ages whose paths are illuminated by the light of the stars. . . . Even if menacing and incomprehensible forces become felt outside the circle which the stars of everpresent meaning draw round the cosmos to be experienced and formed, they cannot displace the presence of meaning; they can destroy life, but never tamper with being; they can cast dark shadows on the formed world, but even these are assimilated by the forms as contrasts that only bring them more clearly into relief. (29–30)

Epic poeticizes a world in which gods, nature, and humans dwell together, a world in which, in a now familiar formulation, "meaning can be grasped; it can be taken in at a glance" (32). The image of the world presented by epic, like the image presented by the symbol, is amenable to the moment of knowing vision outlined above. Like the romantic symbol, epic denies the distinctions between universal and particular, self and other. Although it may take the form of a quest, this quest is complete at each moment; it could not be further from the allegorical seeking that Goethe describes.[8]

In a survey of nineteenth-century historical thought that sheds light on Benjamin's challenge to "epic" historiography, Laurence Dickey takes as his guiding thread the recurrence in German historiographical writings of the term *Zusammenhang*, which can be translated variously as "connection," "complex," "coherence," "nexus," or "pattern" (796). *Zusammenhang*, Dickey notes, indexes the assumption, after the foundational work of Wilhelm von Humboldt and Barthold Georg Niebuhr, that all knowledge of historical facts is knowledge of something necessarily interconnected (*zusammengehörig*; 798). Niebuhr, for example, in the preface to his *History of Rome* (1811), writes the following of those historians insufficiently attentive to "the general connectedness [*Zusammenhang*] of events" (qtd. in Dickey 801): "Some restrict themselves to the collection of mutilated fragments [*verstümmelten Fragmente*] of reports from antiquity without attempting to solve their underlying riddles; they resist the impulse to strain their view in order to see the form of the whole to which the pieces belonged. Such a lifeless compilation of fragments is of no use" (qtd. in Dickey 800). The *zusammengehörig* body of history, then, ought not to be mutilated, fragmented; rather, it should be grasped as an integral, living unity. Versions of the same supposition appear nearly a century later in the writings of the neo-Kantian philosophers Wilhelm Windelband and (Benjamin's teacher) Heinrich Rickert. The latter writes in *The Limits of Concept Formation in Natural Science* (1902) that "history as a science can never consist in the mere 'description' of individual facts"; for, he continues, "in history . . . , the elements of the concept must form a unity—in the sense of a coherent entity [*Zusammengehörigkeit*]" (qtd. in Dickey 795).

Just as allegory opposes in Benjamin's *Trauerspiel* study the metaphysics of the symbol, allegory opposes in Benjamin's late writings the epic vision of the general connectedness of events. But if the simple opposition of eternity to temporality was problematized in the earlier work by Benjamin's identification of allegorical vision with history's petrification, this opposition is even less effective in explaining allegory's challenge to traditional accounts of history, accounts of history that are no less temporal for being hopelessly mistaken. Like the symbol, epic presents a *zusammengehörig* whole, one in which "meaning can be taken in at a glance." This meaning, however, is secured not through the suspension of time in favor of eternity but through the prescription of a very traditional notion of temporal development.

What holds history together, what makes history a *zusammengehörig* body and secures its epic presentation, is fundamentally a certain notion of time, a notion first systematically articulated in book 4 of Aristotle's *Physics* and re-

peated throughout the history of philosophy.[9] Two complementary compo-
nents of this notion of time stand out as essential. The first appears already in
its canonical form in Aristotle. Time, Aristotle argues, must be understood as
fundamentally successive. For time to exist, there can be no singular, static instant; time is, rather, always the fact of its own passing on. "The 'now' is the link
of time," he explains, "(for it connects past and future time), and it is a limit of
time (for it is the beginning of the one and the end of the other)" (220a24–25).
Each instant is knowable, therefore, only in its passing from the future to the
present to the past. And yet, what maintains the body of temporal instants is a
soul able to "count" these instants:

> Whether if soul did not exist time would exist or not, is a question that may
> fairly be asked; for if there cannot be someone to count there cannot be any-
> thing that can be counted either, so that evidently there cannot be number; for
> number is either what has been, or what can be, counted. But if nothing but
> soul, or in soul reason, is qualified to count, it is impossible for there to be time
> unless there is soul. (223a20–25)

The soul, as an overarching principle of order, secures time against its (time's)
own nonbeing. The second component of the traditional notion of time receives its most complete determination in the second analogy of experience
of the *Critique of Pure Reason*. Here, Kant demonstrates that the very experience of an objective succession of events is itself transcendentally determined
by a prior concept of causality; indeed, "it is only because we subject the sequence of appearances and thus of all alteration to the law of causality that experience itself, i.e., empirical cognition of [alteration] is possible" (A188/B234).
Together, the representation of time as a continuous succession of counted
instants and the representation of this succession as a causal chain determine
the received image of time (an image that Giorgio Agamben has identified as
the ideology of the "instant" and the "continuum"[10]).

When Benjamin writes against the SPD—the Social Democratic Party of
Germany—that "the concept of mankind's historical progress cannot be sundered from the concept of its progress through a homogeneous, empty time,"
such that "a critique of the concept of such a progression must underlie any
criticism of the concept of progress itself" (*SW* 4:394–395), it is precisely this
notion of time, with its elevation of causal necessity to a transcendental principle, that he targets. Homogeneous, empty time provides epic history with
its infrastructure. Suffice it to say, absent the causal connection of successive

moments assumed by this notion, historicism would cease to exist; moments would not follow one another in a relation of real necessity. History would no longer appear as an organic whole.

Yet, rather than argue that the traditional notion of time is somehow derivative of a more authentic temporality—the solution which, in the wake of Heidegger, my framing of the problem would seem to invite—Benjamin does not present a distinctly allegorical temporality as an alternative. Allegory's force vis-à-vis time, a force only very problematically associated with dialectical negativity, appears to be simply destructive. In this sense, at least, Benjamin's discussion of nineteenth-century allegory continues his discussion of baroque allegory. In each, we discover the "majesty of the allegorical intention: to destroy the organic and the living" (SW 4:172), though only in nineteenth-century allegory does this destructive process take on a decidedly (if sometimes ambiguously) political character. "Baudelairean allegory," Benjamin observes, "unlike Baroque allegory, bears traces of the rage needed to break into this world, to lay waste to its harmonious structures" (4:173). If nineteenth-century allegory sometimes appears on the side of the commodity (4:183), this is only insofar as both allegory and the exchange relation break the object off from its lived context, from the world in which something like "use value" could be ascertained.

Allegory's effect on history, as this history has been written by the nineteenth-century's historians, is no different from allegory's effect on the world of things: "that which the allegorical intention has fixed upon is sundered from the customary contexts of life: it is at once shattered and preserved" (4:169). It is shattered insofar as the logic that binds its moments to one another has been dissolved; it is preserved insofar as its moments do not simply disappear but remain as ruins. When the allegorical intention is fixed upon epic history—as it is in Baudelaire's lyric poetry as well as in Benjamin's own historical materialism—what is shattered is the temporal continuity of moments. The moments themselves are preserved, then, but not as moments, that is to say, not as successive instants in a unidirectional causal chain. What Benjamin calls "allegorical dismemberment" reveals itself in the nineteenth century by cutting (epic) history's temporal joints (AP J78,3).

While baroque allegory presents a world in which, "any person, any object, any relationship can mean absolutely anything else" because the divinely given hierarchy that would establish each thing's place has been lost (OG 175), nineteenth-century allegory translates this evacuation of order from a spatial to a temporal register. The result is a world in which moments formerly ordered as past, present, and future exhibit "no continuity between them" (*AP* N7,7), a world in which the narrative of historical progress has been lost.[11] But if successive, causal time is the condition of every appearance, as Kant has demonstrated, what remains after time's destruction?

## III. Creatures of Pure Intellect

As I suggested at the beginning of this chapter, the question of allegory, of an allegorical vision of the world, cannot be separated from the question—perhaps unanswerable—of what Benjamin's angel sees. Most readings of the *Angelus Novus* have tended to treat it as a figure for the uneasy coexistence in Benjamin's writings of historical materialism and theology. The presence of the latter is established in Gershom Scholem's well-known essay "Benjamin's Angel" and supported by Scholem's own short poem "Gruss vom Angelus," which provides the ninth thesis with its epigraph. On the other hand: the angel as frustrated Marxist revolutionary. Here is O. K. Werckmeister's characterization, from his "Walter Benjamin's Angel of History, or the Transfiguration of the Revolutionary into the Historian," of the sorts of interpretations one encounters among the melancholy left: "As an icon of the left, *Angelus Novus* has seemed to hold out an elusive formula for making sense of the senseless, for reversing the irreversible, while being subject to a kind of political brooding all the more protracted the less promising the prospects for political practice appear to be" (242). So: the angel as a figure of—not defeat, exactly, but of something hard to distinguish from it. There is, finally, the question of why Benjamin's thesis should have needed Klee's original at all, for "in reality, what it describes bears very little relation to the painting" (Löwy 62). What has not been addressed in readings of Benjamin's angel, though, at least not in any sort of detail, is the possibility that the *Angelus* also arrives with a decidedly philosophical pedigree.[12] It is in relation to the latter, though, that the appropriateness of an angel and of an angel's vision to the work of Benjaminian allegory becomes manifest.

Although only in the writings of Kant does philosophy shift its focus from the question of the absolute to the question of the discursive conditions of knowledge, at the time of Kant's "Copernican revolution" precritical philosophers had already labored to establish the proper boundaries of their enterprise. In their attempts to distinguish philosophy from a purely religious form of speculation, angels were an early target.[13] Some lines from Spinoza's *Principles of Cartesian Philosophy* are typical:

> Angels have also been created, yet, because they are not known by the natural
> light, they are not the concern of metaphysics. For their essence and existence
> are known only through revelation, and so pertain solely to theology; and be-
> cause theological knowledge is completely other than, or entirely different in
> kind from, natural knowledge, it should in no way be confused with it. So let
> nobody expect us to say anything about angels. (208)

Spinoza's paraliptic banishment of angels from the realm of metaphysics anticipates the odd role that angels will continue to play in modern philosophy up
to and including Kant's revolution. Angels survive in the passage cited above,
but only as those beings that cannot be known (except by revelation) and thus
cannot be integrated into any metaphysical doctrine.

While in the writings of the precritical metaphysicians, angels belong to
a theological outside that remains (at least possibly) real despite the gap that
separates it from the realm of metaphysics proper, in Kant's transcendental philosophy the role of angels shifts in a manner appropriate to the critical turn.
Angels still stand outside of philosophy, but this outside is now epistemological
rather than metaphysical in the strict sense. Angels represent for Kant those
beings that are not submitted to the conditions of finite human intuition. While
Kant acknowledges the possibility that there could exist an intellect that is not
limited to a spatiotemporal experience of objects, that is, to human intuition,
however, he denies the value of speculating on what an experience of this sort
would be like:

> [F]or they would have us be able to cognize things, thus intuit them, even with-
> out senses, consequently, they would have it that we have a faculty of cognition
> entirely distinct from the human not merely in degree but even in intuition and
> kind and thus that we ought to be not humans but beings that we cannot even
> say are possible, let alone how they are constituted. (*CPR* A277–278/B333–334)

Kant's reluctance to name angels as such in the preceding passage did not fool
his most critical readers. In *On the Basis of Morality*, for example, Schopenhauer writes incredulously that "to talk of rational beings apart from man is
as if we attempted to talk of *heavy beings* apart from bodies. We cannot help
suspecting that Kant here gave a thought to the dear little angels, or at any rate
counted on their presence in the conviction of the reader" (63–64).

Schopenhauer's critique misses the mark, of course. Kant does not present angels as real beings but rather as figures for the negation of humans' epistemological limitations. To imagine the contours of the knowledge that would result from this negation, however, would be to possess it, to be an angel oneself. Angels, then, as those creatures that possess such knowledge, stand in for something like the subject side of the thing-in-itself. While the thing-in-itself plays an epistemological (rather than ontological) role as the hypothetical object of an experience that does not involve spatial and temporal mediation, the angel is the subject of a nonmediated experience, the possessor of an *intellektuelle Anschauung*, which, as Kant writes in a late text, "would immediately present the object and grasp it all at once" ("On a Newly Arisen Superior Tone in Philosophy" 51); it would, therefore, present the object as it is in itself, without the spatial and temporal orderings performed by a finite intuition.

It is to this notion of intellectual intuition that Benjamin's *Angelus* returns us.[14] If in the writings of the nineteenth-century idealists Kant's notion of intellectual intuition is reconceived such that it becomes realizable by finite creatures, either as a model of self-knowledge (Fichte) or as the very means of access to the Absolute (Schelling, and also the young Hegel), for Benjamin it remains an ability of beings that differ from us "not only in degree but as regards intuition likewise in kind," an ability of angels. Benjamin is quite clear in the ninth thesis that we do not share the angel's vision; indeed, he dedicates much of the thesis to distinguishing what we see—"a chain of events," "progress"—from what the angel sees—"one single catastrophe," "*this* storm."

Certainly, Benjamin and Kant differ in their depictions of the object of such an intuition. For Kant, insofar as space and time, the a priori forms of intuition, condition every objective appearance, the object of an intellectual intuition, strictly speaking, does not appear. To "immediately present" something and "grasp it all at once" is, in truth, to present nothing, or at least to present nothing for us. Benjamin's angel, on the other hand, certainly sees something; he sees a world from which time has been subtracted but objects, events, continue to appear. Benjamin's angel thus bears witness to a world that appears without being (temporally) given.

The angel's object is history, and "where a [temporal, causal] chain of events appears before *us, he* sees one single catastrophe," a series of discrete moments now appearing "immediately and grasped all at once." A destructive potential of intellectual intuition unimagined by Kant is unleashed on the historical object as time is cut away from it; the force of the resulting "storm" is almost too much for the angel himself. Because it is a world that we cannot hope to see in its atemporal reality, this world can only be presented to us allegorically, through the unavoidably temporal figures of the ninth thesis.

The ninth thesis is, then, doubly allegorical, or, more precisely, it allegorizes—in a more traditional sense of providing an extended metaphor for—an impossible vision: the effect of the "allegorical intention" that Benjamin describes. What is the angel's intellectual intuition but this allegorical intention manifest in the world? The angel sees the vital progression of human history allegorically; he sees it, then, "under the sign of fragmentation and ruin" (*AP* J56a,6), but to grasp this fact is to move closer to what can only be presented through allegory: the ruins of a history that is both "shattered and preserved."

## IV. Capital Letters

What makes up the ruins of history toward which the angel has (perhaps unwittingly) directed his allegorical gaze? Benjamin provides a clue in his study of the *Trauerspiel*: "[A]t one stroke, the profound vision of allegory transforms works and things into stirring writing" (*OG* 176). The context of this remark is a meditation on allegory as essentially *written*, a view that winds through Benjamin's study for reasons that are at once historical—"with the Baroque the place of the capital letter was established in German orthography" (208)—and formal—"the meaning of [the *Trauerspiel*'s] action is expressed in a complicated configuration like letters in a monogram" (195). As Benjamin's discussion progresses, allegory's essential character appears more and more to be visible only in the "depths of language" (201), a notion that ties the *Trauerspiel* study to Benjamin's earliest writings on an Edenic "pure language." And yet this reference to "depths" is somewhat misleading. Although allegorical script cannot escape its status as a conduit of meaning, this script is always excessive. "Written script," Benjamin notes, "is not cast away in reading, like dross. It is absorbed along with what is read, as its 'pattern.' The printers, and indeed the writers of the Baroque, paid the closest possible attention to the pattern of words on the page" (215). The material fact of the letter, outside of any constative role that it serves in the paragraph, the sentence, or even the word, is a characteristically baroque obsession. "It is not possible to conceive of a starker opposite to the artistic symbol, the plastic symbol, the image of organic totality, than this amorphous fragment which is seen in the form of allegorical script" (176).

If the destructive vision of baroque allegory "transforms works and things into stirring writing," such that isolated words or letters often appear as the telos of the allegorical intention, this is insofar as an equation of linguistic nature with organic nature and, more exactly, with organic nature's death, is already at work in the baroque *Trauerspiel*. "In its individual parts, fragmented language has ceased merely to serve the process of communication," Benjamin writes, "and as a new-born object acquires a dignity equal to that of gods, rivers, virtues and similar natural forms which fuse into the allegorical" (208); nature, however, is never presented "in bud and bloom, but in the over-ripeness and decay of her creations" (179). The letter may be a "natural form," but only insofar as it points us to nature's demise, and finally to the corpse.

The movement between word and corpse emerges, albeit somewhat cryptically, in Benjamin's brief reading of Calderón's Herod drama, *El mayor monstruo los celos* (*Jealousy, the Greatest Monster*). Benjamin describes this play as a superior example of the form precisely insofar as it demonstrates the manner in which "the language of the Baroque is constantly convulsed by rebellion on the part of the elements which make it up" (*OG* 207). In the scene he cites, "Mariamne, the wife of Herod, catches sight of the fragments of a letter in which her husband orders that, in the event of his own death, she should be killed in order to preserve his supposedly threatened honor" (207). Looking upon the fragments, Mariamne speaks: "What do they contain? / Death is the very first word / which I encounter; here is the word honor, / And there I see Mariamne. / What does this mean? Heaven help me!" (qtd. in *OG* 207–208). In an exchange of properties between bodies and script, the fragments of Herod's letter "take on a threatening quality" (208), proleptically doubling the bodily fragmentation that they portend.[15]

Calderón's play is such a superior example of the form not only because of its considerable artistic merit, but also because it brings to light the relationship between the allegorical intention and language, a relationship in which "anagrams, onomatopoeic phrases, and many other examples of linguistic virtuosity, word, syllable, and sound are emancipated from any context of traditional meaning and are flaunted as objects" (208). These objects are, however, always on the side of the corpse, the privileged baroque figure for the ruination of the organic world (218). Thus, after describing baroque authors' construction of new words through the addition of the concrete to the abstract, for example, "*Unschulds-Zedern*" (the cedars of innocence) or "*Freundschaffts-Blut*" (the blood of friendship), Benjamin notes that "the counterpart to such an approach is triumphantly evident when the writer succeeds in significantly dividing a living entity into the *disjecta membra* of allegory" (199). Like nature, language is "personalized" (as a "living entity"), but only to be "deprived of a soul" (187). "Living" language dies under the gaze of the allegorist, loses its *zusammenge-hörig* character, leaving behind linguistic fragments. Benjamin could thus say of language exactly what he says of the corpse: "*Integrum humanum corpus symbolicam iconem nigridi non posse, partem tamen corporis ei constituendae non esse ineptam*" ("The whole human body cannot enter a symbolical icon, but it is not inappropriate for part of the body to constitute it"; 216).

Let us pause for a moment to note that here, amidst the linguistic fragments of the baroque mourning play and almost certainly where we do not expect to meet him, we meet again Paul Klee—perhaps the same Klee whom, along with Adolf Loos, Bertolt Brecht, and Paul Scheerbart, Benjamin presents in "Experience and Poverty" ("Erfahrung und Armut") as the source of "a new, positive concept of barbarism" (*SW* 2:732).[16] Now, Klee's paintings are rarely of violent scenes; they would make poor illustrations for Calderón's dramas (although *Demonstration of the Miracle* [*Vorführung des Wunders*; 1916], which was, in addition to *Angelus Novus*, the other work of Klee's that Benjamin owned, does include in the upper left quadrant a small decapitated figure who presents to the viewer his own head—a scene worthy of Herod). But Benjamin means by "a new, positive concept of barbarism" something a bit different, something that he associates with those "creative spirits . . . who begin by clearing a tabula rasa" (2:732). In light of Benjamin's reflections on the destructive vision of baroque allegory, then, we might look elsewhere for Klee's barbarism; we might look to his relationship to language. Comparing Klee to Picasso in 1947, Clement Greenberg noted that the real difference between them is that "[Picasso] sees the picture as a wall, where Klee sees it as a page" (2:149). Greenberg means here something fairly specific, means to oppose Klee's "diminutive" approach to Picasso's more comprehensive style—for "when one paints a wall, one has to have a more comprehensive awareness of the surroundings" (2:149). But he could just as easily have been speaking (literally) literally and acknowledging that Klee does in so many of his works treat the canvas as a page in a book, covering it with hieroglyphs or letters "emancipated from any context of traditional meaning and . . . flaunted as objects" (see figure 1).[17]

At first glance, this notion of linguistic fragmentation does not seem to play a role in Benjamin's discussion of the allegorical vision of the *Angelus* or in his contemporaneous studies of nineteenth-century allegory. References to bodily

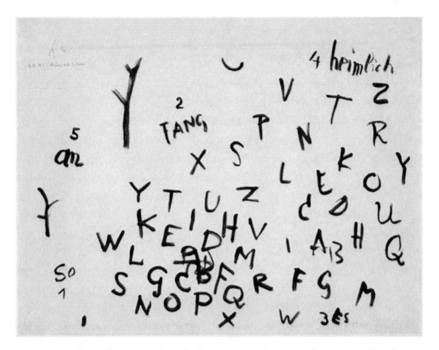

**FIGURE 1.** Paul Klee, *Beginning of a Poem.* © 2015 Artists Rights Society (ARS), New York.

destruction do persist in the latter, as when he writes of Baudelaire's "Une Martyre" that "the allegorical intention has done its work on this martyr: she is in pieces" (*AP* J67a,7); nonetheless, his earlier association of this destruction with a dividing of language is absent. In spite of this apparent shift in his approach to allegory, however, the question of the written word reappears in Benjamin's late writings on the historical materialist method, albeit in a somewhat altered form. "The events surrounding the historian," Benjamin writes, "and in which he himself takes part, will underlie his presentation in the form of a text written in invisible ink"; in short, "to write history . . . means to *cite* history" (N11,3). The empiricist perspective is impossible inasmuch as history exhibits itself only as written and never as a collection of events. And historical materialism alone is able to recognize this fact: "only Marxism can practice great philology where the literature of the previous century [that is, nineteenth-century history itself] is concerned" (N11,6). To take these passages at face value, however, and to read them only as reminders that history is always imparted by someone at some time, is to miss their force altogether. All history is written insofar as all history partakes, more or less, of the epic mode, of the presentation of history as homogeneous and continuous, being determined by the traditional notion of time. This temporal articulation of history is itself a product of a certain narrativization, a fact that Benjamin colorfully addresses in writing that "the historical materialist leaves it to others to be drained by the whore called 'Once upon a time' in historicism's bordello" (*SW* 4:396).

The vocation of the historical materialist is the philological destruction of this historical continuum rather than its narrative recoding; and here, above all, this vocation dovetails with the allegorical intention. For both the historical materialist and the allegorist the object is preserved, but torn from its lived context. Indeed, the object survives, while the context is irremediably lost, as when Benjamin writes of "the art of citing without quotation marks" (*AP* N1,10), an activity in which the writings that make up history are preserved absent any indication that these writings were ever part of some meaningful arrangement. To tear a moment from history, then, is to be left with a collection of fragments; or, since history is only ever cited, only ever truly recognizable to the (materialist) philologist, it is to be left with "stirring writing." Thus, "when, as is the case in the *Trauerspiel*, history becomes part of the setting, it does so as script" (*OG* 177).

Finally, Benjamin returns us to the baroque association of this linguistic disarticulation—in this case, the disarticulation of written history—with putrefaction, writing that "history *decays* into images, not into stories" (*Geschichte zerfällt in Bilder, nicht in Geschichten*; *AP* N11,4; my emphasis). Seen, not read, images are left behind after the allegorical mortification of time. The opposition of these images to stories, far from indicating a larger turn from linguistic to visual media, is simply a reassertion of the tradition of baroque emblematics—one could as easily write that "history decays into letters."[18] These letters (or emblems, or images) do not oppose history's being written—history, Benjamin insists, is always written; they oppose history's being *read* as a meaningful, causal, epic depiction of a chain of events, a "vital progression." In sum, they oppose history's being read as anything but a collection of disarticulated letters. These dead letters, outside any role in sentences or words, are left behind when the vital progression of human history is submitted to the allegorical vision.

Just as Kant's angel bypasses the discursive conditions of knowledge so as to "immediately present the object and grasp it all at once," the *Angelus Novus* bypasses the discursive conditions of epic history—in other words, bypasses history's successive, causal, temporal structure—to see history in what Paul de

**FIGURE 2.** Robert Smithson, *A Heap of Language*. © Holt-Smithson Foundation / Licensed by VAGA, New York, NY.

Man has suggestively referred to as a "material vision" (*Aesthetic Ideology* 82),[19] to see, therefore, the letters that compose history before or outside of their meaningful combination into the temporal progression of words, sentences, and stories (*Geschichten*)—to see, perhaps, what Robert Smithson sketched as "A Heap of Language" (see figure 2). The *Angelus* sees history, in short, without reading it. The vision that results is reducible neither to dialectical negativity nor to the pathos of temporal finitude, though it cannot prevent itself from being read as another metaphor for these philosophical operations. It is, above all, not reducible to the historicism that Benjamin's late writings are dedicated to challenging.

"The interest that the materialist historian takes in the past," Benjamin writes, "is always, in part, a vital interest in its being past—in its being essentially dead" (*AP* J76a,4). Benjamin's *Angelus* sees the dead letters out of which every epic history is written, the linguistic *corps morcelé* that remains when the time that imbues (written) history with life has been (allegorically) subtracted; he is, in this sense, the perfect materialist historian.

CONCLUSION

# THE LIGHTNING FLASH

# AND THE STORM OF PROGRESS

In the fields with which we are concerned, knowledge comes
only in lightning flashes. The text is the long roll of thunder
that follows.

—Walter Benjamin, *The Arcades Project*

**BOTH MY READING** of the works of T. S. Eliot in part 1 of this book and my
reading of the works of Walter Benjamin in part 2 conclude by describing
what we might call—with a nod to the usage established by Paul de Man—a
"textual event" (*Resistance to Theory* 103–104): an inscription marking, without representing, the impossibility of a certain strategy of historical representation. In Eliot, there is the lightning flash that divides *The Waste Land* not
only externally, from the fallen literary history that the poem describes, but
also internally, from *The Waste Land* itself. In Benjamin, there is the storm of
progress, the vision of dead letters piling up at the feet of the *Angelus Novus*
in the ninth thesis of "On the Concept of History." Each appears, when and
where it appears, to indicate that a limit has been reached, a limit, as I have
tried to show, of legibility no less than of historical continuity. Now, whether
this limit is truly a stopping point, whether it is not, rather, a threshold, is
not so clear. Eliot, of course, continued to write. His *Four Quartets* rivals *The
Waste Land* in its ambitions, and some critics would argue that it surpasses
the earlier poem as an artistic achievement (though I would not). At any rate,
and as I suggested above, the later poem is not (as *The Waste Land* is) a crisis
poem—it reflects, rather, its author's choice of an easier variety of transcen-
dence. As for Benjamin, we cannot know for sure what he would have given
us after the theses; and so we are left wondering if the angel's vision, however
horrible, could not still somehow have been reimagined as—in Klee's terms—
the beginning of a poem.

Having reached the limits of historical representation, then, are we returned to history as a brute, empirical fact? One possible reading of Eliot's lightning or Benjamin's storm is that each marks, within the text in which it appears, what lies outside of the text. "History," Jameson tells us, "is what hurts" (*Political Unconscious* 102); or, more pointedly, history, like Lacan's Real, "resists symbolization absolutely" (qtd. in Jameson, *Ideologies of Theory* 107). This seems to me correct, but only up to a point. Eliot certainly forces an encounter with what lies outside of his text when he tries to incorporate within it its own condition of possibility—the lightning flash as pen stroke, the act of inscription that gives us *The Waste Land* in the first place or the editorial mark that bounds it. Benjamin, for his part, produces in the ninth thesis, and by way of the angel's allegorical vision, an image of history as what resists (absolutely) historicization. We need to take care, though, to keep in mind the processes by which the texts of Eliot and Benjamin arrive at these insights. Here we might recall (if only to creatively misread) the Hegelian dictum that something false as a starting point can, nevertheless, be true when arrived at as a conclusion. To state simply that Eliot's lightning or Benjamin's storm is a figure for history itself, or for the "Real" of history, misses the point if what is meant is that one or both of these images refer to some *thing* outside of any conceptual or rhetorical construction—the construction I have associated with history's lyrical, satirical, anecdotal, or allegorical casting. It seems, rather, more accurate to say that the lightning or the storm is itself (conceptually, rhetorically) constructed as a textual outside—or at least that it is the effect of such a textual construction.

*A textual construction*: in no way do I mean to claim—as in some caricatured version of poststructuralism—that there is, finally, only language. I do, however, want to stress the role of construction in even those instances of ostensible immediacy—instances that Eliot's lightning and Benjamin's storm seem to want to index. Benjamin saw this fact very clearly, so even when he appears perhaps to claim—as in the above epigraph—a division of (historical) lightning from (rhetorical) thunder, he can always be relied on to return to the necessity of a moment of (allegorical, constellatory) construction. (And this is likely why the vision of the *Angelus*, though an impossible vision, is still *a* vision, *a* vantage, the effect of a particular sort of seeing and not an objective view from nowhere.) There is history, but it is reached only through a certain labor.

Truly critical attention to this history—to the history that Eliot or Benjamin constructs or to the history into which Eliot's or Benjamin's works fall—cannot rest when it has pointed to its object. History is both (transcendental) scheme and (empirical) event; the two must be taken up together. It requires of the critic, therefore, a certain sort of vision—not the annihilating vision of Benjamin's angel but a double vision, a vision able to take in history's own doubleness as both representing and represented. When this doubleness is ignored or forgotten (as, I have claimed, it almost always is), something truly significant is missed: the resources, the tools, for a different critical practice, one for which the familiar opposition of the formal to the historical can no longer be maintained. In the preceding pages, thinking alongside Eliot and Benjamin, I have tried to show what this practice might look like and thus what it might mean to locate the writings of Eliot and Benjamin within modernism's history (and the latter ought to be taken in both senses of the genitive). Modernism inherits from the nineteenth century history (in the emphatic sense); we inherit this inheritance, which seems to me a good argument for reading it carefully.

# NOTES

## Preface

1. See also Foucault's characterization of Flaubert's and Manet's projects in the 1967 afterword to Flaubert's *La tentation de Saint Antoine* (1849, 1856, 1872). Here Foucault notes that, with *La tentation*, "Flaubert produced the first literary work whose exclusive domain is that of books: following Flaubert, Stéphane Mallarmé and his *Le Livre* became possible, then James Joyce, Raymond Roussel, Franz Kafka, Ezra Pound, Jorge Luis Borges." An equivalent development, roughly coterminous, took place in the visual arts with Manet's *Déjeuner sur l'herbe* (1862–1863) and *Olympia* (1863). These, Foucault goes on, "were perhaps the first 'museum' paintings. The first paintings in European art that were less a response to the achievements of Giorgione, Raphael, and Velazquez than an acknowledgement . . . of the new and substantial relationship of painting to itself, as a manifestation of the existence of museums and the particular reality and interdependence that paintings acquire in museums." The library and the museum: Flaubert, Manet, and their epigones "erect their art within the archive" ("The Fantasia of the Library" 107); history becomes their essential possibility.

2. See in particular the last sections of de Man's *Allegories of Reading*, as well as the posthumous publications *The Rhetoric of Romanticism*, *The Resistance to Theory*, and *Aesthetic Ideology*.

## Introduction

1. Adorno's remark on the barbarity of poetry after Auschwitz reads, in its entirety: "The critique of culture is confronted with the last stage in the dialectic of culture and barbarism: to write a poem after Auschwitz is barbaric, and that corrodes also the knowledge which expresses why it has become impossible to write poetry today" (*Prisms* 34). Lyotard describes the ethical dimension of artistic representation in terms

of the "aesthetics of the sublime" in the essays included in *The Inhuman*. Here he writes that "what is at stake in the arts is their making themselves witness to the fact that there are things which are *indeterminate*" (101; italics in original [henceforth, to be assumed if not otherwise noted]) and, as "indeterminate," unrepresentable. For an opposed reading of the ethics of artistic representation, see Jacques Rancière, *The Future of the Image*.

2. Compare to this remark the challenge set to Phaedrus by Socrates: "But surely you will admit at least this much: Every speech must be put together like a living creature, with a body of its own; it must be neither without head nor without legs; and it must have a middle and extremities that are fitting both to one another and to the whole work" (*Phaedrus* 264c).

3. For Hegel's discussion of empiricist "pointing," see the dialectic of "Sense Certainty" as it unfolds at the beginning of the *Phenomenology of Spirit*.

4. In a recent essay that deals with the philosophical significance of aesthetics, Christoph Menke opposes Aristotle's and Hegel's theories of poetry and philosophy as the difference between "almost already" and "not yet." For Aristotle, Menke writes, poetry is "almost already" philosophical, while for Hegel poetry is "not yet" philosophical and is incapable of ever being so. Though Menke's essay is suggestive, we cannot accept the conclusion that for Aristotle poetry is "in motion, on its way" from history to philosophy (35), while for Hegel this movement is impossible. For this argument to work, one would have to demonstrate that for Aristotle a (historical, temporal) development could see one discourse transform into another. This possibility only exists, however, if one assumes a model of historical development akin to Hegel's self-education of spirit. This model would have been foreign to Aristotle.

5. Royce is cited more often than he is read. His characterization of the *Phenomenology of Spirit* as a bildungsroman has become quite influential, however, with Jean Hyppolite (*Genesis and Structure* 11), M. H. Abrams (229), and Judith Butler (240) all endorsing Royce's argument (though Butler attributes the argument to Abrams).

6. For a discussion of Whitman, Rimbaud, and Marx, see Parker. For a discussion of Marx, Trotsky, and the situationists, see Puchner.

7. In "The Tragic Farce of Marx, Hegel, and Engels: A Note," Bruce Mazlish provides a compelling account of the Hegelian source of the opening lines of *The Eighteenth Brumaire*, in which Marx writes that "Hegel remarks somewhere that all great world-historic facts and personages appear, so to speak, twice. He forgot to add: the first time as tragedy, the second time as farce" (Marx and Engels 11:103). Mazlish does not, however, address how Marx's discussion of poetic representation's self-overcoming could also be informed by Hegel's writings.

8. Marx is said to have made this remark in an 1869 letter to the positivist historian Edward Spencer Beesly. In his *Reflections on Violence*, Georges Sorel attributes this information to the economist Lujo Brentano (128).

9. See, for example, the writings of Robert Kaufman, especially "Red Kant" and "Lyric Commodity Critique, Benjamin Adorno Marx, Baudelaire Baudelaire Baudelaire."

10. I say "temporarily" resolved, first, for the obvious reason that Marx's pronouncements in *Capital* on the form and development of history have not been the last Marxist

word on history, and have been interrogated endlessly over the last century and a half; and second, because Marx himself continues to struggle with history in the years following the publication of *Capital*, as evinced by his defensive remarks in response to the charge of historical idealism in the afterword to the second edition of *Capital*, where he takes pains to distinguish his method of inquiry (empirical) from his method of presentation (dialectical) (Marx and Engels 35:19). The effect, in any case, is to invite the question of whether the dialectical progression of history is a concept applied to more or less nondialectical historical events or whether it exists, immanently, as the law of these events' development.

11. For a discussion of the importance of Shelley's writings to a later (and mostly German) radical tradition—a tradition that includes Marx, Engels, Adorno, Brecht, and Benjamin—see Robert Kaufman's essays "Legislators of the Post-Everything World" and "Intervention & Commitment Forever!"

12. The effect that the whole affair ultimately had on Nietzsche is an open question. In 1872, Nietzsche's then close friend Erwin Rohde responded to Wilamowitz-Moellendorff on Nietzsche's behalf with a pamphlet titled "Afterphilologie," a mocking reference to Wilamowitz-Moellendorff's backward method that plays on the German term for the posterior. Wagner himself replied in an open letter published in the *Norddeutsche Allgemeine Zeitung*, in which he criticized the method prescribed by Wilamowitz-Moellendorff for its dullness. In his recent biography of Nietzsche, Julian Young describes these exchanges, noting that, in their wake, "Nietzsche fell ill with stomach and bowel problems" (154).

13. There is no evidence that Nietzsche was familiar with Vico's writings, though the affinity between some aspects of their projects—the elevated role of philology, for example, as well as the notion of a cyclical history—has encouraged critics to speculate on the possibility of an influence. See, for example, Ernst Behler's discussion in "Vico and Nietzsche." See also the discussion of Vico and Nietzsche in Timothy Brennan's *Borrowed Light*.

14. Nietzsche's proximity to Kant is not terribly surprising, as Nietzsche's most productive years coincided with the regnancy of neo-Kantianism in Germany. Indeed, against those critics who take Nietzsche as a sui generis thinker, both Tsarina Doyle and R. Kevin Hill have recently demonstrated that the "skeletal structure" of Nietzsche's thought remains "broadly Kantian" (Hill 3), a fact attributable to the influence that Arthur Schopenhauer and especially Friedrich Lange (the mentor of the Marburg School neo-Kantian Hermann Cohen) exerted on Nietzsche during his formative years. Nietzsche may target Kantian moral philosophy and aesthetics in his later writings; nonetheless, his understanding of the cognitive-linguistic conditioning of experience is hardly thinkable without reference to the critical revolution effected by the "Sage of Königsberg."

15. Although the actual phrase "will to power" (*Wille zur Macht*) does not appear in Nietzsche's published writings until 1883, in *Thus Spoke Zarathustra* it is anticipated by references to the "desire for power" (*Machtgelüst*) in *The Wanderer and His Shadow* (1880) and *Daybreak* (1881). In any case, the association of the organism with a striving for power or for mastery is a constant in Nietzsche's works from the earliest period.

16. Although it goes beyond the scope of this discussion, it is worth noting that, as a principle of selection directed at historical becoming, the superhistorical anticipates the doctrine of eternal recurrence that Nietzsche would present in aphorism 341 of *The Gay Science* (1882).

17. This turn to rank is likely to appear both arbitrary and disturbing; and to a certain extent, it should. It is, however, important to keep in mind that rank, the judgment of certain "specimens" as "high" or "low," is only determined immanently. In other words, the highest specimens would be those able to bear the knowledge of themselves as artistically creative subjects. No other standard, and certainly no racial standard, could decide in advance one's rank.

18. The conception of art that informs Nietzsche's treatment of history-as-art in this text anticipates the more direct challenge to traditional aesthetics voiced in *On the Genealogy of Morality*. In the latter, Nietzsche notes that all philosophers—and Kant is here exemplary—have "thought about art and the beautiful from the viewpoint of the 'spectator'"; and he suggests instead "starting from the experiences of the artist (he who creates)" (*GM* 72). Kant, then, is to be opposed to Stendhal. Tellingly, Nietzsche passes over in silence Kant's own discussion of genius. The latter concept complicates the opposition that Nietzsche presents, not least because it proves foundational both for a romanticism and for a metaphysics of will from which Nietzsche never entirely extricates himself. Here Martin Heidegger's discussion of Nietzsche's identification of art with will and with life in the first volume of his *Nietzsche, The Will to Power as Art*, is particularly relevant.

## Chapter 1

1. In the spring of 1914, before Pound passed "Prufrock" on to Harriet Monroe, Conrad Aiken had presented the poem to the similarly named Harold Monro, the editor of *Poetry and Drama*. Monro, however, rejected the poem as "absolutely insane" (Gordon 68).

2. For a good treatment of Pound's efforts to define himself in the prewar London context, one that helps us to understand Eliot's appeal, see Rainey's *Institutions of Modernism* (10–41).

3. This remark is included in Lewis's autobiographical *Blasting and Bombardiering*. The full passage reads:

> It is not secret that Ezra Pound exercised a very powerful influence upon Mr. Eliot. I do not have to define the nature of this influence, of course. Mr. Eliot was lifted out of his lunar alley-ways and *fin-de-siècle* nocturnes, into a massive region of verbal creation in contact with that astonishing didactic intelligence, that is all. "Gerontion" (1920) is a close relative of "Prufrock," certain matters filtered through an aged mask in both cases, but "Gerontion" technically is "school of Ezra." (285–286)

4. Explaining these divisions through recourse to a more familiar notion of Eliotic irony (or of poetic impersonality more generally) is not, I think, terribly helpful, not because irony plays no role in the practice that I am describing but because the concept has, in readings of Eliot's work, been domesticated. We all know what irony means,

then, for Eliot and in Eliot, and I hope that by avoiding this term I can go some way toward defamiliarizing Eliot's critical and poetic practice. There are, of course, treatments of irony that elude the limited and limiting frame that I am describing. See, for example, de Man's "The Concept of Irony," included in *Aesthetic Ideology*, as well as Kevin Newmark's *Irony on Occasion*.

5. Fredric Jameson discusses this aspect of the formalist program in *The Prison House of Language*: "In his essay on 'Tolstoy's Crises' [Boris] Eichenbaum [shows] how in a sense Tolstoy's religious conversion itself could be considered a 'motivation of the device,' in the manner in which it provided new raw material for an artistic practice on the point of exhausting itself" (84–85).

6. See, for example, Schuchard's discussion of Eliot's anxieties in *Eliot's Dark Angel* (13), as well as McIntire's discussion of these issues in *Modernism, Memory, and Desire* (75–78).

7. In a letter to John C. Pope dated 8 March 1946, Eliot writes of "Prufrock" the following: "When I went to Paris in the autumn of [1910] . . . I had already written several fragments which were ultimately embodied in the poem . . . but the poem was not completed until the summer of 1911" (*IMH* 176). It was completed, then, only a month or so before Eliot "[began] to worry."

8. In "Judgment and Being" ("Urteil und Sein") Hölderlin writes of judgment (*Urteil*) that it is "in the highest and strictest sense, the original separation of object and subject, which are most deeply united in intellectual intuition, that separation through which alone object and subject become possible, the arche-separation [*die Ur-teilung*]" (37).

9. Another text from the same period that might be placed in dialogue with "Tradition and the Individual Talent" and "The Perfect Critic" is the fourth of Eliot's "Reflections on Contemporary Poetry," printed in the July 1919 issue of *The Egoist* and never reprinted. In his *The Breaking of the Vessels*, Harold Bloom suggests that Eliot's failure to reprint this essay in *The Sacred Wood* is symptomatic of Eliot's inability to deal with the alternative conception of tradition that the essay expresses, a conception closer to his (Bloom's) own. Here Bloom is particularly interested in what Eliot discusses as "personal intimacy, with another, probably a dead author. It may overcome us suddenly, on first or after long acquaintance; it is certainly a crisis" (39). Eliot, Bloom implies, recoiled from this conception of tradition (as the source of crisis) and settled instead on the relatively safe notion of "tradition" with which he has become associated. I agree with Bloom that Eliot figures the encounter with the tradition as a moment of crisis in the "Reflections"; I do not, however, believe that this characterization is, finally, at odds with the one Eliot presents in "Tradition," "The Perfect Critic," and elsewhere. Indeed, these essays—which Eliot did decide to reprint—present the struggle with history in terms stronger than those of the "Reflections." That Bloom misses this when, developing his own conception of the "anxiety of influence," he opposes himself to Eliot is itself telling.

10. Eliot's duties as a lecturer included developing courses on the history of Western literature, if not quite "from Homer," then at least from the medieval period. Ronald Schuchard has made the syllabi from Eliot's courses widely available. The intensive reading this required of Eliot no doubt determined his direction as a critic and a poet. But

as Eliot's letters to his family indicate, it also interrupted his writing. In early 1919, for example, in a letter to his brother, Eliot notes that he has "had so little time to write" and, consequently, that he hopes "to give up lectures next year" (*L* 1:324). And when he finally does give up lecturing, he describes to his mother his "great relief" (1:353).

11.  Richard Shusterman points to the "ludicrous" image in "Tradition" of monuments that are somehow both fixed in their truth and able to be moved by the introduction of a new work among them: "The great and sturdy existing monuments, firmly established in their assigned places as cornerstones of our literary tradition, suddenly start shuffling and nudging each other about so as to accommodate the new work to form a 'complete' order, only to be upset again" (159). It is unlikely, though, that Eliot, trained in philosophy by idealists indebted to the writings of Hegel, would have found this image so ludicrous. Compare Hegel's remarks from the beginning of the *Phenomenology of Spirit*:

> The more conventional opinion gets fixated on the antithesis of truth and falsity. . . . It does not comprehend the diversity of philosophical systems as the progressive unfolding of truth, but rather sees in it simple disagreements. The bud disappears in the bursting forth of the blossom. . . . Yet at the same time their fluid nature makes them moments of organic unity in which they do not only not conflict, but in which each is as necessary as the other; and this mutual necessity alone constitutes the life of the whole. (2)

12.  In a 1920 letter to the editor of *The Athenaeum* regarding the publication of "The Perfect Critic," Eliot distinguishes his own critical practice from the philosophical aesthetics that he associates with Hegel, writing that "Hegel's *Philosophy of Art* adds very little to our enjoyment or understanding of art, though it fills a gap in Hegel's philosophy" (*L* 1:485). Most likely, Eliot had in mind the transitional status of the aesthetic in Hegel's philosophy of history. For more on this topic, see my discussion of Hegel in the Introduction to this book.

13.  The likelihood that Eliot's theorization of the tradition originated in the neo-Hegelian philosopher F. H. Bradley's organic holism, on which Eliot wrote his doctoral dissertation, has been well documented. In *The Invisible Poet*, Hugh Kenner notes that we find in Eliot's writings "evidence for his unqualified ingestion of certain perspectives of Bradley's which one does not discover him ever to have repudiated" (45); while in a more recent book, M. A. R. Habib identifies this turn to Bradley with an intraphilosophical resistance to cultural fragmentation, writing that "the philosophies of Bradley, Royce and other [late nineteenth- and early twentieth-century] neo-Hegelian idealists might be viewed as a last ditch attempt to retain the larger unifying synthesis against the disintegrative onslaught of positivism and realism" (13).

14.  Wyndham Lewis describes "Gerontion" as "a close relative of 'Prufrock,' certain matters filtered through an aged mask in both cases" (*Blasting* 285–286). From the earliest years of Eliot criticism, it has been common to speak of these two poems in the same breath, as in John Crowe Ransom's remark that "I have usually felt that 'Prufrock' and 'Gerontion' were Eliot's most successful poems, because the best composed of his important ones" (295).

15. Pound writes, "I do *not* advise printing Gerontion as preface. One dont miss it AT all as the thing now stands. To be more lucid still, let me say that I advise you NOT to print Gerontion as prelude" (*L* 1:630). I address the significance of Pound's advice in Chapter 2 of this book.

16. As it appears in *Measure for Measure*, the line reads: ". . . Thou hast nor youth nor age, / But, as it were, an after-dinner's sleep, / Dreaming on both . . ." (3.1.32–34). And it continues:

. . . for all thy blessed youth
Becomes as aged, and doth beg the alms
Of palsied eld; and when thou art old and rich,
Thou hast neither heat, affection, limb, nor beauty,
To make thy riches pleasant. (34–38)

17. Indeed, Stephen's remark is often coupled with Eliot's characterization of history in "Gerontion." Thus, Lawrence Rainey writes the following:

"History is a nightmare," wrote Joyce. "History has cunning passages, contrived corridors / And issues," murmured T. S. Eliot. History characterizes the epic, thought Pound, whose own "epic" might seem to have been written to vindicate his modernist confreres, so much does it abound in nightmares, contrived corridors, and cunning passages. The modernists were obsessed with history and with their place in it. They mourned it, damned it, and contested it as tenaciously as Jacob wrestling with the image of God: "I will not let thee go, except thou bless me." Yet if the deity of history had ever deigned to reply to them, it might have said: "Behold, I set before you this day a blessing and a curse." (*Institutions of Modernism* 77)

18. Probably the strongest version of this claim appears in Joyce Hamilton Rochat's "T. S. Eliot's Companion Poems," in which she suggests that the two poems describe "the same character at different stages of development. Prufrock is a character in process, making the choices that will decide a destiny. Gerontion, at the point of death, reviews those choices and the factors that governed them and evaluates their importance" (73).

19. I am associating this notion with Hertz, who describes it in detail in his essay "The Notion of Blockage in the Literature of the Sublime." Similar analyses appear in Paul de Man's "Anthropomorphism and Trope in Lyric" and Jonathan Culler's "On the Negativity of Modern Poetry." In the latter, Culler describes in Baudelaire's "Spleen II" a process comparable to the one that interests me: "[O]nce the excess of heterogeneous materials is resolved into a single figure through negative categories, there is potential for reversal or recuperation" (201).

## Chapter 2

1. See Chinitz; Faulk; Johnson; Schuchard.

2. I am less convinced, though, by Chinitz's assumption (which is also the assumption of so many contemporary critics) that to endorse mass forms or to create art that borrows from mass forms is itself an especially radical or "anarchic" activity. Addressing

this issue would mean entering into debates that developed during Eliot's lifetime and that are still going on today, debates that concern, most generally, the relative political efficacy of "difficult" and "accessible" art. Additionally, it would mean distinguishing more carefully between mass-produced art and authentically popular art, a distinction that was certainly relevant to Eliot during the 1920s. These issues are, however, beyond the scope of my project.

3. The philosopher and art historian Thierry de Duve uses this remark as a way of entering into a discussion of the relationship between Greenberg's well-known 1939 discussion of "Avant-Garde and Kitsch" and his 1950 essay on "Self-Hatred and Jewish Chauvinism." For our purposes, one of de Duve's passing characterizations of kitsch—it is not clear if de Duve is here speaking in Greenberg's voice or his own—is especially relevant: "[T]he love of kitsch is nothing other than the pleasure taken in the corruption of one's own taste, and therefore, indeed, the aesthetic expression of self-hatred" (41). Again, the pleasure taken in kitsch is complicated.

4. "Good Bad Books" is the title of a short essay by George Orwell first published in a November 1945 issue of the *Tribune*. In it, Orwell writes that "the existence of good bad literature—the fact that one can be amused or excited or even moved by a book that one's intellect simply refuses to take seriously—is a reminder that art is not the same thing as cerebration" (21). Orwell attributes the phrase itself—"good bad book"— to G. K. Chesterton, most likely thinking of Chesterton's 1901 *The Defendant* (though the exact phrase does not actually appear in this text).

5. The distinction between "mention" and "use" originates in the writings of Quine, but Richard Strier has explained its relevance to literary studies, focusing in particular on the way it helps us to understand the distinction between formalist and historicist reading practices:

> Formalists are concerned with the uses to which details in literary (and other) texts are put. Their premise is that the work provides the initial context for understanding the significance of any particular item in a text. The question is "How is feature X used in this text?" New historicism, like very old historicism, is concerned with mentions. The fact that some item that is taken to be culturally or politically significant is mentioned in a text—in passing, in a metaphor, it doesn't matter how—is sufficient to get the machinery of "archeology" and archive-churning going. Much that is rich and strange is turned up in this way, but the object of this kind of study is not literature, or any text, but some aspect of culture in general. Ultimately, I think, the question of formalism is tied up with the question of whether a literary approach is valuable and worthwhile—both "in itself" and in relation to the whole world of texts, including "documents." (213)

6. Aldington's own discussion of Joyce was published in *The English Review* (April 1921). Aldington, however, had already invited Eliot to respond to his criticisms of Joyce before their publication, in September 1920. And so, despite the fact that Eliot's response would not appear until 1923, the exchange between the two men can be considered roughly contemporary with Eliot's composition and publication of *The Waste Land*. I will discuss this exchange at greater length in the next chapter.

7. See Lyndall Gordon, *T. S. Eliot's Early Years* (appendix 2, "Dating *The Waste Land* Fragments"); Hugh Kenner, "The Urban Apocalypse"; Lawrence Rainey, *Revisiting "The Waste Land"*; Grover Smith, "The Making of *The Waste Land*."

8. This reading of the poem—that it essentially doubles the incoherence of the modern world—is affirmed by Eliot's friend Conrad Aiken in an early review: "We reach thus the conclusion that the poem succeeds—as it brilliantly does—by virtue of its incoherence, not of its plan; by virtue of its ambiguities, not of its explanations. Its incoherence is a virtue because its 'donnée' is incoherence" (152). Already in his 1941 essay "The Isolation of Modern Poetry," the poet-critic Delmore Schwartz could note the thinness of this explanation of poetic difficulty:

> [T]he complexity of modern life, the disorder of the traffic on a business street or the variety of reference in the daily newspaper is far from being the same thing as the difficulties of syntax, tone, diction, metaphor, and allusion which face the reader in the modern poem. If one is the product of the other, the causal sequence involves a number of factors on different levels, and to imply, as I think Mr. Eliot does, that there is a simple causal relationship between the disorder of modern life and the difficulty of modern poetry is merely to engender misunderstanding by oversimplification. (152)

9. The connection between these two sections was first noted by F. R. Leavis (183).

10. Here I refer to the fact that the notes were added at the behest of Eliot's American publishers, Boni and Liveright, with the sole purpose of making *The Waste Land* long enough to be published as a stand-alone text (Rainey, *Revisiting* 37–38).

11. For a discussion of these lines that relates them to Lewis's notion of a nonmoral satire, see T. Miller 47–49.

12. Pound described himself as the "sage homme" of *The Waste Land* in a short poem of the same name included in a letter he sent to Eliot in December 1921. The first three stanzas of "Sage Homme" read:

> These are the Poems of Eliot
> By the Uranian Muse begot;
> A Man their Mother was,
> A Muse their Sire.
>
> How did the printed Infancies result
> From Nuptials thus doubly difficult?
>
> If you must needs enquire
> Know diligent Reader
> That on each Occasion
> Ezra performed the caesarean Operation. (*L* 1:626)

## Chapter 3

1. *Ulysses* was, of course, still incomplete when "The Influence of Mr. James Joyce" appeared, a fact that Aldington acknowledges, writing that "[o]bviously no valid criticism can be made of Mr. Joyce's *Ulysses* until the whole work has been published in book

form. It seems to me that the serial publication has lasted an abnormally long time, and that there is some excuse for my impatience in speaking of *Ulysses* while it is still fragmentary" (331).

2. We do not find Eliot criticizing Aldington's own verse, perhaps because this verse was—it seems uncontroversial to claim—slight compared to what Eliot was attempting and accomplishing during the period in which he was in closest contact with Aldington. Nonetheless, Eliot does, in one of his letters to Aldington from late November of 1921, target the poetry of H.D., writing to Aldington that "I think you overrate H.D.'s poetry. I do find it fatiguingly monotonous and lacking in the element of surprise." In the same letter, Eliot writes that he expects Aldington to "abhor the poem on which I have been working" (*L* 1:606).

3. For Eliot's relationship to Maurras, see Julius, who overstates the matter in referring to Maurras as "Eliot's mentor" (108).

4. At the beginning of his notes on *The Waste Land*, Eliot describes the centrality to his poem of both Jessie Weston's retelling of the grail myth in *From Ritual to Romance* (1920) and the anthropological writings of Sir James Frazer in *The Golden Bough* (1890). He begins his notes with the following lines:

> Not only the title, but the plan and a good deal of the incidental symbolism of the poem were suggested by Miss Jessie L. Weston's book on the Grail legend: *From Ritual to Romance*. Indeed, so deeply am I indebted, Miss Weston's book will elucidate the difficulties of the poem much better than my notes can do; and I recommend it (apart from the great interest of the book itself) to any who think such elucidation of the poem worth the trouble. To another work of anthropology I am indebted in general, one which has influenced our generation profoundly; I mean *The Golden Bough*; I have used especially the two volumes *Adonis, Attis, Osiris*. Anyone who is acquainted with these works will immediately recognize in the poem certain references to vegetation ceremonies. (*TAWL* 71n)

5. For a fascinating reading of temporality in *Four Quartets*, one that challenges the poem's own supposed privileging of the transcendent moment, see Martin Hägglund's "Dying for Time: T. S. Eliot's *Four Quartets*."

6. In recent years, James Miller has developed the most detailed and compelling discussions of Eliot's debt to Whitman. See his *T. S. Eliot: The Making of an American Poet, 1888–1922*. Harold Bloom, however, has provided this debt with its canonical formulation. In his 1981 Wellek Library Lectures, later published as *The Breaking of the Vessels*, Bloom notes that "Eliot's true and always unnamed precursor was not Dante or Donne or Jules Laforgue or Baudelaire, but an uneasy composite of Tennyson and Whitman, with Whitman being the main figure" (21). And he repeats this claim, now with greater specificity, in a 1983 interview with Robert Moynihan. Here Bloom states that "it seems clearer and clearer that a poem like *Maud* or a poem like *In Memoriam*, or perhaps more than any poem ever written, Whitman's "When Lilacs Last in the Dooryard Bloom'd," are the real precursor texts for Eliot's poetry" (58).

7. This beginning of the *Cantos* is not, of course, how Pound had initially planned to have them begin. The first of "3 Cantos" published in the June 1917 issue of *Poetry* be-

gins "Hang it all, there can be but one *Sordello!*" Note that Pound's revision between 1917 and 1925 is similar to Eliot's revision of *The Waste Land* insofar as the ancient is moved to a place of privilege and the near contemporary demoted (in this case, relocated to canto II).

8. After Crane's death, Williams himself wrote of Crane the following: "I cannot grow rhapsodic with him, the evangel of the post-war, the replier to the romantic apostle of *The Waste Land*" (qtd. in Mariani 328).

9. An excellent treatment of the modernist turn to primitive sources as a racial masquerade is found in Michael North's *Dialect of Modernism*.

10. Following his conversion to Anglicanism, Eliot revised this note in later editions of the poem to read: "'The Peace which passeth understanding' is our equivalent to this word." I am interested, however, in the form that the poem (and the notes) took upon its (and their) first appearance.

## Chapter 4

1. Benjamin refers to Kant three times over the course of his dissertation, each time in passing. Only in the last of these references does Benjamin say anything about Kantian aesthetics, noting that the romantics shifted to "the side of the object or structure that very autonomy in the domain of art that Kant, in the third *Critique*, had lent to the power of judgment" (*SW* 1:155). In the first two references, Kant appears only as an obstacle to the romantics' attempt to infinitize reflection.

2. Some of Rebecca Comay's work is an important exception to this inattention: "When the young Benjamin finally decides, in 1917 [*sic*], to jettison Kant for the Romanticism of Friedrich Schlegel and Novalis as the topic for his doctoral dissertation at the University of Bern, the choice reflects no arbitrary shift of interest" (134); indeed, Comay goes on, "Benjamin's renunciation of Kant during the war years is linked, at least in his own mind, to the conformism he sees implicit in the latter's portrayal of history as an endless inexorable progress toward a pre-established goal" (134). The turn from Kant, Comay suggests, signals Benjamin's burgeoning political sensibilities, sensibilities necessarily at odds with the conservative Kantian worldview. It is this position that I will attempt to complicate in what follows.

3. Stathis Kouvelakis presents a particularly compelling version of this narrative in his *Philosophy and Revolution: From Kant to Marx*. An unquestioned faith in the same narrative is implicit in Fredric Jameson's warning that "attempts to 'go beyond' Marxism typically end by reinventing older pre-Marxist positions (from the recurrent neo-Kantian revivals, to the most recent 'Nietzschean' returns through Hume and Hobbes all the way back to the pre-Socratics" (*Ideologies* 434). Here, rather than challenge the philosophical validity of Kantian and pre-Kantian positions, Jameson points to their untimeliness, to their failure to conform to a Hegelian-Marxist development that culminates, unsurprisingly, in Jameson's own Hegelian Marxism. This path—from Kant to Marx—was indeed followed by a number of Benjamin's contemporaries, by Lukács, for example, as well as by Bakhtin/Voloshinov. But typicality is not the same thing as historical necessity.

4. *Von Kant bis Hegel* was a work published by the German Hegelian (and acquaintance of Benjamin) Richard Kroner in 1921. Since its appearance, variations on its theme and its title have become common—for example, Dieter Henrich's 1973 lectures *Between Kant and Hegel*, Frederick Beiser's *The Fate of Reason: From Kant to Fichte* (1987), and Stathis Kouvelakis's *Philosophy and Revolution: From Kant to Marx* (2003).

5. Scholem describes "On the Program of the Coming Philosophy" as an "elaboration of ideas" expressed in the October 1917 letter. Perhaps Benjamin understood it in the same way—hence the appropriateness of his having presented the essay to Scholem as a birthday gift. At any rate, it makes sense to think of this essay as a kind of culmination of the study of Kant that Benjamin undertook alongside Scholem in the 1910s.

6. As a philosophical movement, neo-Kantianism resists summary description. It comprises at least three separate schools—the Marburg School, the Southwestern School, and the Göttingen School—and there is much disagreement on who should and should not be counted as a neo-Kantian. Most historians of philosophy would probably accept that it was christened if not conceived in the wake of speculative idealism's collapse, in Otto Liebman's *Kant und die Epigonen* (1865), a book in which each chapter concludes with the exhortation "Also muss auf Kant zurückgegangen werden!" (So we must return to Kant!). The decline of neo-Kantianism was as rapid as its ascent. By 1959 Theodor Adorno could note that "the school that dominated the German universities until around forty years ago has become a dead dog" (*Kant's "Critique of Pure Reason"* 3). More recently, Peter E. Gordon has echoed Adorno's verdict: "Generally speaking, neo-Kantianism today has become in great measure a philosophical ghost, and like many such ghosts it has taken up a home in the history of ideas, where it troubles no one" ("Science, Finitude, and Infinity" 32).

7. As a term of opprobrium, "psychologism" has a complicated and far-reaching legacy in the nineteenth and twentieth centuries. Martin Jay, for example, describes the generalized antipsychologism of the early twentieth century as follows: "[W]hereas psychological laws could never be more than vague and probabilistic, based as they were on inductive generalizations, the laws of logic and mathematics were valid, timeless, and pure; the latter could not therefore be derived from the former" (95). Logic must be distinguished from psychology lest psychology pollute logic with its vague generalizations. Thus, in his famous "Review of Dr. E. Husserl's Philosophy of Arithmetic," Frege notes "how very difficult it is for the sun of truth to penetrate the fog which arises out of the confusion of psychology and logic" (335–336). The relationship of Husserl to the issue of psychologism, at least as it pertains to the problem of experience, is a bit more complicated. For a reading that brings Husserl's and Benjamin's projects together, see Peter Fenves's "The Paradisal *Epochē*: On Benjamin's First Philosophy," included in his *Arresting Language*. For an excellent historical overview of antipsychologism, see Jay and also Kusch.

8. Momme Brodersen writes that "of all the lectures and seminars that [Benjamin] attended while at the Albert Ludwig University during the summer semester in 1913, the only one that struck him as noteworthy was evidently Rickert's lectures on logic" (52). Benjamin's correspondence with Scholem, though, indicates that he missed as many

lectures as he attended. Concerning Martin Heidegger's own relationship to Rickert and neo-Kantianism, John van Buren writes that "one finds Heidegger's student writings relying heavily not only on Husserl but also on . . . writings by Rickert and Lask, as well as on the thought of the other prominent neo-Kantians, Wilhelm Windelband, Hermann Cohen, and Paul Natorp" (60). See also the work of Howard Caygill and, crucially, Peter Fenves.

9. The importance of neo-Kantianism to nineteenth- and twentieth-century German (and indeed, European) philosophy is only now being addressed in the English-speaking world. A grasp of the basic tenets of neo-Kantianism, however, and of the work of Hermann Cohen in particular, is essential to understanding Benjamin's philosophical development. In *Walter Benjamin: The Story of a Friendship*, Scholem remembers how, in 1918, he and Benjamin "agreed, in view of [Benjamin's] special interest in Kant, to read the fundamental work of the Marburg school, Hermann Cohen's *Kants Theorie der Erfahrung* [Kant's Theory of Experience] (brackets in original). We spent many hours analyzing and discussing this work" (72). And Benjamin's interest in Cohen's work persisted. Referring to the presence of themes from Cohen's *Logik der reinen Erkenntnis* in Benjamin's later *Trauerspiel* study, Werner Hamacher notes that, even there, "Benjamin's critique of Kant is at the same time a critique of Cohen" (508).

10. As Beiser notes:

> Culturally, neo-Kantianism was at odds with the *Zeitgeist*, with all the profound disillusionment and pessimism that came in 1918 with defeat and the loss of a great proportion of the younger generation. For many, neo-Kantianism had become indelibly associated with the "ideas of 1914," which had been deeply discredited by 1918. Although the neo-Kantians were, to be sure, not the only advocates of the war, some of their most prominent spokesmen—Windelband, Cohen and Natorp—had been especially vocal, indeed fanatical, on its behalf. Furthermore, the cultural optimism of neo-Kantianism—its belief in the inevitable progress of civilization toward ideals of reason–had been shattered by the experience of the war, which seemed to vindicate the darkest cultural pessimists. (*After Hegel* 116)

11. Strawson's suspicion of Kant's table of categories is not the most recent questioning of the table's validity. Strawson, however, deserves mention because his version of revised Kantianism has been so important to one of the most vital strands in recent analytic philosophical thought, the strand represented by the neo-Hegelianism of John McDowell and Robert Brandom. The former writes in the preface to his most important work, *Mind and World*, that "I have been more strongly influenced than footnotes can indicate by P. F. Strawson, especially by his peerless book on Kant's First Critique [*The Bounds of Sense*]. I am not sure that Strawson's Kant is really Kant, but I am convinced that Strawson's Kant comes close to achieving what Kant wanted to achieve" (viii). McDowell goes on to present a version of Kantianism very close to that developed by the neo-Kantians a century earlier.

12. In his "Metacritique of the Purism of Reason" (1781), Hamann attacked Kant's attempts to "purify" reason of its experiential content, focusing in particular on the "genealogical priority of language and its heraldry over the seven holy functions of logical

propositions and inferences" (216). "Sounds and letters," Hamann avers, are themselves "pure forms *a priori*" (217). For a good discussion of Hamann's challenge to Kant, see the first chapter of Beiser's *The Fate of Reason*.

13. Benjamin's work on language is some of the most original and complex in the history of philosophy, and I do not want to suggest, by insisting on the subordination of Benjamin's remarks on language to his doctrine of orders that language is, in any sense, ancillary to his central concerns. For the best treatment of Benjamin on language, see Werner Hamacher's "Intensive Languages."

14. A dearth of *explicit* references to Kant: for the continued presence of Kantian themes in Benjamin's writings, see Caygill, Hamacher, and Chapters 5 and 6 of this book.

15. If this is true, if Benjamin found speculating on alien life to be a useful supplement to his reflections on problems within transcendental philosophy, he was not alone. Descriptions of strange, intelligent life have for a long time fascinated those scholars interested in the possibilities and limitations of experience. In "Kant's Aliens," an impressive survey of Kant's references to and reflections on the problem of intelligent extraterrestrial life, David Clark writes of how Kant sought to grasp better "earthly rationality" by "[holding it] up against its unearthly equivalent" (203). Clark has in mind passages such as the following from the distillation of Kant's lectures on anthropology published in 1798 as *Anthropology from a Pragmatic Point of View*:

> The highest concept of species may be that of a terrestrial rational being [*eines irdischen vernünftigen*], but we will not be able to describe its characteristics because we do not know of a non-terrestrial rational being [*nicht-irdischen Wesen*] which would enable us to refer to its properties and consequently classify that terrestrial being as rational. It seems, therefore, that the problem of giving an account of the character of the human species is quite insoluble, because the problem could only be solved by comparing two species of rational beings on the basis of experience, but experience has not offered us a comparison between two species of rational beings. (qtd. in Clark 202; brackets in original)

Transcendental philosophy, as a classificatory enterprise, is limited by the fact that it has only one form of rationality available for study: human rationality. But in the absence of detailed knowledge of nonhuman, nonterrestrial rationality, any knowledge of human rationality is bound to remain partial.

## Chapter 5

1. Dilthey writes in his "Drafts for a Critique of Historical Reason" that "I have designated the basic task of all reflection about the human sciences as a 'critique of historical reason.' The problem that needs to be solved for historical reason was not fully addressed by the Kantian critique of reason" (*Formation of the Historical World* 297).

2. In what follows, my discussion will focus on *The Arcades Project*. Yet, as vast as *The Arcades Project* is—including more than a thousand pages of fragmentary material—its borders are porous, and it is not always clear to what extent the text ought to be separated from the other projects that Benjamin undertook while he was at work on the Paris arcades. Benjamin writes to Scholem in March 1929, for example, that his

(Benjamin's) essay of the same year on "Surrealism: The Last Snapshot of the European Intelligentsia" ("Der Sürrealismus: Die letzte Momentaufnahme der europäischen Intelligenz") is "a screen placed in front of the *Paris Arcades*—and I have many a reason to keep secret what goes on behind it" (*C* 348). Much of Convolute J of *The Arcades Project*—the longest of the convolutes—is incorporated into Benjamin's Baudelaire studies from the end of the 1930s. And portions of the discussions of historiography included in Convolute N are reproduced in Benjamin's theses "On the Concept of History" (1940). I will therefore feel authorized in what follows to move freely between a discussion of *The Arcades Project* "itself" and ancillary writings that Benjamin produced during the same period.

3.  In what follows, when I refer to the dates of composition of different sections of *The Arcades Project*, I am drawing on the method of dating the work suggested by Susan Buck-Morss in *The Dialectics of Seeing*. See in particular the charts included in part 2 of her book (51–53).

4.  I need to be clear that, when I describe Benjamin's attempt to develop a philosophy of history in dialogue with Kant's theoretical writings while avoiding the errors of Kant's historical writings, I do not mean to suggest that distinguishing these two aspects of Kant's own project—the theoretical and the historical—would have presented itself to Benjamin as a redoubtable task. Rather, readers of Kant have for a long time struggled with the quite different challenge of reconciling Kant's relatively loose claims in his writings on history—which tend to be aimed at a popular audience and concerned with contemporary cultural and political events—with Kant's singularly rigorous critical philosophy. Most readers of Kant—and indeed, Kant himself—have tended to approach this problem as principally a practical one, a problem concerning, for example, the viability of the "ethical commonwealth" that is the telos of mankind's this-worldly historical development. Benjamin would, however, still have faced the problem of translating Kant's Copernican revolution into historiographic terms.

5.  I address Kant's essay and the place it occupies in *The Conflict of the Faculties* in detail in Lehman, "Finite States: Toward a Kantian Theory of the Event."

6.  For a critique of attempts to evade epistemological questions, see Brassier. For an excellent (critical) survey of these positions, see Orlemanski.

7.  Lenin later rewrote this aphorism to read: "Dialectical idealism is closer to intelligent [dialectical] materialism than metaphysical, undeveloped, dead, crude, rigid materialism" (38:274). It is a product of his now famous study of Hegel (and Clausewitz, but that is another story), undertaken in the Berne library from September 1914 to May 1915, immediately following the collapse of the Second International. Although this remark appears in Lenin's *Conspectus of Hegel's Book "Lectures on the History of Philosophy"* (1915), it seems more likely that it reflects his reading of the *Science of Logic*. The latter text includes the following remark: "The opposition between idealistic and realistic philosophy is . . . without meaning. A philosophy that attributes to finite existence, as such, true, ultimate, absolute being, does not deserve the name of philosophy" (*SL* 124). What Lenin calls "stupid materialism" is indistinguishable from what Hegel calls "realistic philosophy" and from what Marx in the first of his "Theses on Feuerbach"

calls "contemplative materialism." I belabor this point as a way of providing a larger philosophical-political context for Benjamin's rejection of empiricism.

8. In his own commentary on Adorno and Benjamin's exchange over the Baudelaire essay, "The Prince and the Frog: The Question of Method in Adorno and Benjamin," Giorgio Agamben focuses on Adorno's fidelity to Hegel, citing the well-known discussion of mediation from the *Phenomenology of Spirit* that begins, "The true is the whole . . ." (*Infancy and History* 117). Robert Kaufman provides a very different and very interesting reading of the same exchange in "Lyric Commodity Critique, Benjamin Adorno Marx, Baudelaire Baudelaire Baudelaire." Although Kaufman admits that, in the exchange, "Adorno makes inaccurate, high-handed pronouncements about literary and cultural matters in which Benjamin is far more expert than he (e.g., philological method; the accuracy of Brecht's translations of Shelley; the history—a foreshadowing, by *Benjamin*, of *Habermas!*—of the English coffeehouse's significance for modernity's development of a public sphere)" (212), Kaufman's desire to depict Adorno as, fundamentally, a Kantian Marxist—and as correcting Benjamin by guiding him toward a Kantian Marxism—is not totally convincing, for Kaufman never addresses Adorno's implicit and explicit references to Hegel. This is a significant omission. Acknowledging Adorno's demand that Benjamin embrace a version of the Hegelian dialectic, Kaufman would need to transform his reading completely. See also Karen Feldman's treatment of the Benjamin-Adorno exchange in "Not Dialectical Enough: On Benjamin, Adorno, and Autonomous Critique."

9. We might think of Benjamin's pedestrian, challenged by the carriage, as a distant relation of the tortoise challenged by Achilles in Zeno of Elea's famous paradox. That the carriage easily overtakes the pedestrian, however, while Achilles cannot overtake his much slower challenger, does not falsify this genealogy. For Benjamin, unlike for Zeno, the two competitors do not move through the same time.

10. Michael Friedman, for example, notes that "Kant's original version of transcendental philosophy took both Euclidean geometry and the Newtonian laws of motion to be synthetic *a priori* constitutive principles—which, from Kant's point of view, function as necessary presuppositions for applying our fundamental concepts of space, time, matter, and motion to our sensible experience of the natural world" ("Einstein, Kant, and the Relativized A Priori" 253).

11. I am here, again, indebted to Agamben's analysis of the differences between Benjamin's and Adorno's projects. See, for example, Agamben's remark that "the task of the critic is to recognize in the amazed facticity of the work, which is there as a philological exhibit, the direct and fundamental unity of subject matter and truth content, of structure and superstructure embedded in it" (*Infancy and History* 123). This unity Agamben calls *praxis* (120).

12. This attempt to transfer what is, in truth, a Kantian problematic into the register of lived experience has predecessors in certain versions of philosophical anthropology and, most significantly, in the analytic of *Dasein* developed by Martin Heidegger in *Being and Time* (1927) and ancillary writings during the 1920s. Benjamin never delivers a sustained reflection on his relationship to Heidegger's work, though he does suggest in a letter to Scholem of 30 January 1930 that, in his work on the *Trauerspiel* book, he

anticipates a faceoff with Heidegger, "and I expect sparks will fly from the shock of the confrontation between our two very different ways of looking at history" (*OG* 359–360). And in another letter to Scholem, sent from Berlin and dated 25 April 1930, Benjamin describes how he had "planned to annihilate Heidegger here in the summer in the context of a very close-knit critical circle of readers led by Brecht and me. Unfortunately, however, Brecht is not at all well. He will be leaving very soon and I will not do it on my own" (*C* 365). So, another missed opportunity. For an excellent collection of essays addressing Benjamin's relationship to Heidegger, see Andrew Benjamin and Dimitris Vardoulakis, eds., *Sparks Will Fly: Benjamin and Heidegger*.

13. In a letter to Scholem from 1924, Benjamin writes that "[*History and Class Consciousness*, which begins with the canonical essay 'Reification and the Consciousness of the Proletariat'] is very important, especially for me" (*C* 244).

14. See also Benjamin's remark in "On Some Motifs in Baudelaire": "Although chronological reckoning subordinates duration to regularity, it cannot prevent heterogeneous, conspicuous fragments from remaining within it" (*SW* 4:336).

15. Samuel Weber writes that "one of Benjamin's favorite words, in this context, was *Vexierbild*: a picture-riddle that 'vexes' by puzzling and demands to be deciphered. The 'new angel' . . . is one such *Vexierbild*" (222). Buck-Morss herself recognizes that Benjamin treats the arcades as an example of a *Vexierbild* ("The Flaneur, the Sandwich Man, and the Whore" 135), but she does not extend this designation to the figures who populate the arcades.

## Chapter 6

1. That allegory unfolds temporally is already assumed in the definition standardized by Quintilian in the *Institutio oratio*: "*continua metaphora*" (8.6.4), a "continuous metaphor," where the continuity occurs as the metaphor's temporal unfolding.

2. The notion of allegory as "mechanical" is most fully developed by Samuel Coleridge (under the influence of Goethe's writings) (*Complete Works* 1:437).

3. See also Rainer Nägele's *Theater, Theory, Speculation: Walter Benjamin and the Scenes of Modernity*: "The rhetoric of the symbol opposes [to allegorical fragmentation] a vision [*Anschauung*] that sees the wholeness of form as *Gestalt*, in a whole subject and whole object" (92).

4. Intellectual intuition was the hallmark of post-Kantian idealism, occupying a central role in the writings of J. G. Fichte as well as in the early Jena writings of Hegel and F. W. J. Schelling. Fichte, for example, tries to overcome the subject-object dualism of Kantian philosophy by demonstrating that, insofar as this dualism is itself subjectively produced, the grounding of philosophy can only be established through recourse to the activity of a freely self-positing "I." As he writes in the 1794 version of the *Wissenschaftslehre*: "Das Ich setz sich selbst" (the I posits itself), and it does so absolutely, prior to any engagement with a distinct object-world. Intellectual intuition is thus reserved for the self's knowledge of itself" (97). In the writings of Schelling and Hegel, this intuition is extended to account for the Absolute's own self-recognition. I will address Kant's very different understanding of intellectual intuition in a later section of this chapter.

5. Fredric Jameson has developed the most detailed dialectical treatment of allegory. Jameson, however, has never seemed particularly close to Benjamin in his formulations (see *Postmodernism* 217–259). Attempts to align Benjamin's own writings on allegory with dialectics have been carried out by Sommer in her "Allegory and Dialectics: A Match Made in Romance" and, more recently, by Matthew Wilkens in his "Toward a Benjaminian Theory of Dialectical Allegory." These treatments of Benjaminian allegory remain unsatisfying, however, because they typically ignore Benjamin's own challenges to Hegelian dialectics, instead assuming that when Benjamin writes "dialectic" he means this term in a very traditionally Marxian sense. More seriously, they neglect the extent to which Benjaminian allegory undermines the (proleptic or achieved) identity of thought and being that underlies dialectics. With this, the critical force of allegory in Benjamin's attacks on nineteenth-century notions of historical progress is effectively evacuated. Wilkens, for example, reads Benjaminian allegory as the figure appropriate to uneven historical development, the latter conceived along more or less Weberian lines as a process of secularization. Nothing could be further from the model of history outlined in *The Arcades Project*, the theses "On the Concept of History," and Benjamin's other late writings.

6. I would like to thank Martin Hägglund for bringing this reference to my attention.

7. As Jacques Derrida notes, philosophies that insist on human finitude issue from this same speculative logic: "The unity of these two *ends* of man, the unity of his death, his completion, his accomplishment, is enveloped in the Greek thought of *telos*, in the discourse on *telos*, which is also a discourse on *eidos*, on *ousia*, and on *aletheia*" (*Margins* 121). Following Derrida's formulation, we could say that allegorical finitude—the "end of man" in death—complements the symbolic completion of knowledge—the "end of man" as his philosophical accomplishment.

8. This is not, of course, to argue that epic and symbol are the same thing for Lukács or for the philosophers who preceded him; nonetheless, both epic and symbol partake in the holism that allegory ought to challenge.

9. Martin Heidegger presents the best-known description of the traditional notion of time, tracing this notion from Aristotle to Hegel:

> Aristotle sees the essence of time in the *nun*; Hegel in the now. Aristotle conceives the *nun* as *horos*; Hegel interprets the now as "limit." Aristotle understands the *nun* as *stigme*; Hegel calls the now the "absolute this." Aristotle connects *chronos* with *sphaira*, in accordance with the tradition; Hegel emphasizes the "circular course" of time. Of course, Hegel misses the central tendency of Aristotle's analysis of time: of discovering a foundational connection (*akolouthein*) between the *nun*, *horos*, *stigme*, and *tode ti*. (*Being and Time* 417)

10. See Agamben's *Infancy and History: The Destruction of Experience*.

11. The same understanding of allegory's disruption of time underlies Benjamin's somewhat cryptic assertion that "[w]herever the allegorical intention prevails, no habits of any kind can be formed" (*AP* 59a,4). Habits arise only when instances of the same action can be related to one another; indeed, habit is just the contraction of temporally

distinct actions in a single behavioral fact. Thus, in David Hume's skeptical philosophy, "habit" describes the replacement of faith in an idealist notion of causality with empirically demonstrable evidence of constant conjunction over time. As Kant demonstrates, however, Humean habit must remain bound to a notion of time as continuous and causally ordered. Absent the continuity of time, habit is impossible.

12. Malcolm Bull, in his *Seeing Things Hidden*, is a rare exception, though his reading of the *Angelus Novus* differs from my own.

13. The prehistory of this question would take us back to the mystical writings of the early Christian philosophers. For an overview of the role of angels in philosophy, see George MacDonald Ross's "Angels."

14. That the description of the *Angelus* betrays a debt to Kant is no great surprise given Benjamin's own early philosophical development, as I have described in the fourth and fifth chapters of this book.

15. Compare the following lines from Paul de Man's *Aesthetic Ideology*: "[T]o the dismemberment of the body corresponds a dismemberment of language, as meaning-producing tropes are replaced by the fragmentation of sentences and propositions into discrete words or the fragmentation of discrete words into syllables or finally letters" (89). Immediately following this passage, de Man cites Benjamin's early distinction between the "saying" (*Art des Sagens*) and the "said" (*das Gesagte*). Although this reference is certainly suggestive, de Man's discussion of the materiality of the letter as it presents itself both in the disarticulation of bodies and in the disarticulation of language is so close to Benjamin's discussions of mortification and emblematics in the *Trauerspiel* study that it is difficult to imagine that de Man did not have this work in mind. Indeed, the comparison of de Man's writings from the late 1970s and early 1980s to Benjamin's studies of allegory seems to me more fruitful than the numerous readings of Benjamin in terms of de Man's still profoundly Heideggerian discussion of allegory in "The Rhetoric of Temporality."

Rainer Nägele also associates Benjaminian allegory with the mutilation of the body: "[T]he scene of allegorical anxiety reveals itself as the subject's anxiety of dismemberment, a phantasy of the dismembered body whose limbs and members take on an independent existence" (92). I diverge from this reading, however, insofar as Nägele never ceases to identify this dismemberment with Hegelian negativity, even as he notes that allegory dramatizes the "cut of language through which the imaginary, substantial I is confronted with the grammatical I" (92). For Nägele, as for Georges Bataille and Alexandre Kojève, Hegelian negativity makes man a "living death"; this is, however, not so different from saying that negativity makes man "living time," since negativity is, for Hegel, profoundly temporal. In associating allegory with this negativity, Nägele again affirms allegory's essentially temporal character against the timelessness of the symbol.

16. For a good discussion of Paul Klee in the context of a reflection on Benjamin's baroque imaginary, albeit one that has little to do with the argument developed here, see Buci-Glucksmann.

17. For an excellent discussion of Klee's turn to script, see Annie Bourneuf's "A Refuge for Script: Paul Klee's Square Pictures."

18. This equation of letters and images also sheds light on Benjamin's enigmatic assertion that "only dialectical images are genuine images (that is, not archaic); *and the place where one encounters them is language*" (*AP* N2a,3; my emphasis).

19. De Man goes on to describe this material vision as one in which, "to the extent that any mind or judgment are present at all, they are in error" (*Aesthetic Ideology* 127). It is, again, a question of a world that would exist independent of the synthetic operations carried out by the human subject.

# WORKS CITED

Abrams, M. H. *Natural Supernaturalism*. New York: W. W. Norton, 1973.

Adorno, Theodor. *Aesthetic Theory*. Trans. Robert Huillot-Kentor. Minneapolis: U of Minnesota P, 1997.

———. *Kant's "Critique of Pure Reason."* Trans. Rolf Tiedemann. Stanford, CA: Stanford UP, 2001.

———. *Prisms*. Trans. Shierry Weber Nicholsen. Cambridge, MA: MIT Press, 1981.

Adorno, Theodor, et al. *Aesthetics and Politics*. London: Verso, 2007.

Agamben, Giorgio. *Infancy and History: The Destruction of Experience*. Trans. Liz Heron. London: Verso, 1996.

———. *Potentialities: Collected Essays in Philosophy*. Trans. Daniel Heller-Roazen. Stanford, CA: Stanford UP, 1999.

Aiken, Conrad. "An Anatomy of Melancholy." North, *The Waste Land*, 148–152.

Aldington, Richard. "The Influence of Mr. James Joyce." *English Review* (April 1921): 333–341.

———. "Some Reflections on Ernest Dowson." *The Egoist* (March 1915): 36–39.

Althusser, Louis. *Philosophy of the Encounter*. Trans. G. M. Goshgarian. New York: Verso, 2006.

Aristotle. *The Basic Works of Aristotle*. Ed. Richard McKeon. New York: Random House, 2001.

———. *Poetics: With the "Tractatus Coislinianus," Reconstruction of "Poetics" II, and the Fragments of the "On Poets."* Trans. Richard Janko. Indianapolis, IN: Hackett, 1987.

Badiou, Alain. *Being and Event*. Trans. Oliver Feltham. New York: Continuum, 2005.

Balibar, Étienne. *The Philosophy of Marx*. Trans. Chris Turner. New York: Verso, 2007.

Bate, Walter Jackson. *The Burden of the Past and the English Poet*. Cambridge, MA: Belknap Press, 1970.

Baudelaire, Charles. *Les Fleurs du Mal.* Trans. Richard Howard. Boston: Godine, 1982.

——. *The Painter of Modern Life and Other Essays.* Trans. and ed. Jonathan Mayne. London: Phaidon Press, 1995.

Baumgarten, Alexander. *Aesthetica.* Hildesheim: Georg Olms, 1986.

——. *Reflections on Poetry.* Trans. Karl Aschenbrenner. Berkeley: U of California P, 1954.

Beckett, Samuel. *Waiting for Godot.* New York: Grove, 1954.

Behler, Ernst. "Vico and Nietzsche." *New Vico Studies* 14 (1996): 65–73.

Beiser, Frederick C. *After Hegel: German Philosophy, 1840–1900.* Princeton, NJ: Princeton UP, 2014.

——. *The Fate of Reason: German Philosophy from Kant to Fichte.* Cambridge, MA: Harvard UP, 1993.

Benjamin, Andrew. *Present Hope: Philosophy, Architecture, Judaism.* London: Routledge, 1997.

——, ed. *Walter Benjamin and History.* London: Continuum, 2005.

Benjamin, Andrew, and Dimitris Vardoulakis, eds. *Sparks Will Fly: Benjamin and Heidegger.* Albany: SUNY Press, 2015.

Benjamin, Walter. *The Arcades Project.* Trans. Howard Eiland and Kevin McLaughlin. Cambridge, MA: Harvard UP, 1999.

——. *The Correspondence of Walter Benjamin, 1910–1940.* Ed. Gershom Scholem and Theodor Adorno. Trans. Manfred R. Jacobson and Evelyn M. Jacobson. Chicago: U of Chicago P, 1994.

——. *Gesammelte Briefe.* Ed. Christoph Gödde and Henri Lonitz. 6 vols. Frankfurt am Main: Suhrkamp, 1995–2000.

——. *Gesammelte Schriften.* Ed. Rolf Tiedemann and Hermann Schweppenhäuser. 7 vols. Frankfurt am Main: Suhrkamp, 1972–89.

——. *The Origin of German Tragic Drama.* Trans. John Osborne. New York: Verso, 1998.

——. *Selected Writings.* Ed. Michael W. Jennings et al. 4 vols. Cambridge, MA: Harvard UP, 1996–2003.

Bergson, Henri. *Creative Evolution.* Trans. Henry Holt. Mineola, NY: Dover, 1998.

——. *The Creative Mind: An Introduction to Metaphysics.* Trans. M. L. Andison. New York: Citadel Press, 1946.

——. *Matter and Memory.* Trans. N. M. Paul and W. S. Palmer. London: Zone Books, 1988.

Blasing, Mutlu Konuk. *American Poetry: The Rhetoric of Its Forms.* New Haven, CT: Yale UP, 1987.

Bloch, Ernst. "Nonsynchronism and the Obligation to Its Dialectics." Trans. Mark Ritter. *New German Critique* 11 (1977): 22–38.

Bloom, Harold. *The Breaking of the Vessels.* Chicago: U of Chicago P, 1982.

——. "Interview with Harold Bloom." By Robert Moynihan. *diacritics* 13.3 (1983): 57–68.

——. *A Map of Misreading.* New York: Oxford UP, 2003.

Bogel, Fredric. *The Difference Satire Makes*. Ithaca, NY: Cornell UP, 2001.

Bohrer, Karl Heinz. "Instants of Diminishing Duration: The Problem of Temporal Modalities." *The Moment: Time and Rupture in Modern Thought*. Ed. Heidum Friese. Liverpool: Liverpool UP, 2001. 113–134.

———. *Suddenness: On the Moment of Aesthetic Appearance*. Trans. Ruth Crowley. New York: Columbia UP, 1994.

Bourneuf, Annie. "A Refuge for Script: Paul Klee's Square Pictures." *Bauhaus Construct: Fashioning Identity, Discourse, and Modernism*. Ed. Robin Schuldenfrei and Jeffrey Saletnik. New York: Routledge, 2009. 105–124.

Brand, Dana. *The Spectator and the City in Nineteenth-Century American Literature*. Cambridge: Cambridge UP, 1991.

Brassier, Ray. "Concepts and Objects." *The Speculative Turn: Continental Materialism and Realism*. Ed. Levi Bryant, Nick Srnicek, and Graham Harman. Melbourne: re.press, 2011. 47–65.

Brennan, Timothy. *Borrowed Light: Vico, Hegel, and the Colonies*. Stanford, CA: Stanford UP, 2014.

Brodersen, Momme. *Walter Benjamin: A Biography*. Trans. Martina Derviş. London: Verso, 1996.

Brooker, Jewel Spears. *Mastery and Escape: T. S. Eliot and the Dialectic of Modernism*. Amherst: U of Massachusetts P, 1994.

Brooks, Cleanth. "*The Waste Land*." North, *The Waste Land*, 185–210.

Bryant, Levi R., Nick Srnicek, and Graham Harman, eds. *The Speculative Turn: Continental Materialism and Realism*. Melbourne: re.press, 2011.

Buci-Glucksmann, Christine. *Baroque Reason: The Aesthetics of Modernity*. Trans. Patrick Camiller. London: Sage, 1994.

Buck, Gene, and Herman Ruby. "That Shakespearian Rag." North, *The Waste Land*, 51–54.

Buck-Morss, Susan. *The Dialectics of Seeing*. Cambridge, MA: MIT Press, 1991.

———. "The Flaneur, the Sandwichman and the Whore: The Politics of Loitering." *New German Critique*, no. 39 (1986): 99–140.

Bull, Malcolm. *Seeing Things Hidden: Apocalypse, Vision, and Totality*. London: Verso, 1999.

Butler, Judith. *Subjects of Desire*. New York: Columbia UP, 2012.

Cassirer, Ernst. "Hermann Cohen and the Renewal of Kantian Philosophy." *Angelaki* 10.1 (2005): 95–108.

———. *Philosophy of the Enlightenment*. Trans. Fritz C. A. Koelln and James P. Pettigrove. Boston: Beacon Press, 1951.

Cavell, Stanley. *Must We Mean What We Say? A Book of Essays*. Cambridge: Cambridge UP, 2002.

Caygill, Howard. *Walter Benjamin: The Colour of Experience*. London: Routledge, 1998.

Chaucer, Geoffrey. *Canterbury Tales*. New York: Bantam, 1982.

Chinitz, David. "T. S. Eliot and the Cultural Divide." *PMLA* 110.2 (1995): 236–247.

———. *T. S. Eliot and the Cultural Divide*. Chicago: U of Chicago P, 2003.

Clark, David. "Kant's Aliens: The Anthropology and Its Others." *CR: The New Centennial Review* 1.2 (2001): 201–289.

Clark, T. J. "More Theses on Feuerbach." *Representations* 104.1 (2008): 4–7.

Cohen, Hermann. *Kants Theorie der Erfahrung*. Berlin: F. Dümmler, 1885.

Cohen, Philip. "*The Waste Land*, 1921: Some Developments of the Manuscript's Verse." *Journal of the Midwest Modern Language Association* 19.1 (1986): 12–20.

Coleridge, Samuel. *The Complete Works of Samuel Taylor Coleridge*. Vol. 1. Ed. W. G. T. Shedd. New York: Harper and Brothers, 1854.

———. *Notes and Lectures upon Shakespeare and Some of the Old Poets and Dramatists, with Other Literary Remains*. Ed. H. N. Coleridge. New York: Harper and Brothers, 1871.

Comay, Rebecca. "Walter Benjamin and the Ambiguities of Romanticism." Ferris, *Cambridge Companion to Walter Benjamin*, 134–151.

Crane, Hart. *The Letters of Hart Crane, 1916–1932*. Ed. Brom Weber. Berkeley: U of California P, 1965.

Crow, Thomas E. *Modern Art in the Common Culture*. New Haven, CT: Yale UP, 1996.

Culler, Jonathan. "On the Negativity of Modern Poetry." *Languages of the Unsayable: The Play of Negativity in Literature and Literary Theory*. Ed. Sanford Budick and Wolfgang Iser. New York: Columbia UP, 1989. 189–208.

Dante. *The Divine Comedy*. Trans. James Finn Cotter. Stony Brook, NY: Forum Italicum, 2000.

Davidson, Harriet. "Improper Desire: Reading *The Waste Land*." *The Cambridge Companion to T. S. Eliot*. Ed. A. David Moody. Cambridge: Cambridge UP, 2004. 121–131.

Dean, Tim. "T. S. Eliot, Famous Clairvoyant." *Gender, Desire, and Sexuality in T. S. Eliot*. Ed. Cassandra Laity and Nancy K. Gish. Cambridge: Cambridge UP, 2004. 43–65.

Deane, Patrick. *At Home In Time: Forms of Neo-Augustanism in Modern English Poetry*. Montreal: McGill-Queen's UP, 1994.

de Duve, Thierry. *Clement Greenberg between the Lines: Including a Debate with Clement Greenberg*. Trans. Brian Holmes. Chicago: U of Chicago P, 2010.

de Man, Paul. *Aesthetic Ideology*. Ed. Andrzej Warminski. Minneapolis: U of Minnesota P, 1996.

———. *Blindness and Insight*. Minneapolis: U of Minnesota P, 1983.

———. *The Resistance to Theory*. Minneapolis: U of Minnesota P, 1987.

———. *The Rhetoric of Romanticism*. New York: Columbia UP, 1984.

Derrida, Jacques. *Margins of Philosophy*. Trans. Alan Bass. Chicago: U of Chicago P, 1982.

Dickey, Laurence. "Philosophizing about History in the Nineteenth Century: The Method of *Zusammenhang* in German Historical Thinking." *The Cambridge History of Nineteenth-Century Philosophy*, ed. A. Wood. Cambridge: Cambridge UP, 2012. 793–816.

Dilthey, Wilhelm. *The Formation of the Historical World in the Human Sciences*. Trans. and ed. Rudolf Makkreel and Frithjof Rodi. Princeton, NJ: Princeton UP, 2002.

———. *Gesammelte Schriften*. Vol. 5. Göttingen: Vandenhoeck und Ruprecht, 1964.

———. *Introduction to the Human Sciences*. Trans. and ed. Rudolf Makkreel and Frithjof Rodi. Princeton, NJ: Princeton UP, 1991.

Donoghue, Denis. *Words Alone: The Poet T. S. Eliot*. New Haven, CT: Yale UP, 2000.

Doyle, Tsarina. *Nietzsche on Epistemology and Metaphysics: The World in View*. Edinburgh: Edinburgh UP, 2009.

Eagleton, Terry. *Criticism and Ideology: A Study in Marxist Literary Theory*. London: Verso, 2006.

Eiland, Howard, and Michael Jennings. *Walter Benjamin: A Critical Life*. Cambridge, MA: Harvard UP, 2014.

Eliot, T. S. *After Strange Gods: A Primer of Modern Heresy*. London: Faber and Faber, 1934.

———. *The Annotated Waste Land with Eliot's Contemporary Prose*. Ed. Lawrence Rainey. New Haven, CT: Yale UP, 2003.

———. *Collected Poems 1909–1962*. New York: Harcourt Brace, 1991.

———. Introduction. Pound, *New Selected Poems and Translations*, 361–372.

———. *Inventions of the March Hare: Poems 1909–1917*. Ed. Christopher Ricks. New York: Harcourt Brace, 1996.

———. *Knowledge and Experience in the Philosophy of F. H. Bradley*. London: Faber and Faber, 1964.

———. *The Letters of T. S. Eliot, Volume 1: 1898–1922*. Rev. ed. Ed. Valerie Eliot and Hugh Haughton. New Haven, CT: Yale UP, 2011.

———. *The Letters of T. S. Eliot, Volume 2: 1923–1925*. Ed. Valerie Eliot and Hugh Haughton. New Haven, CT: Yale UP, 2011.

———. *The Letters of T. S. Eliot, Volume 3: 1926–1927*. Ed. Valerie Eliot and John Haffenden. New Haven, CT: Yale UP, 2012.

———. "London Letter." *The Dial* 73 (December 1922): 659–663.

———. *The Sacred Wood: Essays on Poetry and Criticism*. London: Methuen, 1960.

———. *Selected Prose of T. S. Eliot*. Ed. Frank Kermode. New York: Harcourt Brace, 1975.

———. "Tarr." *The Egoist* 5.8 (1918): 105–106.

———. *To Criticize the Critic and Other Writings*. New York: Farrar, Straus and Giroux, 1965.

———. *The Use of Poetry and the Use of Criticism: Studies in the Relation of Criticism to Poetry In England*. London: Faber and Faber, 1964.

———. *The Varieties of Metaphysical Poetry*. Ed. Ronald Schuchard. London: Faber and Faber, 1993.

———. "War-Paint and Feathers." *Athenaeum* 17 (October 1919): 1036.

———. *The Waste Land: A Facsimile and Transcript of the Original Drafts Including the Annotations of Ezra Pound*. Ed. Valerie Eliot. New York: Harcourt Brace, 1971.

———. *The Waste Land: A Norton Critical Edition*. Ed. Michael North. New York: Norton, 2001.

———. "Whitman and Tennyson." *The Nation and Athenaeum* 18 December 1926: 426.

Ellmann, Maud. *The Poetics of Impersonality: T. S. Eliot and Ezra Pound*. Brighton, UK: Harvester Press, 1987.

Emerson, Ralph Waldo. *Emerson's Prose and Poetry: Authoritative Texts, Contexts, Criticism*. Ed. Joel Porte and Saundra Morris. New York: Norton, 2001.

Epstein, Joseph. "'The Literary Life' at 25." *New Criterion* 26.1 (2007): 4+. Literature Resource Center. Web. 3 May 2015.

Faulk, Barry. "Modernism and the Popular: Eliot's Music Halls." *Modernism/modernity* 8.4 (2001): 603–621.

Feldman, Karen. "Not Dialectical Enough: On Benjamin, Adorno, and Autonomous Critique." *Philosophy and Rhetoric* 44.4 (2011): 336–362.

Fenves, Peter. *Arresting Language: From Leibniz to Benjamin*. Stanford, CA: Stanford UP, 2001.

———. *The Messianic Reduction: Walter Benjamin and the Shape of Time*. Stanford, CA: Stanford UP, 2011.

Ferris, David S. *The Cambridge Companion to Walter Benjamin*. Cambridge: Cambridge UP, 2004.

Fichte, J. G. *Science of Knowledge*. Ed. and trans. Peter Heath and John Lachs. Cambridge: Cambridge UP, 1982.

Fineman, Joel. "The History of the Anecdote: Fiction and Fiction." *The Subjectivity Effect in Western Literary Tradition: Essays toward the Release of Shakespeare's Will*. Cambridge, MA: MIT Press, 1991. 49–76.

Flaubert, Gustave. *The Letters of Gustave Flaubert*. Ed. Francis Steegmuller. Cambridge, MA: Harvard UP, 1980.

Foucault, Michel. "The Fantasia of the Library." *Language, Counter-Memory, Practice*. Ed. and trans. D. F. Bouchard and S. Simon. Ithaca, NY: Cornell UP, 1977. 87–109.

———. *The Order of Things*. Trans. Alan Sheridan. New York: Vintage, 1970.

Frank, Joseph. "Spatial Form in Modern Literature." *The Idea of Spatial Form*. New Brunswick, NJ: Rutgers UP, 1991.

Frege, Gottlob. "Review of Dr. E. Husserl's Philosophy of Arithmetic." Trans. E. W. Kluge. *Mind* 81.323 (1972): 321–337.

Fried, Michael. *Art and Objecthood: Essays and Reviews*. Chicago: U of Chicago P, 1998.

Friedman, Michael. "Einstein, Kant, and the Relativized A Priori." *Constituting Objectivity: Transcendental Perspectives on Modern Physics*. Ed. Michel Bitbol, Pierre Kerszberg, and Jean Petitot. Dordrecht: Springer, 2009. 253–267.

———. *Parting of the Ways: Carnap, Cassirer, and Heidegger*. Chicago: Open Court, 2000.

Gordon, Lyndall. *T. S. Eliot's Early Years*. New York: Farrar, Straus and Giroux, 1998.

Gordon, Peter E. *Rosenzweig and Heidegger: Between Judaism and German Philosophy*. Berkeley: U of California P, 2003.

———. "Science, Finitude, and Infinity: Neo-Kantianism and the Birth of Existentialism." *Jewish Social Studies* 6.1 (1999): 30–53.

Gossman, Lionel. "Anecdote and History." *History and Theory* 42.2 (2003): 143–168.

Greenberg, Clement. *Clement Greenberg: The Collected Essays and Criticism*. Ed. John O'Brian. 4 vols. Chicago: U of Chicago P, 1986.

Habib, M. A. R. *The Early T. S. Eliot and Western Philosophy*. Cambridge: Cambridge UP, 1999.

Hägglund, Martin. "Dying for Time: T. S. Eliot's *Four Quartets.*" *Frakcija: Performing Arts Magazine* 68–69 (2013): 22–34.

Hamacher, Werner. "Intensive Languages." Trans. Ira Allen and Steven Tester. *MLN* 127.3 (2012): 485–541.

Hamann, Johann Georg. *Writings on Philosophy and Language.* Trans. Kenneth Haynes. Cambridge: Cambridge UP, 2007.

Harries, Martin. "Homo Alludens: Marx's *18th Brumaire.*" *New German Critique* 66 (1995): 35–64.

Haughton, Hugh. "Allusion: The Case of Shakespeare." *T. S. Eliot in Context.* Ed. Jason Harding. Cambridge: Cambridge UP, 2011. 157–168.

Hegel, G. W. F. *Aesthetics: Lectures on Fine Art.* Vol. 1. Trans. T. M. Knox. Oxford: Oxford UP, 1998.

———. *The Difference between Fichte's and Schelling's Systems of Philosophy.* Trans. H. S. Harris and William Cerf. Albany: SUNY Press, 1977.

———. *The Encyclopaedia Logic, with the Zusätze.* Trans. T. F. Geraets, W. A. Suchting, and H. S. Harris. Indianapolis, IN: Hackett, 1991.

———. *Hegel's "Science of Logic."* Trans. A. V. Miller. Atlantic Highlands, NJ: Humanities Press, 1969.

———. *Phenomenology of Spirit.* Trans. A. V. Miller. Oxford: Oxford UP, 1977.

———. *The Philosophy of Nature.* Trans. A. V. Miller. Oxford: Clarendon Press, 1970.

Heidegger, Martin. *Basic Problems of Phenomenology.* Trans. Albert Hofstadter. Bloomington: Indiana UP, 1975.

———. *Being and Time.* Trans. Joan Stambaugh. Albany: SUNY Press, 1996.

———. *Hegel's "Phenomenology of Spirit."* Trans. Parvis Emad and Kenneth Maly. Bloomington: Indiana UP, 1988.

———. *Kant and the Problem of Metaphysics.* Trans. Richard Taft. Bloomington: Indiana UP, 1997.

———. *Nietzsche.* Vol. 1. Trans. David Farrell Krell. San Francisco: Harper and Row, 1979.

———. *Off the Beaten Track.* Trans. Julian Young. Cambridge: Cambridge UP, 2002.

———. *Phenomenological Interpretation of Kant's "Critique of Pure Reason."* Trans. Parvis Emad and Kenneth Maly. Bloomington: Indiana UP, 1997.

Hertz, Neil. *The End of the Line.* New York: Columbia UP, 1985.

Hill, R. Kevin. *Nietzsche's Critiques: The Kantian Foundations of His Thought.* Oxford: Clarendon Press, 2003.

Hobsbawm, Eric. *The Age of Extremes: A History of the World, 1914–1991.* New York: Vintage, 1996.

Hofer, Matthew. "Modernist Polemic: Ezra Pound v. 'the perverters of language.'" *Modernism/modernity* 9.3 (2002): 463–489.

Hölderlin, Friedrich. *Essays and Letters on Theory.* Trans. Thomas Pfau. Albany: SUNY Press, 1988.

Hulme, T. E. *Selected Writings.* Ed. Patrick McGuinness. Manchester, UK: Carcanet, 1998.

Hyppolite, Jean. *Genesis and Structure of Hegel's "Phenomenology of Spirit."* Trans. Samuel Cherniak and John Heckman. Evanston, IL: Northwestern UP, 1979.

———. *Logic and Existence.* Trans. Leonard Lawlor. Albany: SUNY Press, 1997.

James, William. *The Principles of Psychology.* Cambridge, MA: Harvard UP, 1981.

Jameson, Fredric. "The End of Temporality." *Critical Inquiry* 29.4 (2003): 695–718.

———. *Ideologies of Theory.* New York: Verso, 2008.

———. *The Political Unconscious: Narrative as a Socially Symbolic Act.* Ithaca, NY: Cornell UP, 1981.

———. *Postmodernism, or, The Cultural Logic of Late Capitalism.* Durham, NC: Duke UP, 1984.

———. *The Prison-House of Language: A Critical Account of Structuralism and Russian Formalism.* Princeton, NJ: Princeton UP, 1972.

———. *A Singular Modernity.* London: Verso, 2001.

Jay, Martin. "Modernism and the Specter of Psychologism." *Modernism/modernity* 3.2 (1996): 93–111.

Jenkins, Nicholas. "More American Than We Knew." *New York Times Book Review* 20 April 1997: 14–15.

Johnson, Loretta. "T. S. Eliot's Bawdy Verse: Lulu, Bolo and More Ties." *Journal of Modern Literature* 27.1 (2003): 14–25.

Joyce, James. *Ulysses: The Corrected Text.* Ed. Hans Walter Gabler with Wolfhard Steppe and Claus Melchior. New York: Random House, 1986.

Julius, Anthony. *T. S. Eliot, Anti-Semitism, and Literary Form.* Rev. ed. London: Thames and Hudson, 2003.

Kant, Immanuel. *The Conflict of the Faculties.* Trans. Mary J. Gregor and Robert Anchor. *Religion and Rational Theology.* Ed. Allen W. Wood and George di Giovanni. Cambridge: Cambridge UP, 2001. 233–328.

———. *Critique of Pure Reason.* Trans. and ed. Paul Guyer and Allen W. Wood. Cambridge: Cambridge UP, 1998.

———. *Critique of the Power of Judgment.* Ed. Paul Guyer. Trans. Paul Guyer and Eric Matthews. Cambridge: Cambridge UP, 2000.

———. "Idea for a Universal History with a Cosmopolitan Aim." Trans. Allen W. Wood. *Anthropology, History, and Education.* Ed. Robert B. Louden and Günter Zöller. Cambridge: Cambridge UP, 2011. 107–120.

———. *Kants Gesammelte Schriften.* Akademie-Ausgabe. 2nd ed. 29 vols. Berlin: Reimer, 1900–1983.

———. *Lectures on Metaphysics.* Ed. and trans. Karl Ameriks and Steve Naragon. Cambridge: Cambridge UP, 2001.

———. *The Metaphysics of Morals.* Ed. and trans. Mary J. Gregor. Cambridge: Cambridge UP, 1996.

———. "On a Newly Arisen Superior Tone in Philosophy." Trans. Peter Fenves. *Raising the Tone of Philosophy: Late Essays by Immanuel Kant, Transformative Critique by Jacques Derrida.* Ed. Peter Fenves. Baltimore: Johns Hopkins UP, 1993. 51–81.

Kaufman, Robert. "Intervention & Commitment Forever! Shelley in 1819, Shelley in

Brecht, Shelley in Adorno, Shelley in Benjamin." *Romantic Circles Praxis Series* (May 2001). http://www.rc.umd.edu/praxis/interventionist/kaufman/kaufman.html.

———. "Legislators of the Post-Everything World: Shelley's 'Defense of Adorno.'" *ELH* 63.3 (1996): 707–733.

———. "Lyric Commodity Critique, Benjamin Adorno Marx, Baudelaire Baudelaire Baudelaire." *PMLA* 123.1 (2008): 207–215.

———. "Red Kant, or the Persistence of the Third Critique in Adorno and Jameson." *Critical Inquiry* 26.4 (2000): 682–724.

Kenner, Hugh. *The Invisible Poet.* New York: Routledge, 1965.

———. *The Pound Era.* Berkeley: U of California P, 1973.

———. "The Urban Apocalypse." *Eliot in His Time: Essays on the Occasion of the Fiftieth Anniversary of "The Waste Land."* Ed. A. Walton Litz. Princeton, NJ: Princeton UP, 1973. 23–50.

Kittredge, Selwyn. "Richard Aldington's Challenge to T. S. Eliot: The Background of Their James Joyce Controversy." *James Joyce Quarterly* 10.3 (1973): 339–341.

Köhnke, Klaus Christian. *The Rise of Neo-Kantianism: German Academic Philosophy between Idealism and Positivism.* Trans. R. J. Hollingdale. Cambridge: Cambridge UP, 1991.

Kouvelakis, Stathis. *Philosophy and Revolution: From Kant to Marx.* Trans. G. M. Goshgarian. London: Verso, 2003.

Kusch, Martin. *Psychologism: A Case Study of the Sociology of Philosophical Knowledge.* New York: Routledge, 1995.

Leavis, F. R. "The Significance of the Modern Waste Land." North, *The Waste Land,* 173–185.

Lehman, Robert. "Finite States: Toward a Kantian Theory of the Event." *diacritics* 39.1 (2009): 61–74.

Leibniz, Gottfried Wilhelm. *New Essays on Human Understanding.* Ed. Peter Remnant and Jonathan Bennett. Cambridge: Cambridge UP, 1996.

Lenin, V. I. "Philosophical Notebooks." *Collected Works.* Vol. 38. Moscow: Progress Publishers, 1961. 85–314.

Levenson, Michael. *A Genealogy of Modernism: A Study of English Literary Doctrine 1908–1922.* Cambridge: Cambridge UP, 1984.

Lewis, Pericles. *The Cambridge Introduction to Modernism.* Cambridge: Cambridge UP, 2007.

Lewis, Wyndham. *The Apes of God.* Santa Rosa, CA: Black Sparrow, 1981.

———. *Blasting and Bombardiering.* London: Calder and Boyars, 1967.

———. *Tarr: The 1918 Version.* Ed. Paul O'Keeffe. Santa Rosa, CA: Black Sparrow, 1990.

———. *Time and Western Man.* Santa Barbara, CA: Black Sparrow, 1993.

Lewis, Wyndham, et al. *Blast I.* Santa Rosa, CA: Black Sparrow, 1982.

Longenbach, James. "Modern Poetry." *The Cambridge Companion to Modernism.* Ed. Michael Levenson. Cambridge: Cambridge UP, 2011. 100–129.

Löwy, Michael. *Fire Alarm: Reading Walter Benjamin's "On the Concept of History."* Trans. Chris Turner. London: Verso, 2005.

Lukács, Georg. *History and Class Consciousness*. Cambridge, MA: MIT Press, 1994.

———. *The Theory of the Novel*. Trans. Anna Bostock. Cambridge, MA: MIT Press, 1971.

Lyotard, Jean-François. *The Inhuman: Reflections on Time*. Trans. Geoff Bennington and Rachel Bowlby. Stanford, CA: Stanford UP, 1991.

Mao, Douglas. *Solid Objects*. Princeton, NJ: Princeton UP, 1998.

Mao, Douglas, and Rebecca Walkowitz. "New Modernist Studies." *PMLA* 123.3 (2008): 737–748.

Mariani, Paul L. *William Carlos Williams: A New World Naked*. New York: McGraw-Hill, 1981.

Martz, Louis. "Origins of Form in *Four Quartets*." *Words in Time: New Essays on Eliot's "Four Quartets."* Ed. Edward Lobb. Ann Arbor: U of Michigan P, 1993. 189–204.

Marx, Karl, and Friedrich Engels. *Collected Works*. 50 vols. New York: International Publishers, 1975–2003.

Mayer, Nicholas. "Catalyzing Prufrock." *Journal of Modern Literature* 34.3 (201): 182–198.

Mazlish, Bruce. "The Tragic Farce of Marx, Hegel, and Engels: A Note." *History and Theory* 11.3 (1972): 335–337.

McDowell, John. *Mind and World*. Cambridge, MA: Harvard UP, 1994.

McIntire, Gabrielle. *Modernism, Memory, and Desire: T. S. Eliot and Virginia Woolf*. Cambridge: Cambridge UP, 2008.

Menke, Christoph. "Not Yet." Trans. Gerrit Jackson. *Nordic Journal of Aesthetics* 39 (2010): 34–47.

Mill, John Stuart. *Autobiography and Literary Essays*. Toronto: U of Toronto P, 1981.

Miller, James E. *T. S. Eliot: The Making of an American Poet, 1888–1922*. University Park: Penn State UP, 2005.

Miller, Tyrus. *Late Modernism: Politics, Fiction, and the Arts between the World Wars*. Berkeley: U of California P, 1999.

Moretti, Franco. *The Modern Epic: The World-System from Goethe to García Márquez*. Trans. Quintin Hoare. London: Verso, 1996.

———. "The Moment of Truth." *New Left Review* 159 (1986): 39–48.

———. *Signs Taken for Wonders*. London: Verso, 1997.

———. "The Spell of Indecision." *New Left Review* 164 (1987): 27–33.

Munson, Gorham. "The Esotericism of T. S. Eliot." North, *The Waste Land*, 156–163.

Nägele, Rainer. *Theater, Theory, Speculation: Walter Benjamin and the Scenes of Modernity*. Baltimore: Johns Hopkins UP, 1991.

Newmark, Kevin. *Irony on Occasion: From Schlegel and Kierkegaard to Derrida and de Man*. New York: Fordham UP, 2012.

Nietzsche, Friedrich Wilhelm. *The Birth of Tragedy and the Case of Wagner*. New York: Vintage, 1967.

———. *The Gay Science*. Trans. Walter Kaufmann. New York: Vintage, 1974.

———. *On the Advantage and Disadvantage of History for Life*. Trans. Peter Preuss. Indianapolis, IN: Hackett, 1980.

———. *On the Genealogy of Morality: A Polemic*. Indianapolis, IN: Hackett, 1998.

———. "On Truth and Lying in a Non-Moral Sense." *"The Birth of Tragedy" and Other*

*Writings.* Ed. Raymond Geuss and Ronald Speirs. Cambridge: Cambridge UP, 1999. 139–153.

———. *Werke: Kritische Gesamtausgabe.* 30 vols. Berlin: De Gruyter, 1967.

———. *Will to Power.* Trans. Walter Kaufmann. New York: Vintage, 1968.

North, Michael. *The Dialect of Modernism.* Oxford: Oxford UP, 1994.

———. *The Political Aesthetic of Yeats, Eliot, and Pound.* Cambridge: Cambridge UP, 1991.

*OED Online.* Oxford: Oxford UP, 2015.

Orlemanski, Julie. "Scales of Reading." *Exemplaria: A Journal of Theory in Medieval and Renaissance Studies* 26.2–3 (2014): 215–233.

Orwell, George. *In Front of Your Nose, 1946–1950.* New York: David R. Godine, 2000.

Österling, Anders. *Nobel Lectures, Literature 1901–1967.* Ed. Horst Frenz. Amsterdam: Elsevier, 1969.

Parker, Andrew. "Poetry of the Future; or, Periodizing the Nineteenth Century." *Modern Language Quarterly* 71.1 (2010): 75–85.

Peacock, Thomas Love. "The Four Ages of Poetry." *Classic Writings on Poetry.* Ed. William Harmon. New York: Columbia UP, 2005. 317–330.

Perloff, Marjorie. *The Poetics of Indeterminacy: Rimbaud to Cage.* Princeton, NJ: Princeton UP, 1981.

Pinkard, Terry. *German Philosophy 1760–1860: The Legacy of Idealism.* Cambridge: Cambridge UP, 2002.

Plato. *Phaedrus.* Trans. G. M. A. Grube and C. D. C. Reeve. *Plato: Complete Works.* Ed. John Cooper. Indianapolis, IN: Hackett, 1997. 506–556.

———. *Republic.* Trans. G. M. A. Grube and C. D. C. Reeve. *Plato: Complete Works.* Ed. John Cooper. Indianapolis, IN: Hackett, 1997. 971–1223.

Plimpton, George. *Writers at Work: The Paris Review Interviews.* Second series. New York: Viking, 1992.

Pope, John C. "Prufrock and Raskolnikov Again: A Letter from Eliot." *American Literature* 18.4 (1947): 319–321.

Pound, Ezra. *The Cantos.* New York: New Directions, 1996.

———. *The Letters of Ezra Pound, 1907–1941.* London: Faber and Faber, 1951.

———. *Literary Essays of Ezra Pound.* New York: New Directions, 1968.

———. *New Selected Poems and Translations.* Ed. Richard Sieburth. New York: New Directions, 2010.

Powell, Charles. "So Much Waste Paper." North, *The Waste Land,* 156.

Puchner, Martin. *Poetry of the Revolution.* Princeton, NJ: Princeton UP, 2006.

Rainey, Lawrence. *Institutions of Modernism.* New Haven, CT: Yale UP, 1998.

———. *Revisiting "The Waste Land."* New Haven, CT: Yale UP, 2005.

Rancière, Jacques. *The Future of the Image.* Trans. Gregory Elliott. London: Verso, 2007.

Ranke, Leopold. "Preface: Histories of Romance and Germanic Peoples." Stern, *The Varieties of History,* 54–58.

Ransom, John Crowe. "The Inorganic Muses." *Kenyon Review* 5.2 (1943): 278–300.

Rochat, Joyce Hamilton. "T. S. Eliot's 'Companion' Poems: Eternal Question, Temporal Response." *Contemporary Review* 227 (1975): 73–79.

Ross, George MacDonald. "Angels." *Philosophy* 60 (1985): 499–515.

Royce, Josiah. *Lectures on Modern Idealism*. New Haven, CT: Yale UP, 1919.

Schaeffer, Jean-Marie. *Art of the Modern Age: Philosophy of Art from Kant to Heidegger*. Trans. Steven Randall. Princeton, NJ: Princeton UP, 2000.

Scheerbart, Paul. *Lesabéndio: An Asteroid Novel*. Trans. Christina Svendsen. Cambridge, MA: Wakefield Press, 2012.

Schelling, F. W. J. *System of Transcendental Idealism (1800)*. Trans. Peter Heath. Charlottesville: U of Virginia P, 1997.

Schlegel, Friedrich. *Kritische Ausgabe*. Ed. Ernst Behler. 35 vols. Munich: Schöningh, 1958–.

Scholem, Gershom. "On Kant." Trans. Julia Ng. *MLN* 127.3 (2012): 443–446.

———. *Walter Benjamin: The Story of a Friendship*. Trans. Harry Zohn. New York: NYRB, 2003.

———. "Walter Benjamin and His Angel." *On Walter Benjamin*. Ed. Gary Smith. Cambridge, MA: MIT Press, 1988. 51–89.

Schopenhauer, Arthur. *On the Basis of Morality*. Trans. E. F. J. Payne. Indianapolis, IN: Hackett, 1998.

———. *The World as Will and Representation*. Trans. E. F. J. Payne. New York: Dover, 1966.

Schuchard, Ronald. *Eliot's Dark Angel: Intersections of Life and Art*. Oxford: Oxford UP, 1999.

Schwartz, Delmore. "The Isolation of Modern Poetry." *Praising It New: The Best of the New Criticism*. Ed. Garrick Davis. Athens: Swallow Press / Ohio UP, 2008. 151–160.

Seymour-Jones, Carole. *Painted Shadow: The Life of Vivienne Eliot, First Wife of T. S. Eliot, and the Long-Suppressed Truth about Her Influence on His Genius*. New York: Doubleday, 2002.

Shakespeare, William. *Measure for Measure*. New York: Penguin, 2000.

Shelley, Percy Bysshe. *Shelley's Poetry and Prose: Authoritative Texts, Criticism*. Ed. Donald Reiman and Neil Fraistat. 2nd ed. New York: Norton, 2001.

Sherry, Vincent. *Ezra Pound, Wyndham Lewis, and Radical Modernism*. Oxford: Oxford UP, 1992.

Shusterman, Richard. *T. S. Eliot and the Philosophy of Criticism*. New York: Columbia UP, 1988.

Sidney, Philip, Geoffrey Shepherd, and R. W. Maslen. *An Apology for Poetry, or, The Defence of Poesy*. 3rd ed. Manchester, UK: Manchester UP, 2002.

Smith, Grover. "The Making of *The Waste Land*." *Mosaic* 6.1 (1972): 127–141.

Smith, Stan. "Proper Frontiers: Transgression and the Individual Talent." *T. S. Eliot and the Concept of Tradition*. Ed. Giovanni Cianci and Jason Harding. Cambridge: Cambridge UP, 2007. 26–40.

Sommer, Doris. "Allegory and Dialectics: A Match Made in Romance." *Boundary 2* 18 (1991): 60–82.

Sorel, Georges. *Reflections on Violence*. Trans. T. E. Hulme with Jeremy Jennings. Ed. Jeremy Jennings. Cambridge: Cambridge UP, 1999.

Southam, B. C. *A Guide to the Selected Poems of T. S. Eliot*. New York: Harvest, 1996.

Spinoza, Benedictus de. *Principles of Cartesian Philosophy. Spinoza: Complete Works.* Trans. Samuel Shirley. Ed. Michael L. Morgan. Indianapolis, IN: Hackett, 2002. 108–212.

Stallabrass, Julian. "The Idea of the Primitive: British Art and Anthropology 1918–1930." *New Left Review* 1.183 (1990): 95–115.

Stallybrass, Peter. "Marx and Heterogeneity: Thinking the Lumpenproletariat." *Representations* 31 (1990): 69–95.

Steiner, Uwe. *Walter Benjamin: An Introduction to His Work and Thought.* Trans. Michael Winkler. Chicago: U of Chicago P, 2010.

Stern, Fritz Richard, ed. *The Varieties of History, from Voltaire to the Present.* New York: Vintage, 1973.

Strawson, P. F. *The Bounds of Sense: An Essay on Kant's Critique of Pure Reason.* London: Routledge, 1995.

Strier, Richard. "How Formalism Became a Dirty Word, and Why We Can't Do without It." *Renaissance Literature and Its Formal Engagements.* Ed. Mark David Rasmussen. New York: Palgrave Macmillan, 2002. 207–215.

van Buren, John. *The Young Heidegger: Rumor of the Hidden King.* Bloomington: Indiana UP, 1994.

Vico, Giambattista. *The New Science of Giambattista Vico.* Trans. Thomas Goddard Bergin and Max Harold Fisch. Ithaca, NY: Cornell UP, 1984.

Ward, David. *T. S. Eliot between Two Worlds: A Reading of T. S. Eliot's Poetry and Plays.* New York: Routledge, 1973.

Warren, Andrew. *The Orient and the Young Romantics.* Cambridge: Cambridge UP, 2014.

Weber, Samuel. *Benjamin's -abilities.* Cambridge, MA: Harvard UP, 2008.

Werckmeister, O. K. "Walter Benjamin's Angel of History, or the Transfiguration of the Revolutionary into the Historian." *Critical Inquiry* 22.2 (1996): 239–267.

White, Hayden. *Metahistory: The Historical Imagination in Nineteenth-Century Europe.* Baltimore: Johns Hopkins UP, 1973.

Whitman, Walt. *Leaves of Grass.* Ed. Malcolm Cowley. New York: Penguin, 1986.

Wilamowitz-Möllendorff, Ulrich von. "Future Philology." Trans. Gertrude Pöstl, Babette E. Babich, and Holger Schmid. *New Nietzsche Studies* 1–2 (2000): 1–33.

Wilkens, Matthew. "Toward a Benjaminian Theory of Dialectical Allegory." *New Literary History* 37.2 (2006): 285–298.

Williams, William Carlos. *The Autobiography of William Carlos Williams.* New York: New Directions, 1967.

Wilson, Edmund. "A Poetry of Drouth." North, *The Waste Land,* 140–145.

Wordsworth, William. *The Prelude: 1799, 1805, 1850.* Ed. Jonathan Wordsworth, M. H. Abrams, and Stephen Gill. New York: W. W. Norton, 1979.

Worringer, Wilhelm. *Abstraction and Empathy.* Trans. Michael Bullock. London: Ivan R. Dee, 1963.

Yeats, W. B. *The Collected Poems of W. B. Yeats.* Ed. Richard J. Finneran. New York: Scribner, 1996.

Young, Julian. *Friedrich Nietzsche: A Philosophical Biography.* Cambridge: Cambridge UP, 2010.